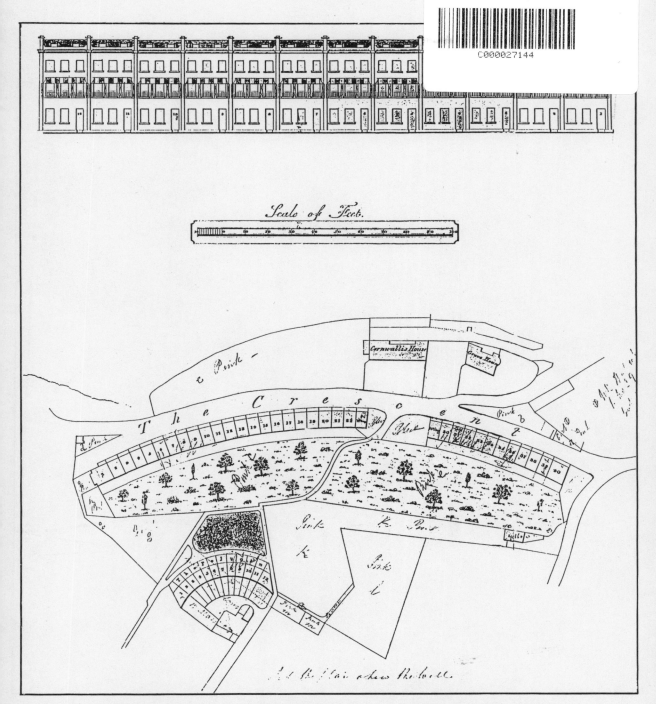

S.M.V. Map 305, drawn in February 1830 by Richard Jones, shows Cornwallis Crescent with a gap through the terrace between nos. 23 and 29. Owing to the bankruptcy of the principal builders in 1793, the original scheme was never completed and the Merchants were still granting leases of unfinished houses in 1827. By this date a right of way had been established through the site. The gap has nothing to do with the view from Cornwallis House.

A History of Clifton

The winning design for the Clifton Suspension Bridge. Isambard Kingdom Brunel won the second suspension bridge competition in March 1831. The 'Egyptian thing I brought down was quite extravagantly admired by all and unanimously adopted'. Egyptian styles were then in vogue and had relaced the 'Gothic' style. The projected span was 630 ft. with an abutment on the Leigh Woods side of the gorge. Brunel's previous designs proposed spans of up to 916 ft. and were rejected by Thomas Telford, first President of the Institute of Civil Engineers.

A History of
CLIFTON

Donald Jones

Phillimore

1992

Published by
PHILLIMORE & CO. LTD.,
Shopwyke Hall, Chichester, Sussex

ISBN 0 85033 820 4

Printed in Great Britain by
BIDDLES LTD.,
Guildford, Surrey

Contents

List of Illustrations

List of Tables

Illustration Acknowledgements

The author would like to thank the following institutions and individuals who loaned photographs and illustrations and gave permission for their publication in this book:

The Society of Merchant Venturers, 5, 6, 8, 14, 35; Alexander Gallery, Blackboy Hill (with thanks to John Cleverdon), 47-52; Bristol Record Office, 30-1, 33, 44, 56; City Museum and Art Gallery, frontispiece, 16, 22, 32, 36, 37, 39-40, 43, 45; Bristol Reference Library, 17-8, 28, 38; P. G. Davey Photograph Collection, 54-5, 57-8; *Proceedings of the Clifton Antiquarian Club*, 1-3, 7; P. G. Stembridge, 13; The M. J. Tozer Collection, 53, 60-1.

Maps of Clifton: 1746, G. E. Hammersley; 1746, Jacob de Wilstar; 1787, M. Hill; 1803, J. Feltham; 1820, Society of Merchant Venturers; 1821, B. Donne; 1836, R. Forrest (of the zoo); 1849, G. Ashmead; 1855, Walker and Boutall (site of Clifton College).

All other photographs are from the author's own collection.

Bibliographical Abbreviations

B.R.O.	Bristol Records Office
Latimer, *Merchant Venturers*	J. Latimer, *The History of the Society of the Merchant Venturers of the City of Bristol*, Bristol, 1903
McGrath, *Records*	P. McGrath, *Records Relating to the Society of Merchant Venturers of the City of Bristol in the Seventeenth Century*, Bristol, 1952
McGrath, *Merchant Venturers*	P. McGrath, *The Merchant Venturers of Bristol*, Bristol, 1975
P.C.A.C.	Proceedings of the Clifton Antiquarian Club
P.R.O.	Public Record Office, Chancery Lane
Seyer	Samuel Seyer, *Memoirs, Historical and Topographical, of Bristol and its Neighbourhood*, 2 vols., Bristol, 1821-3
S.M.V.	Society of Merchant Venturers' Archives
T.B.G.A.S.	Transactions of the Bristol and Gloucester Archaeological Society
U.B.D.	University of Bristol Deeds

Introduction

It is easy to fall between the stools of an academic study and a popular history. Perhaps there is a middle way which may provide much new material that all readers will enjoy, yet providing historians with the necessary academic apparatus. It is widely believed that Clifton's history has not yet been written, and that the evidence with which to do it has not survived. Neither statement is true, although some of the evidence in the Merchant Venturers' Archives has not been available until recently. I gladly acknowledge the debt I owe to the published work of Mary V. Campbell, Patrick McGrath, John S. Moore, Elizabeth Ralph and David Richardson who have studied particular aspects of Clifton's history. My involvement over nearly 20 years in teaching classes in local history for what was called the Extra-Mural Department of Bristol University has made me aware of a widely-felt student need for some help in tracing source material and for some guidance as to its relevance.

Bristol's former City Archivist, Elizabeth Ralph, spent 16 years in cataloguing the Merchant Venturers' Archives. In 1988 she produced her printed guide and, of priceless value to students, her separate catalogues of Deeds 1596-1960, and of Leases of land and property. The Merchants' Deeds are comprehensive for three-quarters of the area of the two Manors involved, and I have been privileged to be allowed to use this material without any restrictions, and in complete freedom. All students will be grateful to Elizabeth Ralph for cataloguing the Merchants' records into archive groups and thus enabling specific references to be identified properly. I owe a similar debt to the late Patrick McGrath's work in examining the history of the Merchant Venturers of Bristol. It is a monumental work of remarkable scholarship which I do not believe has yet received the recognition that it merits.

Another formidable source for this book is the microfilm of the 41 Hall Books of Proceedings which are available in the Bristol Central Reference Library. These record the continuous and persistent application of the Merchants over the centuries to a wide variety of concerns, including the administration of their lands, control over the Hotwells, building developments in Clifton, and the navigation of the Avon and the use of port facilities. Also available in the Reference Library is the microfilm in two reels of the 1851 Census of population for Clifton. For the local historian this is a goldmine of information on the first half of the 19th century.

The history of Clifton cannot, of course, be studied in complete isolation from the background of local and national affairs, or without some attention to a comparative study of South Gloucestershire. Here we are fortunate in having the researches of John Moore, together with that of his Extra-Mural classes, using the Probate Inventories for Clifton and Westbury, 1609-1761, in the Bristol Records Office. The inventories record what actually existed at a given time, particularly the composition of wealth in different social groups within the local population and throw much light on the way capital accumulated. His comparative study of the neighbouring manors in south Gloucestershire has been invaluable.

This book is a history of an important suburb of Bristol. I have omitted a certain amount of 'traditional' social history such as religious life, Poor Law developments and education. I have sought to offer to those interested in the development of Clifton the new material that has become available in the Merchant Venturers' Archives and have sought to put this source material in context by research carried out in the P.R.O. in Chancery Lane, and in the Bristol Records Office. The new source material has in large measure determined my concerns and shaped the book, but I have tried to give a balanced view. Readers now have available references to a much wider range of evidence with which to make their own appreciations of the heritage that is Clifton.

Last, but by no means least, I must acknowledge the expertise and cheerful cooperation of the staff of the Bristol Record Office, particularly John Williams, Sheila Lang, Richard Burley, Margaret McGregor and Anne Bradley. Similarly I am grateful to the Head of the Chancery Division of the P.R.O., Mr. Evans, for his help, and to Bristol University for making available the Deeds of Clifton properties now owned by the University. I should like to thank Tony Robinson, Treasurer of the Society of the Merchant Venturers, for allowing me over a period of two years to study in the Merchants' Archives without any restriction, and in particular I am grateful to Mrs. Pat Denney, Secretary to the Treasurer, who facilitated my work there in so many ways.

APOLOGIA

... if any of you shall observe any slip of pen, number, marginall, or other small mistake (which, I hope, at the most are few, if any), that yee would reforme them favourably and fairly say ... that men and the works of men are not born perfect and with beards upon their chins ...

John Smith

Lives of the Berkeleys,
1618, II, p.444.

Chapter One

The Beginning of Clifton-on-the-Hill

Visitors to Bristol will usually be taken to see the Avon Gorge and the Suspension Bridge. This excursion will often include a short walk to the Observatory Tower from the top of which one can see a panoramic view. As the visitors look down at the immediate foreground they will notice surrounding earthworks of what has come to be known as Clifton Camp. It covers between three and four acres and consists of two ditches forming three ramparts. On top of one of the ramparts, where the turf has been kicked aside, mortar can still be seen, suggesting that there was probably a wall on it. The entrance, which is on the north-east side, is about eight feet wide and at the time when Seyer was writing there was some sort of stone gateway.[1] William Worcester, writing in 1480, says: 'There remain to this day heaps of scattered stones, large and small, lying in order in a large circuit ...'.[2]

On the other side of the Avon Gorge, through the combe called Stokeleigh Slade, one comes across another series of earthworks called Bower-walls. These contain about seven acres and consist of three ramparts. If one can believe Seyer, writing in 1821, the second rampart had a dry wall two feet thick and 'still two or three feet high, and easily to be traced nearly along the whole line'. The attempt to confirm this line has so far defeated some dedicated searchers. Divided from Bower-walls by the great Stokeleigh Combe and a very thick wood is another series of earthworks even larger in extent. Here again in 1821 Seyer saw a stone wall four feet thick, without mortar, and in places still two or three feet high.[3] These early earthworks were probably no more than hilltop fortifications.

Caesar said: 'the Britons call it a town when they have fortified any woods, difficult of access, with a ditch and rampart; where it is their practice to take refuge in order to avoid the assault of their enemies ...'. There, he says, 'they also drove their flocks and herds'.[4] It is clearly significant that 20 ft. above high water mark by Bridge Valley Road, there was a spring of water which could be relied on if armed men surrounded Clifton Camp. It is interesting that Bower-walls has now become Burwalls, apparently indicating a folk memory that in Saxon times it had once been a 'burg' or fortified place. However, in Alfred's scheme for the defence of Wessex against the Danes, there is not even a mention of Bristol amongst the important boroughs.[5] The earliest reference to Bristol in the Anglo-Saxon Chronicle is in the year 1051,[6] and the earliest known Bristol coin yet discovered is a penny of Ethelred II, who reigned from 978-1016. Clearly therefore, in writing of these hilltop fortifications, Seyer is quite wrong to suggest that 'they are evidently the original settlement, from whence the population of Bristol was derived'.[7]

During the Roman occupation of the area, legionaries left behind, at or near Clifton Camp, coins of Nero, Domitian, Trajan, and other emperors. These coins were found in 1784 by workmen digging the foundations of houses, but unfortunately,

1

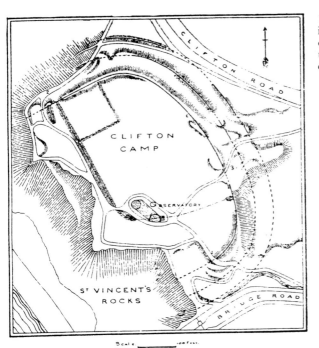

1 & 2. Clifton and Stokeleigh Iron Age camps (Burwalls not illustrated) are dated roughly 500 B.C. to A.D. 43, and they controlled the passage up the River Avon. Clifton enclosed three acres and Stokeleigh six acres. In 1898 two sections of dry stone walling were uncovered at Stokeleigh camp.

CLIFTON CAMP.

STOKELEIGH CAMP.

'a great many more were found by workmen, and embezzled and sold to private gentlemen. A few Saxon coins, silver, were also discovered of Aethelred, with Rex. Angl., and these, with others, are now in my possession'.[8] Very probably, the Romans stationed a detachment of the 2nd Legion at Clifton Camp, as at Blaise Hill and Henbury Hill where similar coins have been found, to act as lookouts. The neighbourhood of such a fortification may have led to a small settlement away from the exposed situation of the hill.

From A.D. 44 to 47, Vespasian's II Augusta legionaries in the south-west fought 30 battles, subjugated two warlike tribes (the Durotriges of Wiltshire and Dorset, and Corio's Dobunni of south Gloucestershire) and captured more than 20 hill strongholds.[9] Vespasian had to rely a great deal on naval support for his legion, and it was once the view that the Roman settlement at Sea Mills, Portus Abonae, had a Claudian origin. However the latest research suggests a Neronian date, matching the evidence of Neronian occupation at the Sudbrook, Gwent, ferry terminal.[10] A probable date for the presence of the fort at Sea Mills is about the mid-50s.

There probably would not have been a Roman trunk road nor a Roman port in the immediate neighbourhood of Bristol had it not been for the Romans' need to subdue the tribe of the Silures across the Severn. Under the bungalows of Hadrian Close on the Portway lie the quay, fort, storehouses and granaries of the supply base of the II Augusta Legion. All kinds of supplies and troops could be assembled here in complete safety and then ferried across to the Welsh shore. The known area of Portus Abonae is about twenty-two acres and it lies between Roman Way, Sea Mills Lane, the Portway and the rivers Trym and Avon.[11]

Crossing the Downs to reach Portus Abonae, and following the present Pitch and Pay Lane and Mariners' Drive, is the Roman road from Hanham and Bitton to Bath (Aquae Sulis). For part of the way, as it crosses the Downs on the left hand side of Stoke Hill Road, the road is within the parish boundaries of Clifton. The road is beneath the turf but it is possible to see the raised line of it as it nears The Old Halt. 'Antoninus' in his Itinerary, written about A.D. 200-250, describes the road as 'Another route from Isca to Calleva, 103 miles: Venta Silurum, 9 miles; Abona 9 miles; Traiectus 9 miles; Aquae Sulis 6 miles'.[12] On at least one occasion a cross section of the road has been examined.[13]

For another two centuries there were Roman legionaries in the area but in the late 260s there was a change. In 255 legionaries and auxiliaries were withdrawn for campaigns in Germany, and the Bristol Channel was under attack from sea raiders, probably from Ireland. Several coin hoards found in the area date from A.D. 270 to 296, implying raids and fear of pillaging. By A.D. 351 there was a large scale withdrawal of troops to support the claims of Magnentius against Constantius II (337-361), and from the 360s sea raiders again appeared in the Bristol Channel. Coins found at the Sea Mills site show continued occupation at the end of the fourth century, but a coin of Constantius II along with four skulls and a quantity of human bones in the well at Brislington Villa, and the destruction of the West wing and the bath suite at Kingsweston Villa, indicate evidence of raids. Plague in A.D. 443 may have been the main agent however in decimating communities in the region.

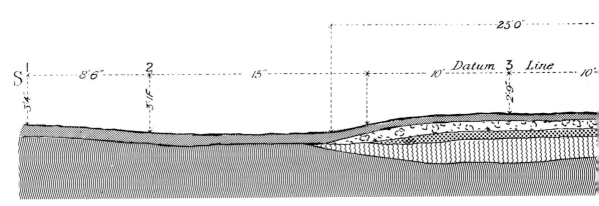

3. Sea Mills was the only urban centre in the Bristol area during the first century and served as a ferry point between the two sides of the Bristol Channel, and as a local market. This Roman road linked Sea Mills,

In A.D. 557 the Anglo Saxon Chronicle records: 'Cuthwine and Ceawlin fought against the Britons and slew three kings, Coinmail, Condidan and Farinmail, at a place which is called Dyrham, and they captured three cities, Gloucester, Cirencester and Bath'.[14] It is from the Anglo Saxons that the names Cliff and tun (an enclosure) come. It means literally the cleft place or place of cliffs, and it is past these cliffs in 1051, and again in 1061 that the Anglo Saxons Harold and Leofwine sailed with their fleet, from Bristol, to harry Ireland and Wales. Shut off from the rest of the country by hills and almost impassable forests, Bristol had developed in the one way open to it – the sea. By the time of the Norman Conquest Bristol had become one of the chief trading ports of the country, and in Domesday Book was assessed at 110 marks of silver. This was a very considerable sum, higher than that paid by any other towns except London, York, Lincoln and Norwich. Its 21 acres were already surrounded by a wall strong enough in 1068 to resist Harold's sons when they sailed up the Avon from Ireland with a large host.[15]

It was Swein, the provost of Bristol, who held the manor of Clifton from Edward the Confessor, and it is he who is mentioned in Domesday Book. The Survey was ordered by William I and completed and laid before him at Winchester, Easter 1086. Within Gloucestershire, in Swinehead Hundred, the Clifton entry reads:

> Roger son of Ralph holds a manor named CLIFTON which Swein the reeve of Bristol, held from King Edward; he could go with this land where he would, and gave no revenue whatever for it. 3 hides. [1 hide in Gloucestershire = 287 acres]. In lordship 3 ploughs; (ploughteams) 6 villagers and 6 smallholders with 2 ploughs. 3 slaves; meadow, 8 acres. The value was 100s; now 60s.[16]

It appears that Swein had the special privilege in Edward's reign of being non-resident, and of not having to give the king any of the produce, by way of tax. Some idea of what these taxes might have been is provided by Offa's Charters, 793-6,

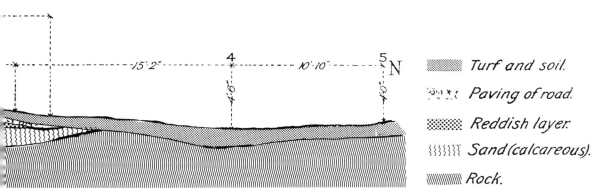

Turf and soil.

Paving of road.

Reddish layer.

Sand (calcareous).

Rock.

through Bitton, to Bath (founded at some date close to A.D. 76). A cross section excavated at the beginning of 1900 revealed a surface area of paving about 20 ft. wide laid on red sand.

granting land at Westbury and Henbury to Worcester Cathedral. They list the only known dues that a Saxon king could draw from his manors: 'two tuns of pure ale [1 tun = 252 gallons], and a coomb full of mild ale and a coomb full of Welsh ale, and seven oxen and six wethers and 40 cheeses'.[17] The value of the land had deteriorated since King Edward's time, and after the Conquest it continued as one of the royal estates. Despite its very small population of 15 working males and their families, the Domesday entry supposedly refers to the whole, undivided, manor of Clifton. Much later, in 1463, it was split into two parts by John Carpenter, Bishop of Worcester and Westbury. The manor was coterminous with the existing parish boundaries.[18]

When Sir Robert Atkyns wrote his *History of Gloucestershire*, he referred to another passage in Domesday Book, folio 163, which he supposed to relate to Clifton. Recent research has shown that the Clifton referred to, together with Chire, Noeunt and Ladeuent, are a schedule of lands seized from the See of Worcester by the Danes in 1041. This was a consequence of a revolt against Danegeld in the time of Ethelred the Unready. The Clifton referred to is Clifton on Teme.[19] Had Robert Atkyns found so unimportant a parish as rural Clifton more interesting, with an ancient family seat of an historic estate like Ashton Court within its boundaries, he might have taken more trouble in tracing its descent.

The manor of Clifton followed the boundaries of land grants in the Saxon period, affecting particularly Westbury and Stoke Bishop. The Charter of 883, witnessed by King Alfred, is the first to state boundary marks. It was followed by the Charters of 969 and 984, the latter describing 10 boundary markers. The exact present location of some of these boundaries is open to some debate.[20] When Clifton's boundaries were surveyed in 1627, in the third year of King Charles I's reign, they followed fairly unchanging landmarks, for the most part:

.LXXV. **R** Terra Rogerij Filij Rad.
Rogervs filius Rad ten uñ Maneriũ *noe Clistone In Sineshoved Hd.*
qd tenuit Seuuin ꝑpoſit de Briſtou de rege. E. 7 poterat
ire cũ hac tra quo uoleꝧ. nec aliquā firmā inde dabat.
Ibi. iii. hidæ. In dñio ſunt. iii. car̃. 7 vi uiłłi 7 vi. bord
cũ. ii. car̃. Ibi. iii. ſerui. 7 viii. ãc ꝑti.
Valꝧ. c. ſolid. Modo. lx. ſolid.

75   **LAND OF ROGER SON OF RALPH**

   In SWINEHEAD Hundred
1   Roger son of Ralph holds a manor named ᴄʟɪꜰᴛᴏɴ which Saewin,
      the reeve of Bristol, held from King Edward; he could go with this
      land where he would, and gave no revenue whatever for it. 3 hides.
      In lordship 3 ploughs;
         6 villagers and 6 smallholders with 2 ploughs.
         3 slaves; meadow, 8 acres.
      The value was 100s; now 60s.

4. Domesday Book entry relating to Clifton in Swineshead Hundred.

From the passage of Rownham by the water of Avon [the swing bridge of the Cumberland Basin], to the Chapel of St Vincent [along the Hotwell Road], and thence by the aforesaid water to Wallcam Slade [the Gully], and thence to a place called the Hawthorne [the site of the water tower on Durdham Down], thence to a certain stone called a Merestone, lying between the Chapel of St Lambert and the Royal Road [Blackboy Hill], and thence by aforesaid road to Smock Acre [roughly Whiteladies Road], and thence to the Whitestile and thence to Dedistone stile [both probably between Tyndall's Park and Berkeley Place], and thence to the Lyme Kyles [the bottom of Jacob's Well Road], and thence by the water of the aforesaid Avon to the aforesaid passage [along the river to Rownham].[21]

The Chapel of St Vincent was described by William Worcester in 1481 as 120 ft. from the top and 240 ft. from the foot of St Vincent's Rock, and as being 27 ft. long and 9 ft. wide. It stood upon a projecting ledge of rock which has either been dislodged or deliberately brought down. In the *Survey Viewe and value of the Manor of Clifton (nigh the Cittee of Bristol)*, made in 1625, it is stated that Ralph Sadleir had retained for 100 years 'St Vincent's Chapel with all commodities thereunto belonging ... and all manner of haukes'.[22] The Avon Gorge was famous as a breeding ground for hawks, and Sir Ralph Sadleir had been the chief falconer to Queen Elizabeth. By retaining the Chapel and its surroundings, while letting out the rest of the manor by indenture in 1579, he had preserved his sporting area and training ground for hawks.

The area of Clifton mentioned in the Domesday survey is three hides. The average area of a hide in the whole shire of Gloucestershire was 287 acres. Sometimes only arable land was registered, so Clifton Wood, which then covered 100 acres, would not have been included. Thus, in the Domesday survey, Clifton covered 861 acres, whereas Robert Atkyns described Clifton as having 984 acres. Even in his day there was little more than one human being to every two acres, but in 1086 the population was very small indeed. It consisted of six tenant farmers or villeins and their families, six 'bords' with their dependants who provided the lord's table with poultry and eggs, and three serfs who were slave labourers. The serfs and their children were part of the manor, like cattle, and would pass in transfer with the land.[23]

These villagers would have lived in simple homes without chimneys and with thatched roofs. The cottages would have been single-storey dwellings with, perhaps, hurdles separating the cow or pigs at one end. Examples of such buildings can be seen at the Open Air Museum at St Fagans. Outside would be a yard or 'backside' with some structure to shelter the oxen. The eight acres of meadow referred to in the Survey would almost certainly have been Rownham Meads.

The commissioners in 1085-6 also learnt from the jury that Clifton was held from the king by a Norman called Roger fitz Ralph. It has been conjectured that he may have been a younger son of Ralph de Berkeley and therefore nephew to Roger de Berkeley who farmed the King's Barton and was reeve of the great royal estate of Berkeley. He was succeeded in the possession of the manor by William de Clifton. It is not likely that there had been a church at Clifton before this time but in 1154 the right to appoint clergy to the church was given by William de Clifton to the Dean and Canons of the Abbey of St Augustine in Bristol.[24] The Abbey itself had only been consecrated on Easter Day 1148, and founded six years before that. The right of appointing clergy was confirmed to the Canons by William's son John.[25]

The relationship is not clear, but a lord of the manor, Roger de Clifton, the heir of Elias de Clifton and presumably the grandson of John, gave the Abbey rights to watercourses at Jacob's Well. The charter concerned gave the Abbey 'the common or pasture in his manor of Clifton, and all the water courses between the croft and the house which Adam his bailiff held'. This house is believed to have been at the foot of Honeypen Quarry where the gates of the old churchyard are. He also gave the Abbey all the courses which were upon (or led to) the Canons' conduit at Wodewell (Jacob's Well), towards the hill, which they were at liberty to draw to their conduit from his land at Clifton. Also he gave them the right to have stone from his quarries at Clifton, to build anything within the Abbey gate, provided they did no injury to his own arable land or wood.[26]

It would seem that the Abbey already had a water supply from a conduit on Brandon Hill. Now the monks were obtaining permission to divert additional water-courses from the other side of Jacob's Well road, which was at that date a wooded and rocky valley with a lane running side by side with the Sandbrook stream down to the Avon. In 1987 the long-lost Jacob's Well, a spring used by Bristol's Jewish community for ritual bathing in the 11th century, was discovered by accident. Builders converting a shop at the corner of Jacob's Well Road and Constitution Hill smashed down a wall and found the bathing spring, known as a Mikveh Bath. It is the only one in this country and dates back to between 1000 and 1290. It is made of Bath stone and on the lintel at the entrance is an inscription in Hebrew which reads 'To Give One Health and Long Life'.[27] The whole area of the hill was dotted with springs and at that date heavily wooded, with many wild animals. The monks of St Augustine's actually kept a pack of hounds to enjoy hunting, and were reprimanded for this by their bishop in 1320. Ignatius de Clifton, who was probably Roger's son, was a witness in 1239 to the important agreement in Bristol's history whereby part of Canon's Marsh was conveyed to the town to enable a new channel to be cut for the Frome.[28] He had been Lord of the Manor for at least four years before this.[29] In 1255 the custodian of the manor of Clifton for the new heir enclosed some of the Common to make a warren. This had implications not only for the people of Clifton but also to the citizens of Bristol who had hitherto exercised their customary right to graze their working cattle on the Common land of Clifton on the annual payment of two pence for each animal.[30] This young heir was the son of Sir John St Lo of Newton St Loe, who had died in 1254.

The manor remained in the hands of the St Lo family for four generations until the fifth Sir John St Lo was survived by three daughters and coheirs, Joan aged eleven, Ela aged six, and Elizabeth the youngest. The manor was divided into thirds. The eldest sister married Sir John Chideock of Dorset who died in 1391. By 1423, his grandson, Sir John Chideock, had inherited one third of the manor. The second daughter, Ela, had been married twice, firstly to Thomas de Bradstone and then to Sir Richard Seymour. Her son and heir, Sir Richard Seymour, died in the same year as his mother, 1409, but he left an heiress, born posthumously, called Alice. Her uncle looked after her estate until she grew up and she married Lord Zouche of Harryngworth. Her grandson, John, Lord Zouche, inherited one third of the manor but at the age of eight he was attainted by Henry VII in 1485 for supporting Richard III at Bosworth Field. His estates were forfeited but restored in 1509. He then sold his third of Clifton manor to John Brook and his wife Joan. This was described as one third of 300 acres of land, 60 acres of meadow, 100 acres of wood and 200 acres of pasture, with appurtenances.

The youngest of the St Lo daughters, Elizabeth, married William de Botreaux of Cornwall who died in 1394. Their heir, William, was made a baron and was described as 'lord of Clifton'. His daughter and heiress married Lord Hungerford, and the family shields of the Botreaux and the Hungerfords hung in Clifton church tower.[31] We now need to bring these thirds of the manor together again.

The third belonging to Sir John Chideock had by 1470 been acquired by Richard Amerycke, one of the wealthy customs collectors of Bristol at the time of John Cabot. In August 1470 he sold it to John Brook and Joan, his wife. Joan was, in fact, the daughter of Richard Amerycke, and his co-heiress. On Richard Amerycke's death on 9 June 1501 John Brook became an even more wealthy man, and in a position in 1509 to buy another third of the manor of Clifton from John, Lord Zouche. In the previous year Brook had purchased from John Oldemixon some demesne lands in Clifton which must have formed a part of the remaining third, but not the lands styled 'a manor of Clifton' and attached to St Andrew's church, with the right of appointing the clergy. This last ecclesiastical manor had been acquired in 1463 by John Carpenter, Bishop of Worcester and Westbury, and given to Westbury College.

John Brook was a Justice of Assize and sergeant-at-law to Henry VIII. He is buried in St Mary Redcliffe church and commemorated there by a brass. Most of the details about the early history of the manor of Clifton have come from an inquest into his lands held on 25 September 1526 after John Brook's death. His son and heir was Thomas Brook, then aged 36, and there were at least two other sons and two daughters. However, the two thirds of the manor came to Joan Brook, John's wife. She died in December 1539, and her grandson and heir, Hugh, was the son and heir of the Thomas Brook who had died during his mother's lifetime.

Hugh Brook, aged 22, inherited not only Clifton, but lands in Long Ashton, Portishead and Backwell. He chose to live at Lower Court in Long Ashton and is buried in the parish church there. He left four daughters as co-heiresses, Elizabeth, Frances, Susan and Alice. In 1676 the Society of Merchant Venturers purchased three quarters of the manor of Clifton from the descendants of these four daughters. This is described in detail in chapter three and will not be repeated here.

From 1463 to 1544 Westbury College appointed curates to serve St Andrew's, Clifton. These curates had no freehold in the church and were probably as poor as the tenants in the farms around St Andrew's. They were essentially parish priests, not vicars. The lands around the original home farm by the church were tenancies of the Dean and Chapter of the newly revivified Westbury College. Bishop Carpenter (1444-76) gave St Andrew's to the college with the proviso that the Dean and Chapter should find a master to teach grammar to those ministering in the church, and to anybody else who came to him, free of charge, and he was to be given free board in the college.[32] The bishop gave them the parish church of Kempsey and its dependent chapels, and King Edward IV in 1464 gave the college the manor of Elmstree in Tetbury, in 1465 the custody of the hospital of St Lawrence, Bristol, and in 1468 the manor and church of Astley in Worcestershire. It must have helped from 1469-74 to have the very rich and powerful merchant William Canynges, five times Mayor of Bristol, as dean of the college.[33] Bishop Carpenter chose to be buried in the chancel of Westbury church in 1476, rather than in Worcester Cathedral.

When the Reformation Parliament was summoned by Henry VIII and began its meetings on 3 November 1529, few people could have imagined the vast changes that would sweep through religious institutions in the next few years. Within 10 years the wealthy and powerful religious houses whose buildings had dominated the Bristol skyline had ceased to exist. In 1534 Dean Barlow, and the fellows of Westbury College, and one of the prebendaries, acknowledged the royal supremacy.[34] On 10 February 1544 the college was surrendered into the king's hands. The possessions of the college, apart from the ecclesiastical manor of Clifton, included the manors of Westbury, Wormington, Foxcote, Dowdeswell and Elmstree in Gloucestershire; Astley, Shelve, Monehills, Greveley and Longborough in Worcestershire; Bereford in Warwickshire; the hospital of St Lawrence, Bristol; and the rectories of Westbury and Kempsey.

The rents from all these lands supported a dean, five prebendaries, a sub-dean, Bishop Carpenter's chaplain, a schoolmaster, eight Fellows, four clerks, six aged priests, twelve choristers and the almshouses for six poor men and six widows.[35] Jobs were found for some of the clerics. Dean Barlow, for instance, was appointed by

Nicholas Thorne to supervise the foundation of Bristol Grammar School. In 1542 a new diocese of Bristol was created, with its own bishopric, and parish clergy were needed to serve within the new structure. What happened to the lands of the ecclesiastical manor of Clifton now that the college was dissolved? This is to form the subject of the next chapter.

On 24 March 1544 Henry VIII granted to Sir Ralph Sadleir and to Ellen his wife, for 1,000 marks, the whole site of the college of Westbury together with the 'manors, lordships, lands, tenements and other premises ... arising from thence', including 'a manor in Clifton previously belonging to the Dean and Canons of Westbury'. Sir Ralph Sadleir married Ellen Mitchell, a laundress in Thomas Cromwell's service, while her former husband was alive. The offspring of this marriage were illegitimate at the time but Sir Ralph secured a special Act of Parliament in 1546, the 37th year of Henry's reign, which set the matter right. Sir Ralph was a great survivor. He was appointed a privy councillor and Secretary of State by Henry VIII, and like Talleyrand's aristocrat in the French Revolution, he 'survived' the reigns of Edward VI and Mary, to emerge as chief falconer to Queen Elizabeth. He was knighted for bravery at the Battle of Musselburgh, and was made custodian of Mary Queen of Scots at Tutbury Castle in 1585. He died at Stondon in Hertfordshire.[36]

Thomas Sadleir, his heir, succeeded to the estate, and at his death on 5 January 1606, his son Ralph inherited the manor of Clifton. Ralph Sadleir sold the manor in 1659 to Frances Chamber, a widow, who then married John Good of Clifton. His sons, John and Arthur Good, sold it in 1668 to Gabriel Deane and Abel Kelly. It was from the heirs of Deane and Kelly that the Society of Merchant Venturers acquired the manorial rights to the wastes, the Common, the springs and the quarries, but not to the enclosed lands which were retained. From March 1694 the Society ordered that the manorial court should be held, and that the perambulation of the parish boundaries should take place.[37] Thus the Society was able to bring together once more the historical manor of Clifton and was henceforth able to regulate much of the development in the environs of the Hotwell and Rownham Meads as well as that of Clifton-on-the-Hill.

Probably not much had really changed. The old church of St Andrew seems to have survived the slings and arrows of the Reformation more successfully than the much more important church at Westbury. Whereas at Westbury Bishop Carpenter's tomb was desecrated and the alabaster figures from the high altar were broken up and the fragments thrown into the small crypt chapel under the chancel, at St Andrew's no such damage was recorded.[38] While from All Saints' church in the centre of Bristol 21 loads of stone rubble were taken from the nave in 1550,[39] it is not until 3 June 1729 that the Vestry Books of St Andrew's state that it was proposed 'to take down the Screen on the passage into ye Chancel'. It had evidently survived through all the religious upheavals. Despite all the changes of ownership of the manors, the small dairy farms clustered around St Andrew's and the Green, the field boundaries, the limekilns and quarries, remained largely recognisable until the middle of the 18th century.

Chapter Two

Clifton from the Time of Thomas Cromwell until the end of the 17th Century

At the beginning of Henry VIII's reign one of the two manors of Clifton, together with the manors and lands of St Lawrence's hospital, was attached to the collegiate church and college of Westbury-on-Trym. When Thomas Cromwell's agents visited places like Westbury they asked 86 questions about numbers, finance, good learning and professionalism. Colleges like Westbury argued that their main function was to offer prayers 'for the souls of the said founders and their heirs'. Similarly they argued that they were important as sources of hospitality for travellers, in their alms-giving to the poor and as educational establishments, but this did not save them. In 1536, 220 were closed.[1] Some heads of Houses retired to the universities like Abbot Austen of Rowley who went to Trinity Hall, Cambridge, or Abbot Alynge of Waverley who became Head of an Oxford College. Some became bishops or deans in the new sees.

At Westbury, as we saw in the last chapter, Dean Barlow was appointed by Nicholas Thorne to supervise the foundation of Bristol Grammar School. Ordinary monks were offered transfer to 'capacities' (becoming secular clergymen) and the P.R.O. has the records of over 3,000 pensions paid out by the Court of Augmentations and its successor, the Court of Exchequer. However, one recent estimate puts the number of unpensioned religious as high as 10 per cent.[2] We can be more precise about what happened to their lands. On the 24th day of March, in the 34th year of his reign, Henry VIII granted to Sir Ralph Sadleir and to Ellen his wife, for 1,000 marks, ... the whole site of the collegiate church of Westbury-on-Trym, together with the lordship, manors, rectories and lands of the College, the manor of Clifton, the rectory and church of Westbury and Henbury, with the tithes and also the tithes of Lawrence Weston, Aust etc., and the site manors, lands etc. of St Lawrence hospital.

The papers of the Sadleir family, which would have thrown much light on these early events, have been dispersed and probably lost. The Sadleir's chief residence was at Stondon, Herts., and a fragment of their papers, preserved by the Hertford solicitors, Hare and Sons of Much Hadham, probably represents part of these archives.[3] These concern Stoke Bishop, Henbury-in-Salt Marsh, Lawrence Weston, Stowick and Compton Greenfield. Other fragments have survived among the records of the Astry and Smyth families who eventually purchased the manor of Henbury. The author found further Sadleir records in a box of unsorted papers, ostensibly concerned with the Victoria Rooms. These were leases relating to a commonfield called Hawefield in Henbury.[4]

Robert Atkyns tells us that Sir Ralph Sadleir's grandson, Ralph Sadleir, was lord of the Clifton ecclesiastical manor in 1608.[5] During the time Ralph owned the manor, Henry Lilly produced his remarkable *Survey of the Manor, 1625*. He died in 1638. The Survey records that William Newce was the lord's tenant of the manor from 1579 and it would appear, from the evidence of the earliest surviving lease of 1596, that it was during the late Tudor period that the final stages of the enclosure of Clifton's old open fields occurred.

> One peece or parcell of pasture ground conteyninge by estimation one acre and a halfe ... lying in a place called the Great Poole, in a Close of pasture there lately inclosed out of the Northffield of Cliffdon aforesaid, together with six acres of arrable ground ... lyinge in the said Northffield, called or known by the name of the Six Acres ...[6]

Lilly described 12 acres still to be enclosed as '... a peice of stoney, Rockey ground, lyeing on Durdom Downe called Shortgrove, reputed as Common, and may be inclosed at the Lord's plesure'.[7] This same area of 12 acres had been described in the lease of 1596 as 'woods and woody ground'.

The former open field known as Northfield was also called Greatfield in a lease of 1690: 'Two grounds called Nyne Acres, One ground called Causeway Close conteyning seaven acres ... And one ground in the Greatfield, alias Northfield, lying next to Landsfield, conteyning seaven acres'.[8] There are several references to the Greatfield in 1652, 1676, 1677 and 1690.[9] It seems also to have been known as Furtherfield. On several occasions at the end of his 1625 Survey, Lilly, when describing Closes without names, refers to them as being in Clifton's Netherfield, or to 'Further Clifton Field', as, for example: 'One piece or plot of arable land lying in Clifton's Netherfield, containing, by estimation, 3 roods and 20 perches ...'.[10]

Dividing the two great medieval fields was the wayne way for horse and cart called Millmote Lane or later Gallows Acre Lane, described by Henry Lilly in 1625. This lane or wayne way divided Gallows Acre and Six Acres on the one side from Westfield on the other. Running nearly parallel with Millmote Lane was another 'common field way' along the line of the present College Road and Lansdown Road. Lilly called this 'a wayne way leading from Durdom Downe into Netherfield'. Running between the two wayne ways was Ten Acres which comprised two enclosed pieces of meadow 'abutting east on Millmote Lane ... and extendeth in length betweene a common field way and A. Hodges' land on the North part ...'. He describes another wayne way 'in further Clifton Field' when describing a little Close called Pitt Acre, bounded on the south by Millmote Way.

Although the lands of the Clifton manors had been enclosed by 1625, Lilly is able to continue referring to the older field patterns of wayne ways and lanes, which would have changed very little, if at all, since the Dispersion of the Church lands. Useful in this context is a less well known map of Clifton, by G. E. Hammersley, hanging in the Merchant Venturers' museum. It was drawn in 1746, the same year as de Wilstar's map, and emphasises wayne ways and footpaths (F.P.), around and into the two great fields on either side of Millmote Lane. It also reveals boundaries and the sites of the meer stones across Durdham Down. I have not found any reference in the Hall Books as to who commissioned the map, but it is helpful in revealing the major field patterns in a way that Wilstar does not.

Nearby, the village of Westbury appears to have been surrounded by two open fields, Eastfield and Westfield, the names of which survived into the 19th century. Moore shows that some open field agriculture still remained on the fringes of the

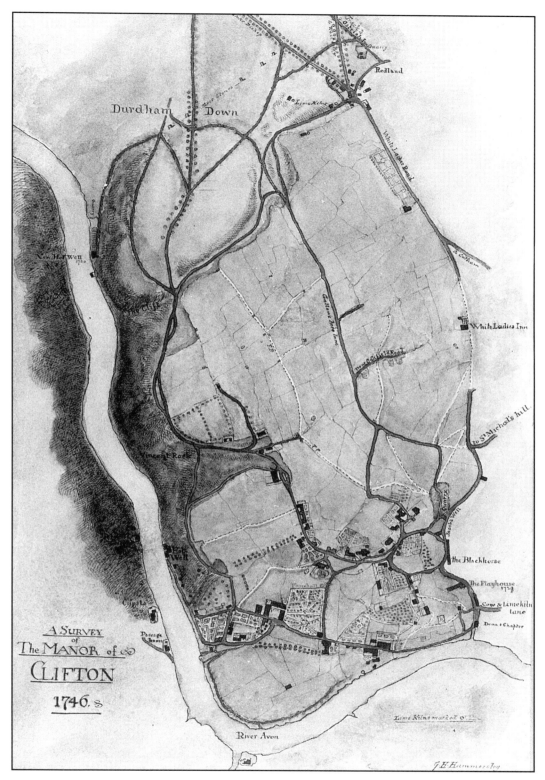

Durdham Down

New Hot Well
1700

Redland

Lime Kilns

White Ladies Road

White Ladies Inn

to St Michael's hill

the Blackhorse

The Playhouse
1744

Cow & Limekiln lane

Down & Chapter

Vincent Rock

Hot Well

Cupilo

Passage house

A SURVEY
of
The MANOR of
CLIFTON
1746.

Lime Kilns market

River Avon

J. E. Hammersley

5. A Survey of the Manor of Clifton, 1746. This survey, by G. E. Hammersley in 1746, was given to the Society of Merchant Venturers by J. Osborn. It reveals the Meere stones across Durdham Down to the water tower, the lime kilns near Blackboy Hill, the playhouse at the bottom of Jacob's Well Road, the new hotwell, the great wayne ways for horse and cart and 'Cupilo', which may have been an early brassworks.

area into the 17th century at Henbury, Kingsweston and Shirehampton, but were enclosed during the 18th century.[11] This process of agricultural change occurred because of the need for greater efficiency in food production. In the great open fields one holding consisted of many strips, each a furrow-long (furlong), scattered between each of the open fields.

It may be that the origin of the division in the open fields arose as the land was gradually taken into cultivation, the strips being shared among those undertaking the task. It was the furthest outlying land, like Shortgrove, that was the last to be enclosed. After the crop had been lifted, the land was a common pasture, either for a month or so (when the winter wheat was followed by spring barley) or more than a year (when spring barley was followed by a year's fallow and then winter wheat). This required common regulation through an elected 'hommage' or council. The hommage of the manor arranged the times of the communal ploughing and sowing thoughout the year. The open field method of farming was typified therefore by excessive subdivision and dispersion of holdings. Moore makes the point that this system was inevitably orientated towards arable farming and that meadow and woodland were scarce.[12] Animals were herded together indiscriminately on the common waste, or in one of the great fields, making selective breeding of stock impossible.

Greater efficiency in food production was made necessary because of a number of factors affecting the region as a whole. Bristol had become a major centre for many industries by the 17th century and its greatness depended on its trade. Over 80 skilled trades were present in Bristol in the Elizabethan period, and many other trades existed which did not require a formal apprenticeship.[13] These trades provided a wide range of finished goods, both from locally produced articles, or from those imported from overseas or London. Proximity to such a regional centre for the collection and redistribution of goods provides a partial explanation for Clifton's population changes and for the absence of many skilled trades in the village.

By analysing the evidence in John Smyth's *Men and Armour for Gloucestershire in 1608*, John S. Moore has drawn our attention to the significance of Thornbury as a market town to the north of Clifton. Proximity to such a redistribution and industrial centre as Bristol, together with a flourishing market town like Thornbury, explains why 71.4 per cent of Clifton's working inhabitants in 1608 were able to specialise in agriculture, 14.2 per cent in maritime occupations, 9.5 per cent in the clothing trades and only 1.5 per cent in food and distribution. Moore's analysis of Smyth's occupational census for the surrounding rural villages in south Gloucestershire, such as Henbury, Almondsbury, Alveston, Stoke Gifford and Westbury for example, shows a percentage for all parishes in agriculture as 82.2 per cent, 2.6 per cent in maritime occupations, 6.5 per cent in the clothing trades and 2.8 per cent in food and distribution.[14] The overall impact of Bristol as 'the metropolis of the West', together with Thornbury's market, was clearly felt throughout south Gloucestershire.

Another factor which limited the rapid development of industry in the Clifton area was lack of accessible raw materials. Moore's extra-mural classes used the probate inventories in the B.R.O. for the period 1609-1761, to provide evidence to enlarge our knowledge of the development of the Clifton – Westbury-on-Trym area. These inventories reveal the fascinating fact that coal only very gradually came into use as a domestic fuel. During the period, only eight inventories out of 246 studied contained revealing items such as: 'One pair of Grates, One pair of Andirons, two pair of Tongs and one fire shovell, 10s. 0d.'.[15] Coal would have had to be brought overland by carts, or by barge down the Avon, from the Kingswood coalfield, and this made it expensive compared with wood. A small amount of lead mining on the Downs, and some lime burning for mortar, were virtually the only industries, apart from agriculture, until the development in Lower Clifton of port employments, the glass industry and lime kilns. This is the subject of another chapter.

Nearly half of the inventories studied by Moore's group relates to the non-agricultural section of the local population and so does not represent a true reflection of the occupational distribution of the Clifton – Westbury area. Many workers at the lower end of the social scale possessed less than the minimum £5's worth of moveable goods which was the level below which it was not necessary to go through probate. Nevertheless these inventories provide an insight into the range of occupations, although the occupation groups are very unevenly recorded. Moore's work in analysing south Gloucestershire villages as a whole shows a similarity with the general conclusions that can be drawn from the inventories about Clifton's housing. The largest houses, having nine or more rooms were, with one exception, occupied by the richer yeomen and gentry. Houses from six to nine rooms were mostly occupied by yeomen's families. Husbandmen generally had four to seven rooms per house. The very poorest recorded generally lived in two-storey cottages with two to four rooms.[16]

The specific sizes of houses on the west side of Jacob's Well Road were recorded on map 5 of de Wilstar's maps of 1746. Much additional information is to be found in the Merchant Venturers' archives on the size and cost of houses in Clifton. The larger messuages and the public house *The Sign of the Crown and Anchor* for example, were 43 × 34 ft., 60 × 34 ft., 57 × 25 ft. Yeomen's families occupied houses typically 28 × 26 ft. and 29 × 25 ft., while the third group occupied tenements 19 × 16 ft., 19 × 14 ft., 20 × 16 ft. All the houses would have had two storeys and the larger ones probably three. There is a hint that tiled roofs were superseding thatched roofs by the end of the 17th century.[17]

The village green was roughly in front of where Goldney House stands today, but was much larger in area. The pound, in which stray cattle were placed until claimed, was clearly marked on the de Wilstar map of 1746. Fronting the green were two large houses and a number of cottages. The most important of the houses was the old Manor House, purchased in 1607 for £369 by the Hodges family as part of an estate of 17 acres, from the descendants of William Clarke and Francis Brooke.[18] By the time the Merchants' Hall bought the larger manor it was hardly recognisable:

All that the scite or ruins of the late Great House or Capital Messuage situate in Clifton aforesd. and parcel of the said Manor, which were heretofore burnt down by ffire and were afterwards in the holding of Mary Hodges, Spinster, called the Old Castle, but the same has been sometime since converted into a Messuage or Tenement and is now in the tenure of the said Joseph Wakley Phippen ...[19]

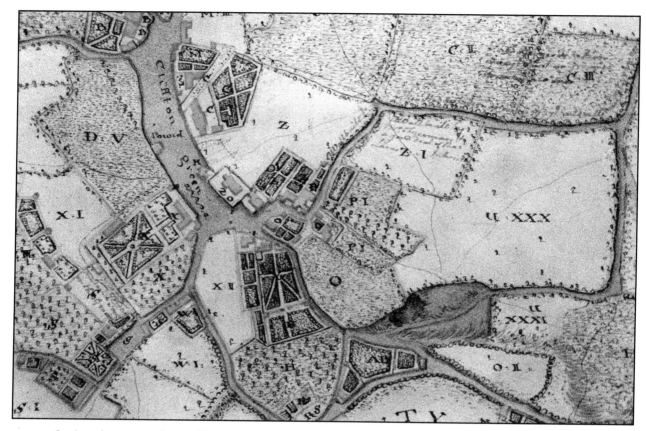

6. An enlargement of part of Jacob de Wilstar's map 4 of the estates belonging to the Merchants' Hall. The map shows Goldney House and estate in the centre (X, XI and XII), the village pound for stray animals, and St Andrew's (20). At the end of the Green and marked 'O' is the site of Hodges' old Manor House, orchard and close, owned in 1746 by Mrs. Wakley Phippen.

It was on the site of the old Manor House that John Hodges subsequently built his Queen Anne house which is now Church House. Adjoining this were the three acres of meadow known as Home Close, and the estate also contained the church and churchyard of St Andrew's. The second substantial house, to the west of St Andrew's, was known as the Parsonage, and in 1625 it was occupied by Andrew Whittington. The Parsonage had a courtyard, barn, stables, wainhouse and garden together with 59 acres of land. It was bounded by the green to the south, by the church to the west and by a lane on the east side of the church which must be Clifton Road. The northern boundary was a six-acre field called Home-Leys which must be the present churchyard.

The other subtenants and customary tenants lived in buildings described in the 1625 survey such as the one depicted as:

a dwelling house with Barne, Orchard, Garden and Backside, abutting north uppon Clifton Wood and the lands of A. Whittington, Gent. towards the west, the customary land in the tenure of John Hodges, Gent. towards the east, 1 acre 33p.[20]

This house was the original building on the site of what is now Goldney House and formed one of the two buildings held in 1625 by Richard Hilling and John Hodges. John Hodges' house was occupied in 1677 by Lord Folliott, who was accused that year in the manor court of encroaching on the waste.[21] In 1692 the two houses 'wherein the said Thomas, Lord Folliott did formerly inhabit and dwell', were settled on Rowland Baugh of Lower Aldon, Shropshire, who married Mary, one of Lord Folliott's daughters.[22] In 1694 Roland Baugh, who had obviously decided to remain in Shropshire, let the property to Thomas Goldney the younger, grocer, for £150 and a yearly rent of 2 shillings. Goldney was to have the first option on the property and in June 1705 he bought it.[23] Clustered around the green therefore, forming the nucleus of the village, were the two substantial buildings, two lesser ones and about twelve farmsteads with yards, backsides, wainhouses and stables. The whole population of the parish, including those living along the river, was estimated in 1712 to be about 450, of whom 10 were freeholders. The total number of houses in the parish then numbered 90, probably five-sixths of the parishioners residing on the low ground.[24]

This was the scene that greeted Prince Rupert's 14 foot regiments, two wings of horse, his life guards and nine troops of dragoons, when they arrived from Oxford on 23 July 1643. On 13 July 1643 William Waller had been defeated at Roundway Down by Prince Maurice and his army was destroyed as a fighting force. It seemed the opportune moment to recapture Bristol, described by Prynne as 'a place of the greatest consequence of any in England, next to London, as the metropolis, key, magazine of the West'.[25] On the eve of the Civil War Bristol's population was about fifteen thousand which was not large when compared with London, but it was a flourishing port trading to Ireland, Spain, Portugal and France. The city had endeavoured to remain uncommitted on both religious and political matters and was not anxious to place its fortunes at the disposal of either King or Parliament.[26] On 9 December 1642, however, parliamentary forces had managed to occupy the city. Some citizens risked their lives in March 1643 to win back the city. It is not possible to guess how far this was due to genuine commitment to the royalist cause, but the plot was betrayed and the ringleaders were hanged.

Prince Rupert's forces numbered between 14,000 and 20,000 men when he set up headquarters at the College at Westbury-on-Trym on the afternoon of 23 July 1643. He only had eight cannons however.[27] The attack on the city occurred well before dawn on Wednesday 26 July and Washington's breakthrough took place between 3 and 4 a.m., and by 5 p.m. the city had surrendered at the cost of some 500 royalist lives. For two years a royalist garrison occupied Bristol and the surrounding countryside. It cannot be imagined that the dairy farms that formed the village of Clifton escaped the taxation or seizure of produce needed to maintain the garrison. Bristol paid £150 each week. The Hundreds of Somerset were compelled to pay £850, Wiltshire £500 and the southern part of Gloucestershire £300.[28]

The villages around Bristol were also required to provide labour to build the new fortifications. Workmen were drafted by force from the surrounding countryside, and parishes as far as 15 miles away were issued with warrants for labourers. Latimer found among the State Papers a warrant to one Hundred in Gloucestershire requiring the sending of 60 able men for a 'few days', provided with good shovels and pick-axes, their wages being levied on the Hundred.[29] Further levies upon the inhabitants to increase the trained bands to 1,000 men were enacted in May 1644 and Clifton would not have been exempt. Plague made its appearance in the autumn of 1643 and at first the Corporation attempted to isolate the infected people in Knowle House. However, by the middle of May the plague had reached epidemic pro-portions. There are no trustworthy statistics on this subject, but it is reported that one fifth of the trained bands disappeared and one of the Calendars stated that there were 3,000 victims. By October 1644, however, the weekly total of victims was down to thirty-two.[30] It is apparent that through constant and excessive taxation, uncleared filth, the spread of infection, hunger and the strain of the troops in their houses, the people in the city and nearby villages were in desperate straits.

On 18 August 1645, a year after the king's defeat at Naseby, Sir Thomas Fairfax and the parliamentary armies laid siege to Bristol. As the parliamentary armies approached, all the cattle in the surrounding countryside were driven into the city and large supplies of grain and beer were brought in from Gloucestershire and Wales.[31] Prince Rupert ordered all the villages around the city to be burnt to the ground so as not to provide shelter for the advancing army. Clifton went up in smoke. We must presume that all the farmsteads were destroyed. The Manor House and Parsonage were left as blackened ruins. St Andrew's church was apparently not destroyed, but in 1654 it was in such a dilapidated state that it had to be largely rebuilt, except for the tower. It is possible to assess the extent of the devastation to the village since the manor court met on 3 October 1646 and the copyhold tenants, John Batten and William Bayly (son of Agnes Bayly) and Nicholas Tilly, swore on oath how much damage had been done. Ralph Sadleir had sustained losses amount-ing to at least £845.[32] This probably represents all the buildings on the hill apart from the church, but it is unlikely to include those riverside dwellings where the bulk of the population lived and which may well have escaped the torch. The inventories for John Good, Gent. made on 30 November 1661, for Richard Yeamans, Gent. made on 3 May 1662 and for George Northover, innkeeper, taken 4 December 1667, suggest this to be likely.[33] Either their dwellings had survived with all their possessions intact or they recouped their losses and rebuilt their houses remarkably quickly.

Unfortunately there is a gap in the church registers of St Andrew's between the years 1637 and 1669, so the impact of the plague on Clifton is unknown. Plague was still in the city when the parliamentary armies surrounded Bristol and after the successful attack some of the troops were quartered in infected areas. However the parliamentary armies lost only one man from plague.[34] Victory cost the lives of 200 soldiers and 400 more parliamentary soldiers were wounded.

Two members of Parliament, deputed by the Commons, spent some time in Bristol looking at local problems in 1645. Their Reports to the Speaker throw some light on the country areas around the city. Roving bands of soldiers had taken away

Wee the Tenannts of the Manor of Clifton in the County of Gloster whose names are here subscribed and inhabitants in the Pish of Clifton or neare thereabouts being chardged by the Steward of the said Mannor of Clifton at a Court there holden for the said Mannor the Third day of October 1646 to inquire and to retourne upon our oathes what Losse is fallen unto Raphe Sadleir of Stondon, in the County of Hertford Esqr by ye burninge of his houses or Tenements in the said Manor of Clifton which were burnt by the comands of Prince Rupert a little before his surrenderinge up of Bristoll unto Sir Thomas ffairefax Beinge now uppon the place and well viewinge and consideringe the damage that the said ffire hath done in the said howses or tenements by the buringe theirof doe upon or othes pesent that the Losse which the said **Mr. Sadleir** hath theirby susteyned doth amount unto the value of eight hundred fforty-ffive pownds at the least **In witness wheirof we have all sub-scribed our names or sett our hands this ffirst day of October in the yeare of or Lord God 1646.**

John Batten
Nicholas Tilly
William Bayly

7. A Civil War return of the jury for Clifton, 1 October 1646. Such forms were evidently prepared beforehand, the amounts and dates being filled in and signatures added. John Batten and William Bayly lived in Clifton at the time of Henry Lilly's survey of 1625. This return was bought from a London bookshop in the 1880s by Col. J. R. Bramble, FSA, together with those for Westbury-on-Trym and Stoke Bishop.

the livestock and provisions.[35] The Deputies complained about the cruel pressures, such as beatings, woundings and imprisonment, used in the countryside with no regard to its impoverished state. The sheep, pigs and dairy herds up on Clifton Down would long since have been requisitioned by one or other of the armies. The farm buildings were burnt down in a hurry so the tenants' possessions were mostly destroyed with the cottages. That John Batten and William Bayly were present to swear the oath about damage to Clifton in the manor court on 1 October 1646 indicates that some of the inhabitants were returning. Although in 1700 the Manor House was still a ruin, St Andrew's was rebuilt in 1654 and suggests a community, supported by five-sixths of the parish who lived in the low-lying area by the river, that continued to worship and were optimistic about the future of Clifton.

Evidence for meaningful population figures is hard to find. No returns have survived for the Hundred of King's Barton from the Poll Tax of 1377. Some returns for the county of Gloucestershire have survived for the Poll Tax of 1381, but not for Clifton.[36] Lists of names exist for taxes on subjects' wealth from the reigns of Edward II[37] and Henry IV[38] which do include the Hundred of King's Barton, but do not differentiate the Tything of Clifton. Sixteen such subsidies were granted to the Crown by Parliament between 1290 and 1332, and for some parts of Gloucestershire the names of taxpayers have survived. After 1334 the assessments named only the place paying the tax and not the names of the taxpayers. It is not until 1524-5 that specific taxable individuals in Clifton can be noted with any certainty,[39] and 1535 when able-bodied men between 16 and 60 had to appear, carrying their weapons, for the Militia Muster.[40]

Another source for population figures is the Hearth Tax, devised in the reign of Charles II and abolished after the deposition of James II in 1689.[41] It was levied on all householders and hearth owners within the houses, although exemptions could be claimed on grounds of poverty. The numbers of inhabitants or communicants in each parish were also required for various purposes by the church, from time to time, and some of these estimates have survived.[42]

Clifton is particularly fortunate in that it was described in the 1608 Muster Roll, *Men and Armour for Gloucestershire*, by John Smyth of North Nibley. Born in 1567 he entered the service of the Berkeleys as a boy of 17. He was sent to study at Oxford and the Middle Temple and became Steward of the Hundred of Berkeley in 1597. The whole county was covered by his clerks in three folio books, covering 28 Hundreds and about four hundred manors. Smyth himself was aware of some defects in the Muster Roll. Of Berkeley he said 'many ... made default in this Hundred and appeared not'.[43] If there were defaulters in Berkeley there must have been many more elsewhere.[44] Nevertheless, John Smyth's information is much superior to that available in many other counties.

In 1711 Robert Atkyns gives the number of houses and a population estimate for each parish in Gloucestershire.[45] John Moore has shown that most parishes in south Gloucestershire experienced a moderate population growth during the 16th and the first half of the 17th century. The second half of the 17th century saw a small overall rise in the population of some parishes, while some even saw a slight fall.[46] Clifton's population, on the other hand, doubled during the 16th century, increased again by three-quarters in the first half of the 17th century and trebled by the end of the century. These are trends, and population estimates are as follows:

Date	1524-5	1608	1650	1662	1672	1711
Population	37[47]	78[48]	135[49]	113[50]	324[51]	450[52]

The crucial records for the period are the parish registers of St Andrew's which survived the fire in the 1940 blitz, although the heat caused the parchment in the two early volumes to curl up into a ball. The P.R.O. have done a wonderful job in flattening the pages but many words are indecipherable. Fortunately Dr. Arthur B.

Prowse, M.D., F.R.C.S., churchwarden for 27 years from 1888, transcribed the registers up to 1681.[53] Recently in 1987 and 1989 Mary V. Campbell transcribed and edited these volumes anew for the Bristol Record Society. The early registers 1538-1763, covering baptisms, marriages and burials, are incomplete. The years 1541 and 1542 and from 1641-69 inclusive, are missing, as also are parts of 1638, 1639, 1640, 1670 and 1680. However, Elizabeth Ralph has transcribed the Marriage Licence Bonds granted for Clifton during part of the period covered by the 1538-1681 register.[54] In most instances these give the occupations of the male partner. Mary Campbell's summary of the numbers of entries for each year in the register is included here, as Table I.[55]

By no means all the occupations are mentioned in the marriage registers for these early years. Those recorded include a weaver in 1540 and two miners in 1574:

> Richard Dunstan and John Langton, Straungers, being Myners of Mendippe, did myne and digge for lyme and lead upon the Downe, (by ShortGrove), and being stifled with smoake, dyed, and were buried, the 20 day of Aprill in the yeere above said. (1574)

A merchant was married in 1575, a hooper in 1576, tailors in 1608 and 1636, a saddler in 1610, a parchment-maker in 1618, two husbandmen in 1632 and 1633. Four sailors were entered in 1597, 1613, 1620 and 1675, and four glasshouse workers between 1673 and 1676. A chimneysweep was entered in 1678 and 20 servants and five parsons were either married or buried during the period. From time to time, as in 1619 or 1632, were buried:

> A poore man, no man knew whence he came, nor whither he woulde, died upon the heighway and was buried in Clifton the 2nd day of September 1619.

> 1632, Aug. 2, was buried John Yoonge, a poore wayfaring man.

> 1632, Aug. 9, was buried John Williams, a poore vagrant youth.

Local landowners like Stephen Stringer were married in St Andrew's, although the natal parish of both partners was in the city: '1680, July 13, Stephen Stringer and Catherine Winstone, both of the parish of All Saints, were married'. Our information about the occupational structure in Clifton is slightly increased by the Bristol Marriage Licence Bonds between 1661 and 1700 and the following occupations of grooms or their bondsmen were listed if they resided in Clifton: seven yeomen, five limeburners, two carpenters, eleven sailors, one farmer, four tailors, two glovers, one clergyman, one shipwright, one ship's carpenter, one cordwainer, one millwright, one servant, one surgeon, one winecooper, one sergeweaver, one silkweaver, one chandler, one blacksmith and two gentlemen (Ayliffe Green and Thomas Power). This, however, is not a large enough, nor a random, sample from which to draw any firm conclusions. Not all of those who were married in Clifton necessarily lived there and in 1672-3 for example, out of 12 marriages, over half the parties lived outside Clifton.

On at least four occasions in the register the incumbent at the time wrote alongside the burials 'the plague time'. This occurred in 1553 (22 buried), 1565

Table I

Summary of the number of entries for each year in the register

Year	Marriage	Baptisms M.	Baptisms F.	Burials M.	Burials F.	Year	Marriage	Baptisms M.	Baptisms F.	Burials M.	Burials F.	Year	Marriage	Baptisms M.	Baptisms F.	Burials M.	Burials F.
1538	0	1	2	0	3	1577	2	1	0	1	1	1616	5	2	1	4	2
1539	0	2	1	1	2	1578	5	1	1	1	0	1617	7	2	4	1	1
1540	0	4	4	1	1	1579	3	1	1	2	0	1618	8	1	2	3	0
1541						1580	0	1	2	1	1	1619	8	4	1	4	0
1542						1581	2	0	2	0	1	1620	4	0	1	2	1
1543	0	4	0	1	0	1582	2	2	1	2	1	1621	5	6	4	0	1
1544	0	5	1	0	0	1583	2	3	2	2	0	1622	3	0	0	2	1
1545	0	1	2	2	4	1584	2	0	3	0	2	1623	0	1	3	3	0
1546	0	0	0	2	4	1585	2	1	2	0	1	1624	2	2	3	4	2
1547	0	0	0	1	3	1586	6	3	2	0	2	1625	5	2	1	5	1
1548	1	1	1	2	1	1587	1	4	2	1	1	1626	2	3	3	2	4
1549	2	4	1	4	5	1588	2	3	0	3	3	1627	3	3	2	1	1
1550	1	1	1	0	0	1589	2	5	0	2	1	1628	1	2	3	1	2
1551	3	1	1	1	3	1590	2	2	1	2	0	1629	8	2	1	2	6
1552	1	4	1	0	0	1591	0	0	2	4	4	1630	4	4	4	4	2
1553	4	1	4	14	8	1592	2	3	1	0	1	1631	3	2	1	1	0
1554	2	5	4	1	3	1593	0	0	0	0	2	1632	6	2	2	5	1
1555	1	1	3	1	0	1594	1	1	0	4	0	1633	3	5	1	4	2
1556	0	2	0	1	0	1595	2	2	2	1	0	1634	6	3	3	2	4
1557	0	1	1	1	0	1596	0	2	3	1	2	1635	8	2	1	5	2
1558	1	0	0	3	0	1597	0	2	0	2	0	1636	8	5	4	3	1
1559	2	0	0	3	2	1598	1	1	1	1	0	1637	4	5	3	5	3
1560	2	1	1	0	0	1599	3	2	3	1	3	1638	3	5	1	5	7
1561	3	4	1	1	2	1600	1	0	3	0	0	1670	1				
1562	1	1	2	0	4	1601	0	2	1	3	2	1671	3	3	5	1	0
1563	0	1	0	1	3	1602	0	3	1	4	0	1672	4	6	5	0	2
1564	3	1	5	0	2	1603	3	0	2	6	6	1673	9	6	8	1	2
1565	0	0	1	12	11	1604	3	3	3	2	4	1674	8	8	5	5	1
1566		0	4	0	0	1605	0	3	3	2	2	1675	17	5	6	7	7
1567	2	1	3	0	0	1606	1	0	3	0	5	1676	11	10	9	3	3
1568	2	1	0	0	0	1607	2	5	2	0	1	1677	12	9	3	1	2
1569	1	0	3	0	0	1608	3	2	1	3	5	1678	10	4	3	0	4
1570	2	2	2	1	0	1609	0	1	6	1	0	1679	9	11	6		
1571	2	0	2	1	0	1610	4	5	1	1	4	1680	7	6	6		
1572	1	0	1	1	0	1611	1	2	4	2	1	1681	9				
1573	1	0	1	1	0	1612	0	2	6	1	6			266	239	205	203
1574	1	1	1	2	0	1613	2	2	1	2	1	111	319	505		408	
1575	1	3	2	0	6	1614	2	4	3	1	4	1	3	5		4	
1576	2	2	1	0	1	1615	7	5	6	1	3						

(24 buried), 1575 (6 buried) and 1603-5 (22 buried). It seems possible that there were no adult burials for four years after the plague of 1565, but the absence of infant deaths is surprising. No burials were entered for 1544, 1550, 1552 and 1560, but the number of baptisms stayed fairly constant. Inevitably it has to be asked whether these registers were being kept properly. If one plots decadal figures for baptisms and burials in Clifton 1538-1681, one can see a small population slowly growing after 1600. After the gap in the register between 1638 and 1669, a marked acceleration in population growth appears to have taken place.

There was probably a vicious braking effect against population increase exerted by visitations of the plague in Clifton. The nearby urban centre of Bristol suffered 2,956 deaths during the plague of 1603-5 and Patrick McGrath's estimate of the total population of the city in 1600 is twelve thousand.56 The number of deaths would amount to 25 per cent. If one accepts that the fit adult male population of Clifton in 1608 was 21, according to John Smyth's occupational census, multiplies that by three and a half to produce a population estimate, adds five for the vicar's family, one arrives at a figure of seventy-eight.57 Twenty-two burials between 1603-5, out of a population of 78, amounts to 28 per cent, which must have been devastating to a small community. In 1553, 22 burials during the plague time would probably have been even more traumatic, and the 24 burials in the plague of 1565 quite desperate. For example Francis Peyton during the first two plague years of 1553 and 1565 lost two wives, four children and two servants. Two more of his servants died in the third plague year, 1575.

Table II

Baptisms and Burials in Clifton, 1538 – 1680

Years	Baptisms	Burials
1538 – 48	29	28
1549 – 58	36	45
1559 – 68	27	41
1569 – 78	24	16
1579 – 88	35	24
1589 – 98	28	27
1599 – 1608	42	49
1609 – 18	60	39
1619 – 28	44	37
1629 – 38	56	64
1639 – 69 (missing)		
1671 – 80 (2 years missing)	134	39+

In a small community, based on the manor court where custom ruled, it is at least an arguable thesis that such visitations as 1553 and 1565 would have necessitated major agricultural change. Land would have remained untilled and animals untended. Communal ploughing and sowing would have been more difficult to practise. The heart of the manor lay in its court which served as a registry for all conveyances of manorial land, and promulgated and enforced by-laws or customs. The court fined those who ploughed into the waste or whose cattle strayed. Its proceedings were entered into a court book kept by the lord's steward. Afterwards it was engrossed on parchment as the court roll. Parts of these have survived for surrounding villages, like Henbury, Stoke Bishop, Stowick and Aust, but not for Clifton, although the Merchants' *Abstract of leases*, 1665-1716, contains similar information.58

When manors were about to be sold, a court of Survey was held. The lord commissioned a surveyor to hold an inquisition and he called upon the steward to summon a special sitting. The bailiff called all the tenants to bring in their deeds, copies of court roll and so on, to the court. These were carefully scrutinised by the surveyor whose records were brought together into a Survey Book. The Merchants consulted one of these survey books during their dispute with John Lambe, the Deanes and the Kellys: '... a copy of the Survey Book of Sadleir's manor was obtained from Mr. Justice Cole, Sadleir's Steward, and it was discovered that 'no certain waste is mentioned in it' ...'.[59] Another such survey is the vellum bound book of 19 pages made by Henry Lilly in 1625. From the Survey Book a rent roll was made and copies of this were handed to the bailiff. A copy of one of these rent rolls for Clifton in 1707 has survived in the Merchants' archives.[60] The survey remained in the estate office where it was in everyday use and amendments and additions to it were taken from the lease books.

Lilly's survey of the smaller manor in 1625 tabulates the tenants' names and their status. William Newce is the lord's tenant and under him come six sub-tenants of the demesne lands whose tenures depend on the length of Newce's life. After these come seven customary tenants. Ralph Sadleir was solely concerned with William Newce who held from him. People like Andrew Whittington, John Satchfield and Richard Hilling, the sub-tenants, held land from Newce and paid their rents to him as lord's tenant. Yet they were quite secure in their tenures. As Eric Kerridge has pointed out: 'Had it been otherwise, had farmers not been secure in their farms, they would hardly have undertaken any improvement, let alone the agricultural revolution they actually achieved ...'.[61]

The seven customary tenants included Richard Hilling again, Anthony Hodges, John Hodges, John Batten and Edmond Watts. They held as title deeds certified copies of entries of their holdings and grants in the rolls of the manor court: 'Richard Hilling, aged about 50, holdeth by coppie of court roll according to custome of the said manor ...'.[62] Almost invariably the copyholder for lives paid for his holding an entry fine which had to be 'reasonable'. If the lord and the heir failed to agree on what was a reasonable fine the manor court had to assess the sum with a jury.

On both of the two Clifton manors customary and indentured tenants held land in each. In 1596 John Satchfield leased from William Clarke and Frances his wife, 74 acres of the larger manor, including some 'lately inclosed out of the Northfield',[63] and he was a sub-tenant of William Newce on the smaller manor for four acres three roods.[64] Andrew Whittington married Margaret Young in 1615, when three-quarters of the larger manor was settled on them by John Young. He also held 59 acres, including Clifton Wood, on the smaller manor.[65] Joan Batten held 43 acres on the main manor,[66] and nine acres three roods on the smaller manor.[67] John Batten, aged about forty, and his son George, aged 12, held 36 acres and three roods on the smaller manor and George held land on the main manor in addition.[68] Anthony Hodges held 24 acres and his 19-year-old younger son, John, 12 acres on a smaller manor, but Anthony bought a quarter part of the larger manor for £369 on 24 December 1607.[69] After Andrew Whittington, he thus became the second largest landowner in Clifton.

It was in the interest of these farmers to try to consolidate their holdings by a process of exchange, rather than to try to work fields scattered widely over the two manors. They might do this by an exchange of several pieces of ground together with some cash, which is the way the Merchants and Stephen Stringer chose in 1695.[70] They might simply purchase the desired lands as Stephen Stringer did in 1690.[71] Stringer had acquired John Lambe's quarter of the larger manor as the result of an unredeemed mortgage, after the death of Mrs. Margaret Hodges. This was the quarter part which had been bought by Anthony Hodges in 1607 from Edward, Thomas, Nicholas and Christopher Clarke, the sons of William Clarke and Frances of Minchin Barrow, Somerset. Anthony's son, William Hodges, inherited the share and when his daughter, Elizabeth, married John Lambe in 1657, William settled the estate on them both. Also Stephen Stringer had bought from William Weare that part of the estate of Gabriel Deane, shared between his daughters as coheirs, that had come to Mary Watts. From Edmond Watts, William Weare had bought Whitestile (one acre), Larridge (four acres), four acres of ground next to Howell's Deane, some ground in Clifton's Netherfield and some in Rownham Mead. He sold these to Stephen Stringer in June 1690.[72]

In 1695 Stringer exchanged some quarter parts of ground he owned and which the Merchants wanted, for some three-quarter parts of lands to the north of Clifton which he wanted. The Merchants made up the difference with £60 in cash. The Merchants exchanged their three-quarter parts in Lidfields and Trinmore (10 acres), in ffoxalls (seven acres), in Shortgrove (four acres) and one and a half acres in the Close called Six Acres. Stringer relinquished his one quarter parts in Home Close and the Old Manor House (three acres), seven acres of Rownham Mead, 12 acres of ground called Millmote, four and a half acres of ground in Clifton's Northfield, 12 acres of Shortgrove ('being heretofore wood but now lying waste on the Downe'), nine acres of Causeway Close and four acres of Mead Close.

The exchange permitted both parties to farm and control whole areas instead of trying to cope with dispersed holdings in the open fields such as '... two acres and an half of meadow or pasture ground lying in the Northfield of Clifton aforesid, inter-mixed with four acres and an halfe there ...'.[73] It also enabled Stephen Stringer to sell an integrated estate on 30 July 1698 for £2,075 to Edward Freeman and Ann, his wife, at what must have been a very considerable profit.[74]

The larger landowners in the area encouraged their tenants to shift from arable to more pastoral farming. When Roger Bathron leased to Thomas Gayner Honeypen Hill, the Deans, and the Whitestile in 1676, he stipulated an additional rent of £5 per acre per year 'for every greater or lesser quantity of the ... fields which shall be eared, ploughed or spitted up, digged or converted to tillage ...'.[75] Similarly the Merchants encouraged Mathias Morgan in January 1677 'not to plow any ground, but what have been plowed for 20 years past (if he does, to pay £10 per acre above the rent.)'[76] and also Thomas Garland who leased from them: 'Over and above the said rent to the Lessor, after the rate of £10 per acre, for so much of the said ground as shalle be plowed or counted to arable'.[77]

This active involvement of landowners in Clifton to discourage arable farming is bound to be impressionistic because of the dearth of examples in the B.R.O. and the Merchants' Archives. Moore, however, has researched better documented estates in the region to throw light on land use between 1452 and 1801. He has found that in another part of south Gloucestershire where the open fields still prevailed in the 15th and 16th centuries, 75 per cent or more of the cultivated area was arable, between 6 and 19 per cent pasture, meadow about two per cent and woodland negligible. He found that in some places like Frampton Cottrell change occurred early, and the proportion of arable was reduced to about fifteen per cent. Elsewhere, as enclosure by agreement occurred in the 17th century, arable was reduced to between 22 and 30 per cent, and still further to 15 per cent in the 18th century. Moore says that in the same two centuries he has found that meadow comprised between 10 and 20 per cent and pasture between 20 and 60 per cent of the total area. The major development in the period, he says, was the prevalence of a more flexible interchange of land between arable, pasture and meadow, known as convertible husbandry or up-and-down farming.[78]

On Clifton, the farm bequeathed by John Young, Andrew Whittington and Margaret, his wife, to Anthony Hodges, was the same as that leased by William Clarke of Barrow Minchin, Somerset to John Satchfield in 1596. Both documents describe the land use of each of the fields.[79] The 74½ acres were divided into 14½ acres of arable (19.5 per cent), 41 acres of pasture (55.4 per cent), seven acres of meadow (nine per cent) and woodland 12 acres (16.1 per cent). This was one of Clifton's earliest post-enclosure farms. It comprised:

> Home Close (5 acres of pasture)
> Mead Close (4 acres of pasture)
> The Twelve Acres (12 acres of pasture)
> Lydfield (9½ acres of pasture)
> Trinmore (6 acres of pasture)
> Causeway Close (3 acres of pasture)
> Great Pool (1½ acres of pasture)
>   41 acres of pasture (55.4 per cent)
>
> Rownham Mead (7 acres of meadow)
>   7 acres of meadow (9 per cent)
>
> Northfield (4½ acres and 6 acres arable)
> Shortgrove Close (4 acres arable)
>   14½ acres arable (19.5 per cent)
>
> Shortgrove (12 acres woods)
>   12 acres woods (16.2 per cent)

Lilly's *Survey* of the 208 acres of the smaller manor shows a very similar distribution of land use: arable constituted (20 per cent); meadow, 'meadow or pasture', or pasture (60 per cent); woodland (16 per cent). Moore has pointed out the significance of the flexibility of 'meadow-or-pasture' implying that convertible husbandry was well established by 1625. His wider survey of south Gloucestershire showed that at Olveston in 1610 the Rectory manor contained 86 per cent of 'meadow-or-pasture', and that in 1649, tested by the strains of the Civil War, this flexibility came into its own. It was able temporarily to revert to 30 per cent arable and 20 per cent 'arable-or-pasture'. The trend in south Gloucestershire was towards convertible husbandry biased towards pastoral farming. In this way agriculture in the region became more efficient in supplying food for the Bristol area. New crops were being planted in Flanders with beneficial results for the soil, and local landowners like Edward Southwell of Kingsweston were to cross the Channel to see for themselves.[80] Increasing efficiency and specialisation were a prerequisite for the continued industrial and commercial growth of the area.

At the time the Merchants were completing the purchase of the two manors of Clifton, Robert Southwell was conducting a correspondence on the subject of 'Limeing, Marling and Sanding' his lands, together with a rotation of crops. His informant recommended:

> ... the first year oates, and two crops of Barley, one cropp of wheat, then a cropp of pease, wch. left for hoggs or Cattle to tread, unmowed or cutt, will remanure ye ground for a cropp of wheat and two crops of Barley, with the last of wch. sowe youre Clover which will last you 3 or 4 years Then that ground is fitt for grass or Corn, and that was not to be valued before the husbandry att eighteen pence an acre: four tun of coals burns Lime to cover an acre, it must not be soe much burnt as for other uses, Also 500 Winchesters shelly sand to an acre ... the shelly things are lighter than pebble or gravell and other moveable contents of the sea ...[81]

John Plomley wrote to him in May 1696 about the new 'ffrench grass' or cinquefoil, planted by Captain Pride, which 'is the best that ever I saw for the first year'.[82] Another correspondent wrote to him on the subject of turnips:

> To sow turnip seed 2 pound is enufe for an acre. If you have any Land sowd. the last yeare with Barley or oates, fallow the said land once or twice and then make the Land finne with Harrowing, and sow your turnip seed sometime before middsummer, two pound upon an acre ...[83]

One cannot generalise from the correspondence of the Southwells in neighbouring Kingsweston to what was actually occurring in Clifton at the time the Merchants decided to acquire the manors. The evidence of the case argued by the Merchants' Counsel in the Chancery 1682-85 suggests that their intention was to provide a steady source of income to finance the improvements to the river and the port. It follows that they would have encouraged their tenants to become more efficient, as had the Whittingtons and Roger Bathron before them. The fact that the Merchants subsequently chose to provide this source of income through building leases and ground rents does not mean that in the 1690s they were not concerned to encourage new farming methods.

Unlike the farms at Kingsweston, however, situated on rich alluvial soil, much of the ground at Clifton was rocky limestone, very shallow and most suited for pasture. Whereas elsewhere in Gloucestershire farms were steadily enlarged at the turn of the century and later, at Clifton small holdings were able to survive as grazing land, with market gardens growing vegetables for the Bristol market.

Chapter Three

The Merchant Venturers' Purchase of the Two Clifton Manors

Towards the end of the 17th century the Society of Merchant Venturers became a significant landowner. Besides acquiring a number of premises in Bristol itself, the Society purchased three-quarters of one of the manors of Clifton with its considerable manorial waste, water courses and quarries for stone and ore. A few years later the Society purchased the Lordship, commons and waste of the smaller ecclesiastical manor of Clifton.

At a time when the trade of the port of Bristol was growing, the Society built a new quay on the River Frome between 1661-3, and then raised their wharfage and anchorage dues, but unfortunately the new quay fell into the river and had to be rebuilt in 1679-80. This additional expense occurred at a time when the Society was planning further expansion of the facilities of the port, and the construction of another quay which would permit a quicker turn round of ships. It was while these plans were being formulated that the purchase of the manor of Clifton took place, thus tying up much of the Society's capital. Why did the Society want to become a large property owner? Perhaps it was to provide a steady source of income from the leases, producing fines whenever a life was renewed or the lease ran out. Clearly the Hall needed more money in order to improve river facilities and to increase the port's trade.

Such a view was argued by the Merchants' counsel in the Chancery case of 1682-5, before the Lord Chancellor, along the lines that

> the plaintiffs, intending to expend a considerable amount of money in making some works about the banks of the said River, for preserving the Navigation for the benefit of the City and trade thereof, thought it necessary to have a portion of the said waste, between them and the defendants, if they had any title thereunto.[1]

Already the growing awareness of the special qualities of Hotwell water had awakened the Society's interest in the area below Clifton Wood. The wharfage lease of 1661 had required them to build a road along the riverside from Rownham to the Hotwell and at that time tentative negotiations were made to purchase the Hotwell and some waste ground next to it, but this proved abortive.[2] The Hall continued to seek to acquire the manor lands, however, and in June 1676 set up a standing committee for this purpose. In July of that year they were successful in acquiring three-quarters of one of the two Clifton manors for £1,704 4s. 6d. from the executors of a deceased owner, John Bowen.[3]

This was the manor which had been laboriously drawn together by Hugh Brook of Lower Court, Long Ashton and which had been inherited by his four daughters as coheirs in February 1588.[4] In 1593 Elizabeth, the eldest daughter, married Giles

Walwyn Esq., of Herefordshire, and sold her part of the manor to her brother-in-law, Thomas Vatchell of Bagborough, north Somerset. He had gained another share by marrying Alice Brook, another of the sisters. In 1602 Thomas Vatchell and Alice sold their share and that of Elizabeth for £200, to John Young, Gent., of Bristol,[5] 'All that the moiety, halfendeal and half part of the Manor of Clifton'. In 1602 it consisted of half of John Satchfield's holding of 74 acres of arable, meadow, pasture and wood, half of Elizabeth Yates' (widow of Andrew Yates, ropemaker) 61 acres, half of Thomas Hall's 55½ acres, half of Joane Batten's 34 acres and half of eight acres of wood and woody ground; also half of Arthur Lions' 32 acres of land and eight acres of wood, half of Lawrence Steel's 26 acres and Thomas Green's 32½ acres. Other tenants involved were William Bayly and George Batten, and 10 acres of meadow and 12 acres of pasture in the tenure of William Green. There were covenants against himself and against Hugh Brook and Sir David Brook, saving existing leases for terms of years.

In addition to these holdings,

> all the messuages, cottages, mills, dovehouses, demesne lands, tenements, meadows, leases, pastures, feedings, demesne woods, underwoods, coppice, waste, water, watercourses, fishings, fowlings, furze, heath, wasteground, mines, quarries, limekilns, profits, commodities, emoluments and hereditaments whatsoever to the said moiety, halfendeal and half part ... to the only use and behalf of him the said John Young and of his heirs and assignes for evermore.[6]

The following year, John Young acquired another quarter part of the larger manor of Clifton,

> heretofore the property of Susan Hallswell, wife of Hugh Hallswell, and one of the four daughters and coheirs of the said Hugh Brook, and after the death of the said Susan, the land, fourth part amongst other things made by the said Hugh Hallswell and Thomas his son, and heir of the said Susan ... assigned and conveyed ... unto the said William Clarke and Frances his wife, one other of the said coheirs ...

The Hallswell family lived at Goathurst, near Bridgwater, Somerset. William Clarke of Barrow Minchin, Somerset, sold Susan's quarter part to John Young for £100.[7] It consisted of a fourth part of the messuages already listed, held by John Satchfield, Thomas Hall, Joane Batten etc., and it is possible to discover the field names involved by looking at the share of Frances, wife of William Clarke, which was not involved in the transactions of 1602-3. Her share was sold eventually to Anthony Hodges for £369, and involved a fourth share of '11 messuages, 11 gardens, 10 orchards, 38 acres of arable, 34 acres of meadow, 245 acres of pasture, 400 acres of furze and heath, and 3 furnaces with appurtenances, in Clifton'.[8] The field names included Home Close, Mead Close, Rownham Mead, Twelve Acre field, Lydfield, Trinmore, Causeway Close, Great Pool, Northfield, Shortgrove Close and Shortgrove.[9]

John Young now held three-quarters of the larger manor of Clifton, and when his daughter Margaret married Andrew Whittington, in 1615, John settled the estate to the use of Andrew and Margaret and the heirs of her body, granting it to Thomas Young, Christopher Cary and Richard Winter as trustees, and then to the right heirs of the body of John Young.[10] In the event, the estate came to Margaret's son, John Whittington, and then to her grandson William. He sold it to Isaac Morgan in October 1668 for £1,080,[11] 'except such parts thereof as had been lately sold to Ayliffe Green by the said William Whittington'.

Isaac Morgan was the Collector of the Customs in Bristol and, as a guarantee of his good behaviour in that office, he was required by the Farmers of His Majesty's Customs in London to convey the manor of Clifton to them by lease and release, 'to be void on the due performance by the said Isaac Morgan of the office of Collector of Customs of Bristol'.[12] The three-quarters of the manor of Clifton was handed over as a pledge, for 5s. 'consideration', that Isaac Morgan do

> truly and faithfully performe and execute the Office, trust and employment of Collector of the Customs and Subsidies within the Port of Bristoll ... and do also well and truly perform the Condition of one obligation, bearing date 12 June 1669, wherein the said Isaac Morgan stands bound to our said Sovereign Lord the King in the sum of £2,000 of good money ...[13]

Unfortunately, Morgan got into difficulties and appears to have been bailed out by John Bowen, who paid for him what was due to the Farmers of His Majesty's Customs.[14] In the meantime the manor had been impounded by Richard Mountney for the Farmer of the Customs, 'Isaac Morgan failing to give a juxtamount of the execution of his office'. John Bowen now received the manor from Isaac Morgan 'for reimbursing John Bowen such moneys as he had paid for him to the Farmers of the Customs'.[15] John Bowen was a wealthy merchant and a former Master of the Society, but he didn't enjoy the manor for long. Within three years he was dead, and the estate was handled by trustees, including Thomas Moore and Roger Bathron. These executors temporarily mortgaged the property to Thomas Day for £1,000, but when the negotiations between the Society and the executors had been completed, Thomas Day refused to move.[16] The Hall therefore began a suit at Chancery to get him out. Through mediation the dispute ended within the year, and Thomas Day released his rights and titles to the Society.[17]

The other smaller manor of Clifton, which had been acquired by Sir Ralph Sadleir at the dissolution of the college at Westbury-on-Trym, had been sold by his grandson, Ralph Sadleir, to Frances Chamber in 1659. She subsequently married John Good of Clifton, whose two sons, John and Arthur, sold it again in May 1668 for £850 to two speculators, Gabriel Deane, merchant, and Abel Kelly, grocer.[18] The sale incuded:

> all and all manner of houses, edifices, buildings, barns, stables, orchards, gardens, lands, meadows, closes, feedings, pastures, remaining common pasture, remaining mines, quarryes and wayst, waters, watercourses, woods, underwoods, trees, hedges, hedgerows, and the ground and soile of the same woods, underwoods, trees, hedges and hedgerows, Courts Leet, Courts Barron, equities and profits of Courts and fines ... which were at any time the Inheritance of the said Frances Goode, or which, in the time of her widowhood and intermarriage with he said John Goode, her late husband, did by the name of Frances Chamber, widowe, buy or purchase of and from Ralph Sadleir of Stondon in the County of Hereford, Esquire ...[19]

8. Thomas Goldney's house originally belonged to Lord ffolliott but was given to his daughter, Mary, in 1692 on her marriage. Bought from Roland Baugh in 1705, the house was rebuilt for Goldney II *c*.1720-3 by George Tully. The exterior of the house was formerly brick but it has been refaced with Bath stone. The older part of the house (east wing) is separated from the later additions by Alfred Waterhouse's 19th-century tower, but the surviving 18th-century wing has had its Georgian glazing bars removed.

It is worth quoting at some length because, subsequently, there was considerable dispute between the Society and the descendants of Deane and Kelly as to their rights and limits regarding commons, watercourses, quarries and waste, particularly along the banks of the Avon.

On 10 October 1685 the Society purchased from Martha Deane and five of her relatives, Ellis Kelly, his brother and three sisters, for £100,[20] and from John Lambe, Gent., for the sum of £50, paid to each family 'their shares in the wastes or common in the manor or manors of Clifton, and in all rocks and springs of water. Reserving their rights of common, their cottages etc. and their right to dig stone for repairs (except within 300 yards of the Hotwell)'.[21] But the Deanes and Kellys reserved:

> their messuages or enclosed lands in Clifton, and shall for ever hold and enjoy such common of pastures for all their commonable rights ... And all cottages and inclosures belonging to the said vendors within the said waste or Commons as they respectively had or ought to have before the sealing hereof ... And also Digg and raise quantities of stone for repairs, but not within 300 yards of the fountain called the Hotwell.[22]

The transaction was registered in a Deed of 1686, the signatories to which included representatives of the Society such as Edward Tocknell (Master), Thomas Edwards, Francis Yeamans and Thomas Morgan. They added a footnote: 'the power mentioned ... for liberty of digging of stone ... was intended only for them to use in

9. Clifton Court, now the Chesterfield Nursing Home, was built for Martha Goldney and Nehemiah Champion c.1742, but the architect is unknown. Both parties had been widowed and had married again in 1728. Martha bought the site from the Hodges family in 1742. The east side of Clifton Court is composed of black refuse ore, cast into square blocks, from the brass foundry on St Augustine's Back in which Nehemiah had an interest. The eastern supporting wing has blank windows to the upper storey to permit a high ceiling in the ground-floor rooms.

building and enclosing in etc. upon their respective lands and hereditaments in Clifton, and not elsewhere'.[23] Thus, the descendants of the Deanes and the Kellys sold the smaller ecclesiastical manor and its lordship rights, Courts Leet, Courts Baron, mines, quarries, waste, waters and watercourses for what John Latimer described as 'a trifling outlay'.[24]

The de Wilstar Survey of 1746 reveals that the cultivated lands belonging to the Merchants' Hall totalled 184 acres. At that date Francis Freeman's freehold in Clifton was larger than that of the Society, covering 189 acres. The Rev. John Power's estate amounted to 78 acres. The Hodges family's freehold was purchased in December 1607 for £369 by Anthony Hodges from Edward, Thomas, Nicholas and Christopher Clark,[25] the young sons of William Clark and Frances Brook. It included the church and churchyard of St Andrew's and the site of the old Manor House, on which John Hodges built the Queen Anne house which now forms the Lord Bishop of Bristol's official residence.[26] Robert Smith's estate of 20 acres covered the slopes below Goldney's house and, facing south across the Avon, included a vineyard and orchards. Thomas Goldney's lands at this time had not expanded beyond eight acres, while Paul Fisher's freehold covered only an acre, although he leased another 17 acres from the Merchants' Hall. Nehemiah Champion owned the acre freehold on which Clifton Court, now the Chesterfield, was built. Altogether these, and 11 other landowners, account for the 414 acres which were not owned by the Merchants' Hall after the purchase of the two manors. However, as lords of the manor they controlled the 386 acres of common, the 184 acres of arable land and the wastes, quarries and watercourses. The de Wilstar map shows the total area of the manors as amounting to 984 acres.

The Society took counsel's advice as to the best method of resisting the claims of those people who, by virtue of rights acquired from the Sadleir family, were exploiting the Hotwell and other fountains and quarrying stone. The merchants sought the opinions of William Powlett and John Romsey, then Recorder and Town Clerk of Bristol.[27] A copy of the Survey Book of Sadleir's manor was obtained from Mr. Justice Cole, Sadleir's steward, and it was discovered that 'no certain waste is mentioned in it ... '.[28] On counsel's advice, therefore, a Bill in Chancery was issued against Lambe, Deane and Kelly to establish their rights and title to the waste. Apparently John Lambe made 'more profit of his fourth than the Merchants did of the other three'.[29] The Deanes and Kellys were receiving from the City of Bristol

> the sum of £12 yearly, for the use and benefit of a fountain and spring, or well of water, commonly called Jacob's Well ... and William Pope paid 6s. 8d. per annum to the Deanes and Kellys 'for the use and benefit of certain other fountains or Springs ... commonly called or knowne by the name of Hotwell'. Also they were receiving £3 per annum for 'all Quarryes in the Great Rocke that is part of the waste of the said manor of Clifton ... commonly called St Vincent's Rocks'.[30]

The Deanes and Kellys and John Lambe all were able to prove sound titles. The Hodges freehold, purchased in December 1607, had descended to William Hodges, whose daughter Elizabeth married John Lambe. On 18 April 1657 Hodges, by Indenture of Enfeoffment, secured the estate for John and Elizabeth and their heirs and, on the subsequent death of Elizabeth, further assured the estate by another Indenture. The Society sought counsel's opinion on the Intaile as to whether Lambe was tenant in fee simple. Mr. Francis Pemberton's opinion was quite clear:

> If Hodges, the feoffee, were dead before the recovery, I conceive the recovery is good, and hath dockt all the estates and remainders, and made Lambe an estate in fee simple, and his mortgate to Tyndale is, for ought I see, very good, and by assignment of that, or taking in that, he may, I conceive make any mortgage either of the fee or otherwise.[31]

Similarly, the other defendants – Martha Deane, five of her relatives and Ellis Kelly and his relatives – were able to show sound titles to the smaller manor, from Ralph Sadleir through John and Arthur Good to Gabriel Deane and Abel Kelly.[32]

There are at least four copies of the Chancellor's judgement on 22 July and the Court Order, which have survived in the Society's archives. The essence of the Merchants' Bill was reported at length. They contended that when the larger manor was divided into four parts, 'all the inclosed grounds of every the said parts were holden by oath of the said plaintiffs, dividedly and in severalty, but the said wastes were by them holden, and are still kept and enjoyed in Common and undivided'. Similarly, 'their shares in the said waters and rocks thereunto belonging, were never separately enjoyed'; 'the defendant Deane, with other defendants, claim one other entire copyhold Manor of Clifton ... which formerly were the lands and estate of Ralph Sadleir, deceased, under a title distinct from that of the plaintiffs and the said defendant, Lambe'. They contended that the Deanes and Kellys had refused to come to a fair partition of the waste and the quarries, and they had brought a writ of partition against Lambe, to secure for the merchants three-quarters of the wastes, watercourses and springs along the River Avon. The chancellor ordered two arbitrators to be appointed, assisted by three commissioners, to value and divide the waste and rocks into two parts and shares proportional to the value of the several lands and tenements belonging to the parties concerned:

It is this day ordered by the unanimous consent of all the said parties that all matters in controversy or difference and now depending in this suit be referred, and are hereby referred to the award, order and determination of William Powlett Esq. and Nathanial Haggatt Esq., Arbitrators, indifferently elected and nominated, between them. And for as much as they are strangers to, and ignorant of as well of the value of the Manor and lands of and belonging to the defendants, as of the quantities and boundaries of the wastes of them respectively belonging, and of the several Royalties, perquisites and privileges thereunto appurtaining, All the said parties have agreed and do hereby agree that Ayliffe Green, Gent., Arthur Maskell Gent., and John Wickham, or any two of them, shall view survey and value the respective estates and interests of the said parties, and bound and estimate the waste belonging to the said Manors and lands respectively ...

Then they ... or any two of them, are to report the same in writing, under their hands, to the Arbitrators, who may thereby be the better enabled to make their award of and upon the matter hereby to them referred ... the award to be made by the said Arbitrators, when made, shall be ratified and confirmed by the decree of this Hon.ble Court. (Chancery) ... on or before the first day of next Mich.mas Term. And in the meane time all proceedings are hereby stayed.[33]

The merchants' attorney, Thomas Edwards of Cliffords Inn, wrote a note on the front of one of the copies of the Chancellor's judgement, on 22 July:

Sir, Pray peruse this Order this morning if you can, for Mr. Hawkworth, who is for Lambe, will be in towne today, and then Mr. Young and he and I will meet and settle it, and settle Commissioners' names. I have sent you Mr. Powlett's amendments, [Recorder of Bristol, 1683] which I believe will never pass. But however, if you concur with him, then we must apply with haste to the Court to settle it.

It would appear that the Hall did appeal against the arbitrators' decision, against Thomas Edwards' better judgement, but that on 10 November they withdrew their bill:

Upon morrow this day, made unto this Court by Mr. Collins, being of the plaintiffs', Council. It was alleadged that the plaintiffs, since exhibiting their Bill into this Court against the saide Defendants, have found the same to be mistaken in the most material points thereof, for they cannot safely proceed thereupon to a hearing without prejudice. It was therefore prayed that the said plaintiffs' Bill may stand dismist out of Court, paying twenty shillings costs in respect thereof, which is ordered accordingly.[34]

As to the Writ of Partition against John Lambe, on 21 September 1686, Thomas Edwards wrote to various commissioners summoning them to Ridland, and to Sir Robert Yeaman's house, on 8 October, to begin the task of 'dividing the waste within the Manor of Clifton' and giving 14 days notice.[35] Finally, in October 1686, the Master, Edward Tocknell, and the Society of Merchants acquired by deed from John Lambe his rights to the Hotwell Rocks and waste for fifty pounds. For £100 they acquired the similar rights from the descendants of the Deanes and Kellys. Arthur Hart, Stephen Watts, John Tomlinson

Table III

A Particular of the tenements and lands att Clifton, bought of Mr. Roger Bathron.
Survey of the manor of Clifton conveyed 9 July 1689.[38]

John Whittington Esq holds one messuage, garden orchard, and homeclose, containing 11 acres	16 00 00	John Bailey holds a little house, with a wash house, garden and close, containing one acre.	5 00 00
Hill close containing 5 acres adjoining. Lord Ffolliott's house & enclosure bought in fee from Bathron	6 00 00	By his own life only, aged above 40 years. Edward Bond, Senior, Rent of £8, Herriott 6s. 8d. holds a tenement in own possession	8 00 00
Ferney close & Bradmore, 12 acres	16 00 00	Another in possession of John Stokes	5 00 00
Lay bridge containing 3 acres	4 00 00	Another in possession of Edw. Bond Jnr.	2 00 00
The five acres	6 00 00	Another destitute of a tenant	3 00 00
The Deanes, containing 4 acres	4 00 00	Another in possession of Ann Morgan	4 00 00
The Tyning out-field 4 acres	5 00 00	**Total**	**39 00 00**
Two acres by Pittacre	2 10 00	By his own life only, his son John being dead. Aged above 70 years.	
Two grounds called Lyppiatt, 4 acres	5 10 00	Thomas Garland holds a tenement and garden in his own hands	6 00 00
Two grounds called Trinmore containing 7 acres	5 10 00	Another in possession of John Waite	2 10 00
Three grounds called Trinmore Paddock 5 acres	5 00 00	Another in possession of Edw. Morris	2 00 00
Three grounds called Lydfields lying under Vincents Rocks cont. quarries	12 00 00	Another in possession of Richd. Jones	1 00 00
Twenty acres and half, in Rownham Meade which laid to waste	23 06 08	A tenement in possession of Tho. Gayner	4 00 00
Total	**110 16 08**	**Total**	**15 10 00**
3 lives, to witt John Whittington aged 23 years; John Fry, Gent, aged 30 years; Elizabeth, daughter of Edw. Arundell aged 30.		By the lives of Thomas Garland and Tho. Garland, Jnr., Mary Garland, Joane Garland. All young lives.	
John Hodges holds a ruinous messuage, garden and homeclose	5 00 00	Thomas Barnes holds a tenement in possession of Giles Emerson	2 15 00
The Seven Acres	12 00 00	Another in possession of Wm. Morris	2 10 00
The Four Acres	6 00 00	Another in possession of George Worth	1 18 00
Lachels Causey Close adjoining to Holland's leases, 4 acres	4 00 00	Another in possession of Ann Jones	1 15 00
The One Acre	1 10 00	Another in possession of widow Snooke	1 10 00
Great Field containing 7 acres	9 00 00	Another in possn. of Gabriel Collins	1 10 00
Two grounds by the Highwayside leading from Durdham down to Bristol called the Nine acres	14 00 00	Another in possn. of Edith Holloway	2 02 00
Four acres, lying under Shortgrove, adjoining to Poolclose, Trynmore, and containing 9 acres	9 00 00	A small field containing one acre, which field and tenements last mentioned are now in grant to Thomas Barnes	1 06 00
Lydfield with the coppice cont. 4 acres	4 00 00	**Total**	**15 06 00**
Two grounds called Trynmore, cont. 4 acres	2 13 04	William Pope holds a tenement in his possession and a little strip of ground upon the Hill used as an orchard & small garden	1 10 00
Meadeclose, containing 4 acres, opposite Withybed	5 00 00	Another small tenement in his son's possession Lives – William himself, William's sons and daughters	1 10 00
Seven acres, by Shutt, in Rownham Mead	8 03 04	**Total**	**3 00 00**
Total	**80 06 08**	William Nibbs hold one tenement and a little piece of ground in possn. of Charles Chick	1 00 00
(2 old lives, viz. Mr. Hodges and his sister, both over 80 years old.)		Another tenement and a long garden, and about 2 acres under the Hill, reaching to the old mill or Withybed, and in grant to William Nibbs	4 00 00
Thomas Gaynor, A messuage, garden, orchard and homeclose, cont. about 4 acres	12 00 00	**Total**	**5 10 00**
Honeypen hill cont. 7 acres, and excluding Mr. Deane's 2 acres	7 00 00	Richard Sayes holds a tenement on the Waste Wm. Watkins holds a small tenement and garden	2 00 00
The Dean, and Whitestile, 5 acres	5 00 00	The old mill and a quarter acre of ground with many trees	0 10 00
Total	**24 00 00**	The Withey Bedd	2 10 00
By his own life and his wife above 40 years.		The City of Bristol paid for Jacob's Well water	0 08 00
William David, Copyholder, A fair messuage, garden, orchard, court & paddock of ground	12 00 00	The Gulleys and Limekiln and 12 acres of the common	1 00 00
This surrendered and granted to Matthias Morgan — the Court Rolls. By the lives of Robert and Margaret, son and daughter of Lawrence Brown – the lives are above 30 years old.		The Hotwell, with the concessions and privileges thereto belonging	0 10 00
		Total	**6 18 00**

and all others who claim or have the other moiety of the same Manor or lands under title of Abel Kelly, deceased, shall and will, on or before the 20th day of December next, at the charge of the said Master, well and sufficiently convey and assure all their, and every of their right Title, Estate, Interest, share and portion of and in the soil of the Waste and Commons ... And of all rocks, Quarries, issues and Springs ... unto such person or persons, and their heirs, as the Company shall at the next Common Hall appoint, for the sum of £100 to be paid to the said Vendors ...[36]

Thus, finally, the Society purchased the waste and watercourses of the ecclesiastical manor of Clifton and within the next three years a survey was undertaken of the Society's holdings within their Lordship of the two manors of Clifton. If taken together with Henry Lilly's survey in 1625 of the smaller Ralph Sadleir manor, it is apparent that tenants had all along had holdings in both manors. The fourth part of the lay manor, belonging to Lambe, was sold by Indenture (dated 30 May 1677, 28 Charles II) to John Tyndale of Bitton, Glos. Gent. There was a condition relating to his mortgage to John Wimpenny in trust for Stephen Stringer. On 30 July 1698 Edward Freeman paid £2,075 for this quarter of the Manor of Clifton on marrying Ann Asteley of Worcester.[37]

Chapter Four

Clifton Merchants in the First Half of the 18th Century

There was just sufficient of the upper class in Clifton in 1712 to form a whist table, according to the Rev. William Goldwin, head of Bristol Grammar School. Living in Clifton in 1702 were four 'gentlemen' who were each fined 2s. 6d. for failing to attend the Hundred Court. These were Thomas Goldney, John Hodges, John Sandford and Arthur Hart.[1] The Court was held each month and, at the end of the 18th century, was largely engaged in enforcing by-laws and preventing encroachment of the Downs by landowners.[2] There were 450 people living in Clifton in 1712,[3] but most of them lived along the riverside and worked in the limekiln, the dockyards, or made a living in trades associated with a sea-faring city. We can discover much useful information about the village at this time from Gabriel Goldney's copy of a map drawn up in 1746 for the Merchants' Hall.[4]

It shows a dozen houses scattered along the road running from St Andrews and Clifton Green to the Gully and St Vincent's Rocks, but not all of them may have been occupied. A note in Seyer's manuscripts in Bristol Reference Library suggests that, in 1790, out of 20 houses on Clifton Hill, 11 were offered to be let or sold at one time.[5] This was essentially a farming community of perhaps a dozen farms which the map indicates varied in size from two or three of 40 acres to only a few acres, the majority. Some cottages in the neighbourhood of Blackboy Hill reveal the presence of lead diggers and quarrymen, and patches marked 'Z' probably indicate lime-burning kilns.

Detail on the map shows the new playhouse, opened in 1729, at the bottom of Jacob's Well Road, the Hotwell with its pump room, lodging house and billiard room, and Granby Hill with its steep climb up to Clifton. From Dowry Square, which was begun c.1727, a road proceeds to the Hotwell and then stops. There is no indication of even a pathway along the river bank beyond this point. The New Hotwell, where John Wesley spent many lonely months in 1754 recovering from consumption, is marked opposite Leigh Woods. It could only be reached by a precipitate path close to Walcombe Slade, and it had next to no facilities. Across the Downs from the New Hotwell, and radiating from Blackboy Hill, are the two turnpiked roads to Stoke Bishop and to Westbury. Each road has two lines of trees marked, but the turnpike gates, which were frequently broken down and burnt with the connivance of landowners, are not indicated.[6]

The buildings indicated on the map include St Andrew's and the Queen Anne building constructed in 1711 and now known as Church House. The Hodges family had owned the site of the old ruined manor house and built this splendid house on the site. The family lived there until 1776 when it was sold to Samuel Worrall and his descendants remained there until 1900.[7] On the other side of the road and down the hill is Clifton Wood House (1721) and Amherst (1738) which are still standing today.

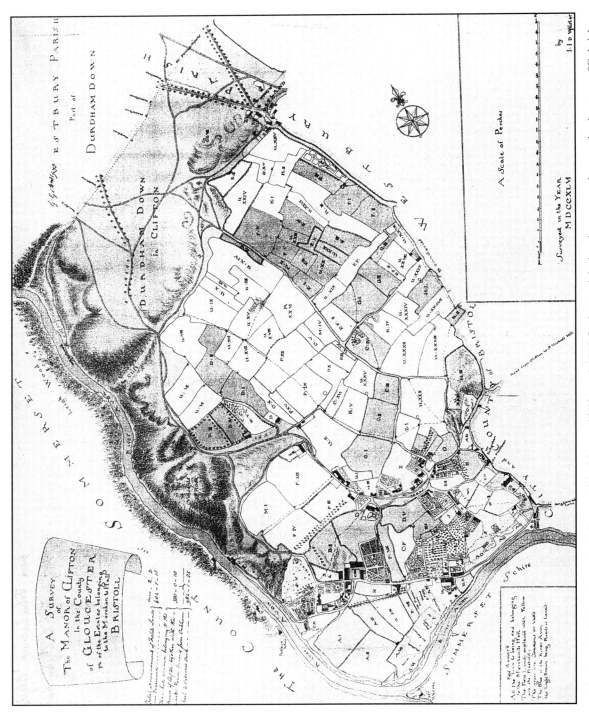

10. Jacob de Wilstar's map 4, 'A Survey of the Manor of Clifton . . .', 1746. In the top right-hand corner can be seen the signature of Gabriel Goldney, whose copy this probably was. The detail on this map is remarkable. The key to this map, showing the owners and tenants in 1746 has survived and is in the Merchant Venturers' archives.

Robert Smith, a wealthy linen draper, employed the architect George Tully to build Clifton Wood House as a speculation, and it was leased first to the Countess of Huntingdon and then to the Farr family, which was still there in 1768. Amherst was also built to rent. The 1746 map reveals the extent of the land owned by Robert Smith (Si to SVI), but in 1747 he was overtaken by misfortune and Thomas Goldney III bought it from him.[8]

Thomas Goldney II had originally leased Lord Folliott's house, marked (x) on the survey, in 1694. Thomas, 2nd Baron Folliott of Ballyshannon, had given it to his daughter Mary in 1692 when she married Rowland Baugh, a Shropshire gentleman.[9] However, by 1705 Thomas Goldney II was wealthy enough through the death of his in-laws to buy the house outright, and George Tully had largely rebuilt it by 1723. Thomas Goldney II died in 1731 after rebuilding the house, and from 1732 Thomas Goldney III began enlarging the estate. The chance came to buy what is now Clifton Hill Cottage, a garden, and all the pasture land to the east of Goldney House where Callender House (1744) and the Fry wing of Clifton Hill House now stand (marked XII on the map).[10]

In the year the map was drawn (1746), the vicar, the Rev. Thomas Taylor, bought 'Homeleaze', which was a large part of the old Parsonage Close, from the Hodges family. He was later to sell part to Nicholas Simpson, apothecary and, since Thomas Paty was a witness to the deeds, it is highly likely that he was involved in the building of Prospect House (1757). Subsequently, Taylor sold the rest to Thomas Manley and Beresford House was built in 1763. Meanwhile, Thomas Goldney III bought adjacent land from Robert Smith to carry out his plans for the grotto (S) and, from Mr. Deverell (DV), 'Hill Close' to the west to keep as open ground. He also bought the paddock (XI) to the south-west for the Fort garden and, from Mrs. Hamilton of *Black Horse Inn*, two large paddocks (WI and WII) for building development. To complete the estate, he bought a freehold called 'Ambra Hill' from Mrs. Bishop (CF).[11]

On the opposite side of the road to Goldney's house was Clifton Court (1742), now the Chesterfield Nursing Home. Martha Goldney had lost her husband, John Vanderwall, a London draper, and since her mother's death in 1722 had probably been mistress of the Goldney household. In 1728 she married her father's business partner, Nehemiah Champion. He was a widower with a grown family and a Quaker like their partners at Coalbrookdale, the Goldneys and the Darbys. He and Martha had the magnificent Clifton Court built in 1742. By 1746, therefore, the evidence of the Merchants' Hall map shows that at least three wealthy families – the Goldneys, Champions and Farrs – had moved out of the main city to the clean and bracing air of Clifton-on-the-hill.

Paul Fisher, a linen draper and ship owner, was building Clifton's most distinguished mansion, Clifton Hill House (marked Y on the 1746 map). His architect was the national Palladian designer Isaac Ware, whose design was reproduced in his *Complete Body of Architecture* of 1756. The mason and carver was Bristol's leading architect, Thomas Paty. The date 1747 and the initials of Paul and Mary Fisher appear above the entrance to the house on Lower Clifton Hill. The pediment on the other side of the building contains the Fisher coat of arms. Paul Fisher senior had

11.   Clifton Hill House. Clifton's most distinguished house was designed by Isaac Ware and reproduced in his *Complete Body of Architecture*, 1756. The mason and carver was Bristol's leading architect Thomas Paty. Paul Fisher, senior (d.1735), a wealthy merchant, had made a fortune from trading with the American colonies and Europe in cloth and sugar, privateering and slaves. Paul Fisher, junior (d.1761), also a merchant, had the house built, and left it, in his will, to Christopher Willoughby.

died in 1735. During the period of Bristol's peak involvement in the slave trade some of his boats, such as the *Post Boy* in 1731 and 1733, carrying on average 344 slaves, and *Scipio* in 1735, carrying 300 slaves, were actively involved. His boats transported slaves from Angola to Jamaica and to South Carolina, and their return cargoes were redwood and cowries.[12]

Paul Fisher junior was co-partner to Slade Baker and William Griffin.[13] Both father and son owned shares in a number of boats and imported linens and cambrics from Dunkirk, rice from Carolina, and Holland linen from Rotterdam. Some of Paul Fisher's boats were engaged in privateering in the war of Austrian Succession (1739-48), such as the *Eagle* (300 tons), the Jamaica (290 tons) and the *North Cape* (306 tons).[14] The *Eagle* made at least one capture, but the *Jamaica*, with about five hundred hogsheads of sugar on board, subsequently foundered off the West Indies in 1746. The *North Cape*, one of the finest ships belonging to the port of Bristol, was captured after a four-hour battle off Antigua.

Normally, privateers did not carry cargo. In the same way that public men-of-war were fitted out by the State, privateers were fitted out by their owners to sail against the enemy and capture prizes, which were sent into port to be sold. They therefore carried large crews, and the men were paid on a share system. Paul Fisher, however, would appear to have tried to have the best of both worlds by fitting out his ships with guns while continuing to pursue his normal trade with the West Indies.

The Fishers were regular worshippers at St Andrew's church, and Paul Fisher junior served as a churchwarden. They owned a family pew; after service the pew doors were locked and even pew owners could only obtain entry through the regular officials – five carefully-chosen widows.[15] A minute in the Vestry Book for 1734 actually particularises 22 February as the date when they were given leave to build their pews.

> 1734, Feb. 22. Agreed that the Rev. John Hodges shall have the liberty of disposing of the part of the Gallery that is the new ile to Robert Smith Esq., Mr. Paul Fisher and Captain Joseph Osbourne, to make three seats as they shall think fit at their own cost.

Paul Fisher's will, dated 16 September 1761, devised all his real and personal estate to Christopher Willoughby, one of the executors of his will. It included:

> All that Messuage or Tenement, Coach House, Stables, Erections and Buildings situate on Clifton Hill in the County of Gloucester, erected and built by said Fisher, deceased, And also all that upper Garden adjoining and belonging to the said Messuage ... And all other freehold Messuages, Lands, Tenements and Hereditaments late of him, said Fisher deceased ... together with all deeds.[16]

The Goldneys, who created Goldney House, originated from a prosperous family of Chippenham. Born in 1620, the second son of Gabriel Goldney, Thomas Goldney was apprenticed in 1637 to a Bristol grocer, Theophilus Behethland. Gabriel Goldney had trading interest in the West Indies, and that may explain why he sent his second son to Bristol. In 1646 Thomas was made a freeman and then married Mary Clements, the daughter of a Bristol merchant. They set up home at Bristol Bridge in the High Street, and were active Quakers. Both Mary and Thomas Goldney were, at different times, imprisoned for their faith. In 1670 Goldney was one of the overseers who had responsibility for the new Friars Meeting House in what is now Broadmead shopping precinct. Goldney was fined £200 for refusing to take the Oath of Allegiance and Supremacy while being an elected Common Councillor. Several other Quakers were treated in this way for refusing to accept office, and the money was used to construct military defences, ordered by the Duke of Beaufort, after the Monmouth Rebellion had been put down.[17] Goldney's business had prospered and, in 1674, he bought a country estate at Elberton, 10 miles north of Bristol. However, he was over-generous in the marriage settlement of £1,500 he made to his daughter Mary in 1678, and was forced in 1681 to lease the farm and estate to his son-in-law, James Wallis, at a nominal rent because he was not able to pay the promised sum.[18] Thomas Goldney I died in September 1694.

His surviving son, Thomas Goldney II, lived at the house in the High Street after his marriage to Martha Speed and the birth of their first child. He became a freeman in June 1688 and leased Lord Folliott's house on Clifton Hill in April 1694. Goldney's sixth child, Thomas Goldney III, was born in this house in July 1696. Goldney II's father-in-law, Thomas Speed, died in 1703, and Martha Goldney inherited money and property. As a result, Thomas Goldney was able, in June 1705, to buy the freehold of the Clifton house, and to indulge in a high-risk capital

12. One of two candlesticks given in 1712 by John Romsey, former Bristol town clerk, to the cathedral. They are to be seen on the altar of the eastern lady chapel and were given in thanksgiving for the safe return, with great profit, of the two privateers *Duke* and *Dutchess* from their voyage round the world 1708-11. Of the 256 shares in the voyage, Thomas Goldney with 36 was the greatest shareholder, but John Romsey owned fifteen. Representations of the ships are shown on a medallion at the foot of each candlestick. The candlesticks have the English hallmark of 1712 with the initials of Gabriel Sleath, a well-known silversmith at the time.

venture which eventually became a privateering voyage round the world.

Captain Woodes Rogers had suffered losses at the hands of the enemy, probably in the Newfoundland trade, and he gave this as his reason for setting out on a privateering expedition in 1708. There had been a proclamation in 1702 which gave the whole interest in captured enemy ships to the owners and crew of the victor, except for custom house duties and 10 per cent to the Crown. Among the Bristol merchants who ventured money in Woodes Rogers' expedition, the man who took the most shares – 36 at £103 10s. each – was the Quaker Thomas Goldney II, and in so doing he was clearly risking the wrath of the Society of Friends.[19] It certainly concerned the Mens' Monthly Meeting, and two Friends were deputed to find out the facts. They reported in October 1708 that no Friends or their sons were involved, except for 'T.G. who is now in prison'.[20] Thomas Goldney was there because of his involvement in an obscure controversy between the City Corporation and John Sanson (junior), who was son-in-law of the town clerk, John Romsey, and had been appointed Collector of the Customs in 1700. In 1707 Sansom was found by His Majesty's Collectors to have defrauded them of £30,351.[21] It took Goldney until 1710 to clear his name of any involvement.

Captain Woodes Rogers' ships, the *Dutchess* (300 tons, 24 guns and a complement of 120 men) and the *Duke* (320 tons, 30 guns and 150 men), set sail in August 1708.[22] The venture was ostensibly to establish 'a Trade to the South Seas', since Rogers was one of the first to advocate trade to the River Plate, but is best known for the recovery of Alexander Selkirk from Juan Fernandez. He became the original for Defoe's Robinson Crusoe. For the Bristol speculators what mattered were the prizes and booty which the *Duke* and *Dutchess* brought back with them in October 1711. The ships had been fitted out to prey on French and Spanish ships sailing from South America and the West Indies to Europe, and the pilot for both ships was the Somerset buccaneer William Dampier, who had already made two voyages round the world.[23] The speculators were not disappointed. Two silver candlesticks on the altar table of the Eastern Lady Chapel in Bristol Cathedral are mementoes of one of the most notable privateering voyages on record. On 23 July the *Duke* and *Dutchess* arrived in Holland, where the treasures taken from 10 prizes were displayed.[24] Latimer tells us: 'Some of the lucky owners repaired to Holland to feast their eyes on the booty, the gross value of which was reported to be £170,000'.[25]

Thomas Goldney had doubled his stake, and received £6,824 for an outlay of £3,726. Goldney II was a generous friend; during 1708, when William Penn was in great financial difficulties due to frauds perpetrated on him in Pennsylvania by a Bristol Quaker named Philip Ford, whom Penn had sent out as his agent, he asked the Friends for help. Thomas Goldney, the Callowhills and others advanced him £6,800, taking as security a mortgage on the entire province of Pennsylvania. This lease and William Penn's marriage certificate may still be seen in Quakers' Friars in Broadmead. Goldney also provided large-scale financial backing for another Quaker, Abraham Darby of Cheese Lane in Bristol, and in the long run this proved even more profitable. Darby moved to Coalbrookdale, and by 1709 kettles, firebacks and iron pots were being transported down the Severn and up the Avon by trow to be sold by Goldney and the Champion family. In 1713 Darby mortgaged half the works at Coalbrookdale to Goldney as security for a loan of £1,700 which he needed to develop his new technique of smelting, which used coke instead of charcoal in the furnace. Darby died in 1717 at the age of 39, leaving Goldney with eight of the 16 £200 shares in the new Dale Company. Goldney travelled round to the large fairs, such as Chester, Nottingham and Manchester, taking orders and receiving payments for iron goods already supplied. Goldney took young Thomas III with him on these journeys and was eventually able to hand this side of his affairs over to his son. Thomas Goldney II was, therefore, as a result of his remarkable good fortune in privateering and his business acumen, able to contemplate building a much more distinguished mansion.

At the old house on Clifton Hill between 1698 and 1707 another six children had been born to Thomas and Martha, but not all survived.[26] One son died as a baby in 1702, and a second son, Joseph, died in 1717. Mary, the eldest girl, also died in 1707, but the Goldneys still had six children living at home in the 1720s. In 1723 half of Lord Folliott's house was demolished, and a much more impressive house began to be built in its place. The unpretentious east wing and the south-east corner are said to be the only parts of the old building remaining, and it is highly likely that the Quaker George Tully was the architect of the new house.[27] Goldney would have seen the building completed before his death at the age of 68 in June 1731.

Thomas Goldney III, who now inherited the estate, had originally worked as the cashier of the Dale Company. He was now part owner of the Coalbrookdale business and, from 1752, became a partner and managing director in Bristol's second bank, Goldney, Smith & Co. in Corn Street.[28] Cast iron was much needed throughout the 40 years of warfare in the 18th century, and the account books of the Dale Company record delivery by trow to Bristol of large consignments of two-, four-and six-pounder guns and casks of shot.[29] Thomas' younger brother, Gabriel, also engaged in privateering, as had his father. He was the principal partner, with Charles Harford, Caleb and Vickris Dickinson, Francis Rogers, David Dehany and Andrews Lloyd, in the *Union* (390 tons, 30 guns and 70 men).[30] The guns from Coalbrookdale works arrived for checking at the quay and some were then sold direct to ship owners like Gabriel Goldney; he paid £260 for guns and shot for the *Union*.[31] Thomas Goldney continued working until a month before his death, aged 72, in December 1768.[32] He was succeeded in Goldney House first by Hannah Ball, his elder widowed sister, and then by Gabriel, his younger brother. Gabriel Goldney and his remaining sister, Ann, ended their association with Coalbrookdale in 1773, selling their holdings to Abraham Darby III for £10,000. Gabriel died in 1786, aged 82, and his sister Ann died in 1796. The house and estate were then inherited by the cousins at Chippenham.[33]

On the opposite side of Clifton Green stands Clifton Court, now the Chesterfield Nursing Home. It is described in the book accompanying the Merchants' Hall map as 'Mr Champion's freehold, (a mansion house and gardens) 1 acre, 2 rods and 20 perches'. Nehemiah Champion II was a ship owner, merchant and partner in the Bristol Brass Wire Company. He was born in 1678 into a Quaker family, but was dis-owned by the Society for taking part in privateering. Nehemiah Champion and Martha Vanderwall (née Goldney) had both lost their spouses. He had at least three surviving children by his former marriage and was well known by the Goldneys, both in the Society of Friends and because he was Thomas Goldney II's business partner in the Coalbrookdale enterprise. Martha had purchased the site from the Hodges family in 1742, and the house which the couple built for their declining years is one of the glories of Clifton. They married in 1728.

Nehemiah Champion II had engaged, during the war of Austrian Succession (1739-48), in privateering on a large scale. He was a partner in the *Dragon*,[34] the *Hawke*,[35] the *Lucea*,[36] the Townsend,[37] and the *Severn*.[38] In the course of the war the *Dragon* captured a number of prizes, sending them into Madeira or Falmouth, or bringing the prizes back to Bristol. Most of the ships survived the war undamaged, but the *Townsend*, after bringing in some rich prizes, was badly mauled by two French privateers in 1745. The *Lucea*, returning to Bristol in August 1743, fired a salute as was the custom: 'Through the carelessness of a gunner, two balls were left in two of the guns, which on their discharge, surprised many of the inhabitants of this city ... It is said one of the balls fell in the garden, late Cheneys, and the other near Cutler's Mill'.[39] For his part in these privateering ventures Champion was proscribed by the Quakers.[40] In times of peace, however, his boats appear to have been busily engaged in importing wines and port from Spain. Nehemiah died on 5 August 1747.

13. The grotto of Goldney House. The surprising variety of shells, fossils, rocks, ores and stones took Thomas Goldney II 20 years to assemble, and it is among the most elaborate examples surviving. Goldney died in 1768, four years after completing it. It had been inspired by Pope's celebrated grotto at Twickenham. Some of the shells came from the West Indies and the Pacific.

His eldest son, John, inherited his shares in the Bristol Brass Company. The second son, William, had little contact with his brother and devoted himself to his own works at Holywell, North Wales.[41] He subsequently became famous as a pioneer zinc spelter and as the owner of the extensive Warmley Copper Works and the brass foundry on St Augustine's Back.[42] The refuse ore, cast into square blocks of almost impenetrable hardness, forms one side of Clifton Court.[43] Cast into a different shape, it also forms the top of the walls along Stoke Hill Road.

William travelled widely in Europe and at the age of 20, in 1730, returned to Bristol and experimented with a new process, heating calamine to 900 degrees centigrade to produce zinc. He patented this method in 1738, and from 1746-61 expanded production at Warmley to such an extent as to require large inputs of capital. Nehemiah's death in 1747 occurred before the works commenced production and, partly as a result of inheritance, William was able to provide by far the largest part of the capital needed. His fellow partners were all Quakers – Thomas Goldney; Thomas Crosby who had married Rachel, widow of the banker Charles Harford; and Sampson Lloyd. Lloyd, from the Birmingham Quaker family of ironfounders, had married William's sister Rachel.

In January 1767 William Champion had proposed an imaginative plan for a floating harbour in Bristol which would have constructed lock gates across the Avon opposite Red Clift House.[44] He had previously built a large dock for repairing ships, near Rownham, but it proved not to be deep enough, and at the instigation of his uncle, Richard Champion, it was eventually purchased by the Merchants' Hall in 1770.[45] William Champion was a local shipbuilder and merchant as well as a contractor for large building works, and his yards were not short of business. However, he very much wanted the contract for building the lock gates at Red Clift, and wrote to Mylne in January 1767:

> ... altho' I wish for no more business than at present falls to my Lot, yet for the Public Good, was willing to undertake it: the more so, as my Dock Gates, Timber-Yards, Masons, Carpenters, Engineers, near the Spot, had furnished me with Opportunities of Experience and Conveniences beyond Others.[46]

Like his father, William was not averse to privateering, and during the Seven Years War (1756-63) he was part owner of a privateer, the *Nancy*, of 100 tons.[47] Among the manufactured items in stock at the Warmley Copper Works were such items as 'Guinea manillas and Guinea rods, kettles and pans, Guinea kettles, Guinea neptunes ... etc.'.[48] As Joan Day concludes, William Champion was clearly 'supplying wares for African barter in the outward journey of the Bristol slave trade'. William had so many business interests that eventually he appears to have over-reached himself, and was declared bankrupt on 28 February 1769. His creditor was his elder brother John Champion, merchant, who was himself declared bankrupt in 1787. Joseph Hornblower, maker of the Warmley engine for William Champion, had found him difficult: 'As to Mr. Champion [William], I think there are few mortals queerer, I hope I shall have done with them soon'.[49]

William's relations with his uncle, Richard Champion, were often strained, and this was shown particularly clearly in 1761 when William was in great need of more capital to expand the Warmley works. Richard was a leading partner in the Bristol Brass Company and a competitor. William complained that he had been deprived of coal when the older company had been able to continue buying supplies from the Warmley area. He said his men had been bribed to reveal the secrets of his spelter process which had then been used by the Brass Company. Furthermore, the Brass Company's unfair discount system made it difficult for Warmley to sell at a profit. Richard was an even more awkward person to deal with than William. He eventually provoked the Kingswood coal owners to combine and demand much higher prices for coal deliveries.

William's cousin, Richard Champion III, a member of the Society of Friends until 1778, found his religious beliefs under challenge from the world of commerce and from the stresses of the War of American Independence. In the second half of the 18th century the Society increased its organisational efficiency through the use of 'Enquiries', according to Deborah Olsen. Within the Society in Bristol she has traced from one to three disownments a year from 1774-7. In 1778 there were seven, and in the following year ten.[50] Richard Champion's relative, George, was 'disowned' for his 'concern in vessels fitted out with Letters of Marque', and Richard was reported in 1777 at a meeting of overseers 'to be fitting out an Armed Vessel'.[51] In 1778 Champion worked out an arrangement with a number of friends and creditors to act as trustees in disposing of his assets, in order to avoid a court declaration of bankruptcy which would have been grounds for disownment by the Society. There was a more serious matter concerning Bristol porcelain manufacture. It appears that when he purchased the patent and porcelain works, from Cookworthy in 1773, he did not satisfy the claims of three of the original Quaker partners. He would not submit to arbitration in 1778, but there is no record of disownment being served on him.[52] However, after 1778 Champion's financial contributions to the Society ceased. He did not stop his donations to other causes, such as the Royal Infirmary, so the evidence suggests that he deliberately chose to end his association with the Society of Friends.[53]

The increasing organisational efficiency of Quakers is also reflected in their campaign against the slave trade. For example, on 12 June 1769:

> Wm. Fry. brot. in from ye Meeting for Sufferings (London) 30 Books Entitled 'Caution to Great Brittain and her Colonies' by Anty. Benizet, wch. Wm. Fry, Jas. Harford, Joseph Fry and Thos. Frank are desired to distribute amongst those of this City who are Concerned in ye Negro Trade. Wm. Fry is desired to write for 40 or 50 more.[54]

This is in stark contrast to the activities of the Merchants' Hall, which frequently petitioned the government for aid or protection of their African trade. Yet, if the Quaker families of Clifton Hill were not involved with that trade directly, the Farr family certainly was.

The fourth of the houses on Clifton Hill previously mentioned is Clifton Wood House, built for Robert Smith. Occupied first by the Countess of Huntingdon, it was leased by the Farr family for much of the rest of the century. Today, the doorway of the 1720s is flanked by bowed-out additions from the Regency period. In 1721 Robert Smith bought about eight acres of land to build a mansion with views across to north Somerset and down the Avon. Inside the house much of the early Georgian work has survived. The hall has an elliptical arch such as that in Church House, and the wooden staircase is one of Bristol's best. Richard Farr I, ropemaker, was a leading agent of Bristol slaving voyages from 1726-45, and was responsible for managing 37 voyages.[55] Richard Farr II, who lived in Clifton Wood House, was Master of the Merchants' Hall in 1762 and Mayor of Bristol in 1763.[56] He was a merchant and ship owner trading to Africa, the West Indies and the American colonies. From 1747-72 he was responsible for managing 20 slave voyages.[57] Eventually, in 1778, he was judged bankrupt and died on 15 May 1782.[58] The whole family were prominent members of Lewin's Mead Meeting.

Richard Farr II had seven sons, two of whom became bankrupt at the same time as their father.[59] They were Thomas, a merchant and ship owner who became Sheriff in 1762 and Mayor in 1775, and Paul, Master of the Merchant Venturers in 1775. The family firm, Richard Farr and Sons, suffered heavy losses during the American war and failed. Thomas Farr had purchased 110 acres of the Blaise estate from Edward Gore, nephew of Anne Smyth, in 1762.[60] With the collapse of the family fortunes Thomas Farr was forced to sell Blaise House and its estate to Denham Skeate, a Bath lawyer, who lived there until 1789.[61]

The family figured prominently in the political life of Bristol. Richard Farr II was a committee member of the Tory Union Club which had sponsored Lord Clare's candidature in 1754 as Bristol's M.P.[62] When Lord Clare withdrew during the 1774 election, Richard Farr would not support either of the alternatives, Cruger and Burke. Thomas Farr, however, became a strong supporter of Burke and was once described by him, in a letter to Lord Rockingham, as his 'particular friend'. He entertained Burke at Blaise in 1774 and 1775. After a distinguished career as Sheriff, Mayor and Master of the Merchant Venturers, Thomas died on 30 August 1791. Paul Farr is often remembered best for the incident on 8 October 1774 when he rode through the night with John Noble to bring the news that Lord Clare had withdrawn to Richard Champion, so keen was he to get Burke nominated as a candidate. Paul, having been Master of the Merchant Venturers, ceased to play an active part in politics after the bankruptcy of 1778. John Farr was one of the sheriffs when war broke out in 1776, to whom Burke addressed the celebrated 'Letter to the Sheriffs of Bristol'. He became Mayor in 1784, after the war had ended.[63]

The Farr family, which had started with comparatively humble beginnings, played an active part in the early and most profitable years of the Bristol involvement in the slave trade. Richard Farr II managed slaving ventures at an early age compared with most instances of tradesmen's sons, who were often around 40 before getting the chance.[64] Colonial Naval Office Shipping Records show that there existed a core of investors who were regular shareholders in the partnerships that financed slave ventures. David Richardson has shown that, on average, two or three partners were involved in a Bristol slaving voyage. Richard Farr I was organising agent 37 times and his son, Richard, 20 times. The duties involved have been listed as selecting the outward-bound cargo of goods, fitting out the ship, corresponding with the master of the vessel, giving detailed instructions to factors in the West Indies or North America on the sale of slaves, and how to remit the proceeds, selling the inward-bound cargo, paying off the crew, and distributing the profits. Agents were often 'sleeping partners' in other slaving voyages, but the activities of an agent do not appear to have produced immediate financial rewards.[65]

In the years of the expansion of the slave trade, from 1698-1729, Richard Farr & Co. organised slaving ventures on the *Henry* and *Little Joseph* between Guinea and Jamaica, landing between 150 and 210 slaves.[66] They continued organising slave voyages in the Mary in the same year with 360 slaves.[67] The company found the slave trade a profitable business and it is not surprising that when the War of Austrian Succession occurred, and the Seven Years War, the Farrs were part owners of privateers which could increase profits even faster. Such privateers were the *Resolution*, the *Phoenix*, the *Anson*, the *Gloucester*, the *Hanover Planter*, the *Indian Queen* and the *True Briton*. The *Marlborough*, of 200 tons and 120 men, continued the slave trade and arrived in Jamaica with 252 slaves despite fighting off a 14-gunned enemy privateer.[68] The Farrs suffered losses however. The *Jason* was sunk, and the *Clifton* was lost at Madeira in 1766. Their other boats survived the hostilities without incident.[69]

Up to the time of the outbreak of war with America, Richard Farr and Sons were annually shipping a wide variety of produce to the American mainland colonies. On 5 June 1773, on board the *Charming Sally* and bound for North Carolina, they shipped:

9 casks of lead and shot; 3 coils cordage; 26 kegs paint; 12 boxes tobacco pipes; 30 casks nails; 1 bundle and 2 casks wrought iron; 54 jars vinegar; 324 iron pots; 36 grindstones; 75 bales woollen stuffs.[70]

On 7 August 1773 Richard Farr and Sons shipped to South Carolina on board the *Liberty* 19 bales of woollen stuffs and one chaise.[71] In November, aboard the *Fortune*, they shipped 2,200 tiles.[72] On 18 November, aboard the *St Helena* and for South Carolina, they shipped '4 casks and 4 bundles wrought iron; 2 casks glue; 4 casks lead shot; 2 casks hair brushes; and 4 coils cordage'. By 1775 Thomas Farr and William Jones were the largest colonial creditors of any of the Bristol merchants trading with America. Jones was owed £80,000 by debtors in Virginia and Thomas Farr was owed £8,200 by debtors in South Carolina.[73] Farr and Jones were sent to London as representatives of the Merchant Venturers in January 1775 to remonstrate with the government over its proceedings. They remained in London until March, but their appeals fell on deaf ears.

1774 had been a prosperous year for Bristol merchants, despite talk of a non-importation scheme. The colonists had decided not to import any goods from Britain after His Majesty's Government, under Lord North, had reacted very vigorously to the incident of the Boston Tea Party in December 1773. When the Boston patriots threw the cases of imported tea into the harbour rather than pay Townsend's duty on tea, the British government had passed a number of measures known as the 'Intollerable Acts'. The Massachusetts Government Act (14 Geo III c.45) suspended the whole machinery of representative government in the colony. The Boston Port Act closed the city to trade until the East India Company should have been compensated for the lost tea. The Administration of Justice Act gave the governors discretion to allow royal officials, accused of murder, to stand trial outside the colony in which the offence had been committed. The Quartering Act of May 1774 gave governors wide powers to billet troops in private houses, and extended the obligation to all the colonies. The colonists therefore had reason to fear that the North government intended to subvert American liberties.

The implementation of the non-importation scheme was so slow that Bristol merchants had plenty of time to prepare for it. One merchant observed on 6 August:

So great has been the exportation to America, particularly to New England, for these six weeks past, that it is the opinion of some merchants conversant in American trade that if the colonies do agree to a non-importation scheme, it will hardly be felt by our manufacturers for six months, or a year ...[74]

It was not until December that non-importation and non-consumption agreements were put into effect by the colonies. Latimer says that after that date '8,000 tons of shipping had to return from America unloaded, the blockade preventing them from landing their cargoes'.[75] Newspapers of the time recorded the closure of one Bristol firm employing 400 people in making serges for America. Another firm that regularly exported 3,000 pieces of Wiveliscombe stuff across the Atlantic reduced the order to 200 in 1774, and to nothing after that. Five or six hundred boxes of pipes were sent each year to the colonies from Bristol, but after 1774 these exports stopped.[76] Bristol's foreign trade rapidly declined. In 1775, Latimer records, the number of ships paying mayor's dues was 529. In 1781 it had fallen to 191. So, with many other Bristol merchants trading with the American colonies, Richard, Thomas and Paul Farr were faced with unpaid debts and a drastic reduction in their trade with South Carolina.[77] They were declared bankrupt.

These four merchant families that chose to live or build on Clifton Hill in the first half of the 18th century can be seen as representative of the mercantile and industrial wealth of Bristol at the time. Their interests were remarkably diversified and, in that respect, typify the manner of the city's growth pattern. One of the families played a leading role in the Merchants' Hall and in city politics. The two Quaker families, excluded from both domains, nevertheless played a very active part in Bristol's industrial development and in banking and trade. All four families found privateering too tempting to ignore, and they were all fortunate in their gamble. Goldney House, Clifton Court, Clifton Hill House and Clifton Wood House, while not ostentatious, are evidence of the growing wealth of Bristol's mercantile community. Wealth gave these merchants the opportunity to move out of the grime and stench of the city to the clean air, the spring water, and the village environment of Clifton.

Chapter Five

The Development of Lower Clifton

The rural character of the village of Clifton-on-the-Hill before 1780, and the elegance of the Hotwell season, have until recently obscured important developments occurring in Lower Clifton along the river Avon. In commenting on the 1746 de Wilstar map, John Latimer says that:

> by an Act passed in 1776, that portion of the parish lying between Hotwell Road and the Avon, from a little brook anciently called Woodwell Lane down to Rownham Ferry, was separated from Gloucestershire and incorporated with the City of Bristol, except as regarded local taxes and the parliamentary franchise of freeholders.[1]

This can be seen as the culmination of the industrial development of Lower Clifton. Effectively, the area south of Hotwells road had become part of the Bristol docks area at least 25 years previously.

The growing reputation of the Hotwell had attracted the interest of the Merchants' Hall soon after the Restoration and prompted them to try to buy the Manor as early as 1661. At this date however, it was not glass-making, nor the manufacture of lime for mortar, nor any of the trades associated with shipping that characterised Lower Clifton. The population of the parish, revealed in John Smyth's occupational census of 1608 as mainly rural, was rapidly transformed in the century following into a largely artisan community of lightermen, limeburners, shipwrights, glassworkers, masons and labourers living along the Hotwells Road.[2] The 1746 de Wilstar map no.5 shows the north side of the Hotwells Road laid out to houses, with gardens behind them, extending up into what had been Clifton Wood. Houses and tenements following the line of the road from the city to Dowry Square, along Avon Row, Avon Street and Love Street, had been erected by the time of the M. Hill map of 1787, and are clearly indicated.[3]

The most valuable recent work to throw light on this aspect of Clifton's history has been that of John S. Moore, using probate inventories for the years 1609-1761.[4] He has pointed out that many of the poorer people possessed less than the minimum £5 worth of moveable goods which necessitated going through the probate process. Therefore the 246 surviving inventories which have been transcribed cannot be a random sample of the total population of Clifton, but comprise the possessions of those householders or individuals with more than the minimum. By the time of Queen Elizabeth I there were over 80 skilled trades in the City of Bristol requiring an apprenticeship.[5] Apart from some lead mining on the Downs, it is not surprising to find that Clifton remained such a rural parish, since it was near such a centre of trade and industry at this time. With the growth of Bristol's port employment and

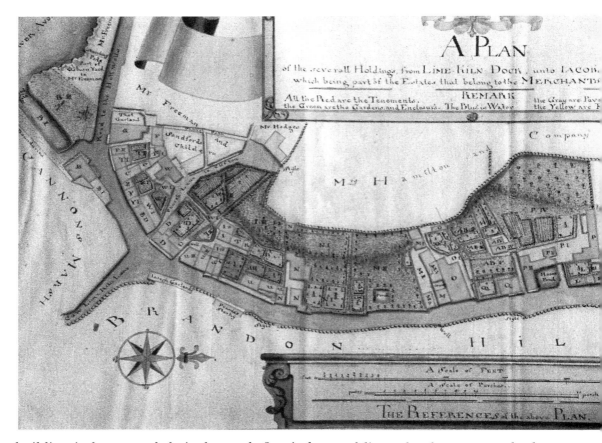

building industry, and their demands for timber and lime, development took place along the line of the Hotwell Road. The same facts explain why Clifton's population trends were so different from the surrounding areas.

By 1712 Sir Robert Atkyns' estimate for the population of Clifton was 450.[6] By 1779 Rudder showed it had trebled to 1,367,[7] and at the turn of the century the first census of 1801 shows it had nearly trebled again to 4,457.[8] One facet of this increase in population is seen in the need to extend St Andrew's church by the addition of a south aisle in 1768, costing £420. Fifteen people subscribed 25 guineas each on the understanding that they should be given pews in perpetuity. These included members of the Goldney, Elton and Hobhouse families and Sir William Draper. Every pew had a door with its lock and key and after services each was carefully locked by one of five widows wearing black dresses and white caps.[9] One hundred years later the ownership of these proprietory pews became a scandal when one was sold by auction for £190. Gradually funds were raised by the church wardens to buy them up. The petition to the Consistory Court for permission to build the south aisle stated: 'the parish of Clifton by reason of the many new Buildings lately erected therein had become very populous and was still increasing'.[10] Within 50 years the enlargements of 1768 were

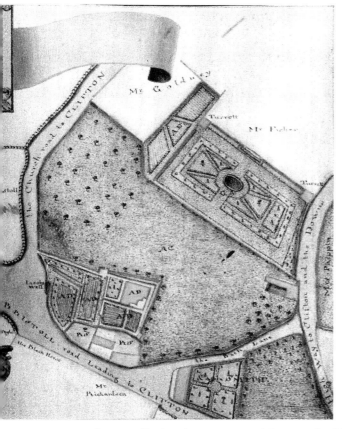

14. Jacob de Wilstar was a surveyor who was frequently employed by the corporation. His splendid survey of Clifton is preserved in the Merchant Venturers' archives and this is map 5. It shows in great detail each piece of ground in Lower Clifton, its size, and the name of the owner. Each plot along the north side of what is now Hotwells Road has a house with gardens to the rear, extending up to Clifton Wood.

seen to be totally inadequate, and it was decided to build a new church, slightly to the north of the existing building. The foundation stone was laid in 1816 and for some years the two churches, that of 1654 and that of 1822, stood side by side. The gorgeous old stones of the 1654 church were then carted away and buried in the quarry adjoining the last house in Harley Place.[11]

Building developments in Clifton had actually started as early as 1645. In 1625 the demesne woodland of Ralph Sadleir's ecclesiastical manor of Clifton amounted to about thirty acres.[12] This area of Clifton Wood was purchased by a Bristol brewer named Robert Hooke and leased in 1638 for 99 years to three men. One small holding amounting to five and a half acres was leased to John Bailey, limeburner, and 'about three acres or thereabouts' was leased to George Garland and William Croome. The rest went to Thomas Barnes, limeburner, 'with libertie and authoritie as well to digg stones on any part ... and to cutt down and moote upp all trees, woods and underwoods growing, or which shall grow in the said demised premises'.[13] John Bailey was also a customary tenant with a house, yard and garden, in the south-east corner of Clifton Wood, and probably was the same John Baylie who rented 'a cottage, lymekill and quarre' in Stokeleigh Slade in 1626 from Sir Hugh Smyth of Long

Ashton.[14] Later tenancies in Clifton Wood required the lessees to leave 12 oak trees standing on every acre they cleared.[15]

After the Civil War, Thomas Barnes began to sublet his 20 or so acres. One strip, 34 ft. broad and '40 yards up the hill leading from Rownham, past the house of William Clarke, yeoman,' was let to William Chandler in March 1665, for 70 years.[16] Another strip 30 ft. wide, running up to Clifton Wood, went to William Barlow, shoemaker.[17] Barnes' lease to John Watts was 100 ft. wide 'leading from Bristol towards Rownham, Southwards, and 444 feet long, back up to the woods'.[18] This was then split up into housing plots and sublet to David Sawyer, shipwright,[19] David Nicholas, lighterman,[20] and William Bailey, shipwright.[21]

Apart from leasing building land, John Watts also purchased part of Clifton Wood from Robert Hooke's son, John, and Frances, his wife, in 1667. This extended 500 ft. along the highway and sloped up to the wood for a depth of 100 ft. at least.[22] After John Hooke's death, his widow continued this policy of building development between Bristol and Rownham Meads on ground sloping up to the wood,[23] and the release of the reversionary rights by John and Frances Hooke to John Watts in February and March 1688 accelerated this process.[24]

Another landowner in Clifton was the Rev. John Power, whose estate amounted to 78 acres.[25] He too began leasing land for 100 years, in plots adjacent to Barnes' lease. In September 1693, he granted to Hugh Williams, 'a piece of woody ground adjoining to the garden, consisting of the length of the newly built wall about 255 feet, and in breadth 100 feet ... to hold for 100 years ...'.[26]

To the west of Jacob's Well Road from 1645, cottages were being built on land leased by Edward Bond, Thomas Garland, Thomas Barnes and William Pope. By July 1689 when the Merchants' Hall received particulars of tenements and lands bought from Roger Bathron, it was clear that Bond had sublet for cottage building five sites at the Limekiln bringing in an annual rent of £22, and Garland had overseen the construction of five more bringing in a total rent of £15 10s. Barnes had built seven cottages producing a total rent of £15 6s. a year and William Pope two more bringing in £3 annually.[27] Thomas Garland's houses were also close to the Limekiln, since he paid ground rent for the Limekiln as well as for the powder mill. Edward Bond in 1664 leased a quarter acre of ground called 'Cattwaies, situate, lying and being near the Lymekiln', paying a fine of £22 for 99 years and an annual rent of 20s.[28] In 1667, from the same landowner, John Whittington, Bond paid a fine of £1 10d. and an annual rent of 10s. for a 'new erected house, with the appurtenances, containing by estimation, 15 foot square (be it more or less)'. Another builder in the area was Nicholas Barnes, Thomas Barnes' father, as is revealed in another grant:

> John Whittington Esq., in consideration of £5, demises to Thomas Barnes, yeoman, a messuage or dwelling house, lately erected and built by Nicholas Barnes, father of the said Thomas Barnes, upon part of a Close called Lymotts Park, within the parish of Clifton aforesaid, with the garden on the North side of the said dwelling house, to hold for 99 years ... and warrants the premises against him and John Young, Esq., his grandfather, and Andrew Whittington Esq., his father.[29]

A VIEW of S.t VINCENTS ROCKS with the HOT WELL's from M.r Warrens House the Opposite South side of the River Avon A : S.t Vincents Rocks B : the Hot Wells C : M.r Warrens House

15.   A view across the Avon to the Hotwell and St Vincent's Rock. This view from the Redcliffe Gate glasshouse which was managed by Richard Warren in the early 18th century, is one of 10 to be found around the margins of John Rocque's plan of Bristol, 1750. Rocque was a Frenchman, living in England, and this was the second plan of the city which he had produced.

It is also clear that the houses varied in size and construction from 'that little tyled messuage or tenement now in the tenure of the said Thomas Cuffe ...' to 'the messuage or tenement 3 stories high, now in the possession of the said Thomas Barnes'.[30] The people who lived in these small cottage holdings soon began to include industrial workers engaged in bottling the Hotwell water for sale to other parts of England, the Continent and also to the West India colonies. Marriages of glasshouse workers are recorded in the Clifton parish registers in 1673, 1675 and 1676, while baptisms of children of workers 'at the Glasshouse' occur from 1675.[31]

The glasshouse was situated in Limekiln Lane, on the bank of the Avon close to Jacob's Well. It supplied the bottles referred to in the *Freeholders' Journal*, 1722, 'Bristol Water for sale in Bottles. The empty bottles at 2s. per dozen. N.B. The bottles are large and London shaped'.[32] One of the workers in the glasshouse, William Wood, voted in 1722 in the parish in which the glasshouse stood, so it was operational at that time. During the second half of the 18th century, the Child family directed the

16.   This watercolour of Limekiln Lane glasshouse by Hugh O'Neill, *c.*1821, is from the Braikenridge Collection. The glasshouse was operational as early as 1722 and it eventually produced 380 tons of glass in one year. During the second half of the century it was owned by the Child family, then Child, Nicholas and Co., and from the late 1780s John Nicholas and Co. Limekiln Lane was at the bottom of Jacob's Well Road.

glassworkers. William Child, who lived at 38 Limekiln Lane, and subsequently Richard Child, took apprentices in the trade.[33] One of the pupils at Bristol Grammar School from 1771 to 1778 was John Nicholas, whose address was The Glasshouse, Limekiln Lane. The later Directories of 1785 and 1787 show the ownership of the glasshouse as Child, Nicholas and Co.[34] By the late 1780s the firm had become simply John Nicholas and Co. Glasscones were quite large structures, built of brick and, on average, 50 ft. in diameter at the base, rising to a height of 100 ft. Workers' wages varied between 3s. 9½d. and 4s. a day for a building craftsman.[35] Glasshouses were exceedingly hot and uncomfortable places. A row of openings existed round the furnace for handling the crucibles which were straight-sided pots holding about a ton of glass each. The tall cone increased the natural draught, acting just like a chimney.[36] Workmen came from other parts of the country, attracted by the high wages, and this caused problems locally. Abraham Elton, Thomas Callowhill and Nathaniel Wade were appointed on 20 April 1700, particularly to look into the likelihood of 'workmen belonging to glasshouses and tydsmen, to prevent their becoming chargeable to the said parishes'.[37] Cleo Witt has described some visits paid by Patty More and her sister, toward the end of the 18th century, to some of these glasshouses:

> The work of a glass-house is an irregular thing, whether by day or by night ... The wages high, the eating and drinking luxurious – the body scarcely covered ... The high buildings of the glass houses ranged before the doors of these cottages, the great furnaces roaring – the swearing, eating, and drinking of these half-dressed, black-looking beings, gave it a most infernal and horrible appearance.[39]

The end process, however, was something quite beautiful and required skill of the highest order from the glasscutters who would take a whole week to make a pair of glass decanters. Eventually production at the Limekiln Lane glasshouse reached substantial proportions, amounting to 380 tons melted in one year.[39]

After 1676 the Bristol Marriage Licence Bonds increase our knowledge of the occupations of Clifton residents. The close association with the sea is indicated by the listing of three ships' carpenters, one sailmaker and three shipwrights between 1675 and 1681. Other Clifton occupations up to 1681 include three coopers, one vintner, a hairweaver and an ironmonger.

Leases of small lots of land for building in Clifton Wood continued into the early 18th century. The Hooke estate was passed on to Frances Hooke's daughter, Hannah Harris, and subsequently to her daughters Elizabeth and Martha. During the 1720s and 1730s, most of the former Clifton Wood came into the ownership of Robert Smith, the wealthy linen draper.[40] He employed the architect George Tully to build Clifton Wood House (1721) and Amherst (1738), as speculations, but financial problems forced him to sell most of his land to Thomas Goldney. Goldney acquired thereby most of the old Clifton Wood apart from the cottage-holdings along the Hotwells Road. The eventual purchaser of John Watt's estate, James Baskerville, together with the Goldneys, continued the extension of buildings along the Hotwells Road in the mid-18th century.[41] In 1736, Bristol Crown Fire Office insured five houses for Samuel Edward of St Augustine's parish. The houses were built or in process of building at the Limekilns and were constructed of stone and tiled.[42] These building activities involved narrow-wheeled carts filled with stone from the local quarries, which caused great ruts in the existing roads. This forced the Merchants' Society to act from the 1730s onwards to conserve the roads to the Hotwell.[43]

The Hotwell's existence and its peculiar properties were known to William Worcester in the 15th century. Society was frequenting the spa in 1634 but its problem was inaccessibility. The Master of Sidney Sussex College, Cambridge from 1610 to 1643, used to have Hotwell water sent to him to drink. It was reputed to be particularly efficacious for 'hot livers, feeble brains and red pimply faces'.[44] Its milky white water gushed out at a temperature of 76°F, roughly where Bridge Valley Road now meets the Portway, close to the Suspension Bridge. However, before the Civil War, there was not even a decent path giving access to the spring.

Having acquired the smaller manor of Clifton in 1676, the Merchants' Hall leased the Hotwell to two tenants for only £2 a year.[45] Latimer tells us however that some very prominent Bristolians, led by Robert Yate, M.P. and former mayor, and Sir Thomas Day, mayor and subsequent M.P., negotiated with the Hall in 1695, to provide suitable access to, and accommodation for, visitors to the spa. In April of that year the Merchants leased the well for 90 years at an annual rent of £5 to Charles Jones, soapboiler, and Thomas Callowhill, draper. These men were required to build a Pump Room and lodging houses and to lay out walks giving better access to the well and shelter to visitors. They promised to spend £500 on the project. The building they erected enclosed the spring, screening it from the tidal flow of the Avon, but looked more like a dock warehouse than a spa. These improvements to the Hotwell soon became known in fashionable circles and attracted people during the months of April to September, who then went on to enjoy the winter at Bath. Tradesmen were able to open bookshops and milliners' shops in both the Hotwell and Bath, so long as the season lasted.[46]

17. The old Hotwell House, 1696. Hot springs emerged on both sides of the Avon but were developed on the Clifton side. In 1695 the Merchant Venturers leased the well for 90 years to Thomas Callowhill, draper, and Charles Jones, soapboiler. They were required to build a pump room and lodging houses, and to improve access and shelter for visitors. They spent £500 and screened the spring from the tidal Avon, but the building looked more like a dock warehouse than a spa.

The Hotwell water was used for many illnesses. Skin diseases such as ulcers were said to be cured and, taken internally, the water was supposed to be very efficacious for scurvy, diabetes, gout and rheumatism.[47] By 1775 Sketchley's *Directory* was claiming Hotwell water cured dysentry, venereal disease and cancer![48] The Hotwell even received royal patronage in 1677 when Queen Catherine of Braganza rode along the rough track to the area, attended by courtiers, but we are not told if they actually descended the '200 slippery steps' to the source of the spring.[49] In its heyday, such elegant society people as the Duchess of Kent and the Duchess of Marlborough visited the spa. Addison, Cowper, Gay, Pope and Sheridan were among the literary figures who were present at different times.[50] It was a seasonal occasion and the strain on lodging accommodation must have been considerable. Bryan Little has pointed out that there is often a time lag between a spa's early social popularity and its major architectural expansion.[51]

By 1727 work had started on houses on the upper side of Dowry Square. By the middle decades of the century, Dowry Parade was built behind a broad pavement edged with pollarded limes, and in 1763 the sloping site of Albermarle Row created Clifton's first real terrace, designed with a central pediment linking the houses. For

Hotwell's visitors, worship at St Andrew's meant a very stiff climb for horses and
carriage up Granby Hill from Dowry Square, so a chapel within Clifton parish was
built by 1746, known as Dowry Chapel. A grimmer note was struck by the provision,
halfway up the hill to Clifton church, of a 'strangers' burial ground'. Inevitably, as
the claims for the healing properties of the Hotwell were spread far and wide,
people in the last extremities from tuberculosis came for a cure. The frequent
deaths lowered the reputation of the spa and another burial ground was found to be
necessary.[52]

There was also need for a new Assembly Room and one was built on the other side
of the road, and is indicated on Hill's 1787 map. These buildings are described on
the map as 'The Rooms'. Evening balls and parties were held there, and it was also
the height of fashion to give public breakfasts, sometimes for up to 200 people, with
cotillions and country dances.[53] These were given once or twice weekly during the
season and admission cost two shillings, including breakfast. (This second 'Long
Room' had to be destroyed quite recently to clear the way for the Cumberland Basin
flyover.) Sketchley's *Bristol Directory*, 1775, lists the managers of both these Long

18.   In May 1786 Samuel Powell leased the ground below Rownham Wood from the Merchant Venturers and
built the Colonnade next to Rock House. It consisted of two storeys; below the living rooms were shops and
Ann Yearsley's circulating library. The Colonnade is still there today.

Rooms. Joseph Norman, at the newer Loggon's long room, whose address is given as 4 Paradise Row, offered lodging and board and the facilities of a tavern and coffee house.[54] Across the road, at 3 Paradise Row, in the old long room, Mrs. Shirley offered simply lodging and board.[55]

Further diversions were provided for visitors in the New Vauxhall Gardens next to the Long Room. In 1757 four concerts a week were given in these gardens and admission was one shilling. There was also a Ladies' Tea Room where one might read the newspapers.[56] Riding on Durdham Down was very popular in good weather, and a covered promenade or 'Colonnade' from the Pump Room had existed since 1786. There had been a protected walk along the bank of the river for some time previously, but now a double row of trees was extended to give cover to visitors. Another favourite pastime was sailing down the river to Avonmouth, and even Portishead, for a picnic, and sometimes musicians accompanied these excursions. The serious business of taking the Hotwell water involved drinking as many as 12 glasses daily. Faced with such a regime, some invalids preferred the entertainments just described, where excitement and diversion provided an alternative cure.

Seasonal visitors to the Hotwells could also find entertainment at the Jacob's Well Theatre, built in 1729 next to the *Horse and Groom*, on the Clifton side of Jacob's Well Road, opposite Brandon Hill.[57] It was situated just outside the city boundaries because, previous to 1728, theatre players had been harassed by constant persecution from the Bristol magistrates. The players were accused of 'lewdness and debauchery' and their presence, it was feared, would 'corrupt and debauch' Bristol's youth. Before 1706 players had performed outside the city walls in Stokes Croft, but then in 1706 they had built themselves a playhouse at St Augustine's Back. The magistrates closed it down, however, after the Bishop of Bristol had denounced it as a 'school of debauchery and nursery of profaneness'. Therefore the players chose the neighbourhood of the Hotwell, outside the city boundary.

In 1726 the magistrates had permitted some actors from Drury Lane, London, to reopen the St Augustine's Theatre to perform Cato, and in 1728 John Gay gave several performances of the Beggar's Opera in the Long Room. This seems to have incensed the magistrates and a new mayor issued warrants against the St Augustine's Company and ordered the actors to be arrested in the midst of a performance. During the ensuing disturbance the actors escaped.[58]

In 1728 George Martin transferred a vacant piece of ground called 'Margaretts' to John Hippisley of Wookey, Somerset, a popular actor in London. Martin was the lessee of the *Horse and Groom* from the Merchants' Hall, under a grant of June 1723, and 'Margaretts' was land adjoining the inn. Hippisley was supported in his theatre project by Abraham Isaac Elton, John Brickdale, John Peach, William Vick and other wealthy Bristol merchants. The theatre was a cramped little building, but because it shared a party wall with another inn, the *Malt Shovel*, it had the advantage of a hole through which liquid refreshment was passed to the actors and to the privileged people who sat on the stage. An actor who left the stage on one side and needed to re-enter on the other, had to walk around the outside of the building. Latimer tells us that instead of footlights the stage was lit by tallow candles stuck in four hoops, suspended above the actors' heads. At one performance of *Richard III*, an actor wielded his sword rather too enthusiastically and cut through the rope of one of these chandeliers and had to be rescued from the hoop![59]

The auditorium of this theatre consisted of one larger front and four smaller side boxes, front and side galleries and an upper gallery to which servants were admitted free. One side of the gallery was called the 'balcony'. On special occasions seats were fitted at the back of the stage as in an amphitheatre and scenery then became an impossibility. Prices ranged from 1s. to 3s. and a full house represented takings of £80. One dare not think of the consequences had there been a fire. As an indication of the public enthusiasm existing in Bristol for the Jacob's Well Theatre, in 1760 ladies and gentlemen were requested to send their servants by 5 o'clock to secure seats. It is said that one pregnant young woman would not be dissuaded from watching a performance of *Romeo and Juliet* and that, while crossing Brandon Hill afterwards on her way home, she gave birth to a boy whom she named Romeo.[60]

So well was the new theatre patronised, that Hippisley prudently obtained from George Martin his entire lease and occupied the *Horse and Groom* as his house. Eventually, in 1746, the Merchants' Hall granted Hippisley the *Horse and Groom* and the piece of ground called Margaretts for the lifetime of his two children, on payment of two rents of 5s. each. After Hippisley died in 1748, Mrs. Green, one of those children, continued to live in the old inn until 1791.

Among the drawbacks of the theatre were its distance from the city and the complete absence of lighting in the neighbourhood. Sometimes on dark nights the manager placed men with torches along the road from Jacob's Well to College Green. As late as April 1792 a local newspaper, reporting an accident in Hotwell Road, spoke of the mud and said that coaches sank into the soft surface and the occupants dreaded being smothered.[61] The Jacob's Well Theatre finally closed in 1779 since by then the theatre in King Street had become firmly established and from 1779 to 1781 Sarah Siddons was playing to packed houses there.[62]

At the height of its popularity the Bristol Hotwell was crowded with genteel society and invalids of all ranks. Three large taverns were constantly full and the two ball-rooms made a profit. From 12 noon to 2 o'clock the Pump Room was so crowded that it was difficult to get to drink the water. The houses that had been built for letting in Dowry Parade, Chapel Row and Dowry Square made fortunes for their owners. They were quite large houses and the *Bristol Oracle* for 22 January 1748, carried an advertisement for 4 Dowry Square which gives a good idea of the size. It was four storeys high and there were four rooms to each floor:

> The house is large and commodious, has a Grand Entrance and a Staircase, a Dining-Room 42' by 16½', four large and necessary Closets, Garrets etc., built on purpose for lodgings, having below Stairs two large kitchens, a Servants' Hall, Laundry, Cellars, Pantries, both sorts of Water, and all other conveniences, and handsome paved Areas six feet wide.[63]

Yet the popularity of the spa did not last and when the end came it was dramatic.

In 1784 the Merchants' Hall had advertised for a new tenant for the Hotwell, without success. The next year they offered leases of from 40 to 60 years. The

Merchants wanted £1,000 to be spent on building a quay wall and £500 on protecting the spring from the tide. Furthermore, they wanted the Pump Room enlarged. A new tenant was not forthcoming on such terms and the Society were forced to carry out the improvements themselves and to appoint Thomas Perkins as caretaker for five years.[64] To cover this expenditure the Merchants' Hall naturally wanted to raise the rent and this caused the new tenant, Samuel Powell, great difficulties from the start. He tried all sorts of ways to raise receipts so that he could pay the increased rent and in so doing he brought about a rapid decline in the spa's popularity. One of the hotels and two of the Assembly Rooms were forced to close as a result of the bankruptcy of their occupiers and many lodging-house keepers also became insolvent.[65] The Merchants allowed Powell to continue his increased charges for three years before interfering in March 1793. By then genteel society had moved to other spas and the damage had been done. With the ending of the long war with France the wealthy were able once more to travel to European watering places. The old Hotwell House was pulled down in 1822 to make way for Bridge Valley Road, and a new Pump Room was demolished in its turn to make navigation of the Avon safer at Hotwell Point.[66]

If the peak period of popularity for the seasonal Hotwell spa was between about 1760 and 1784 when the Merchants renewed the lease, it was during this period that the permanent residents in Clifton rose from 1,367 in 1779 to 2,205 in 1784. One might have looked to the service industries, the ostlers, farriers, saddlers, carriage builders, spurriers, tailors, upholsterers, glovers, haberdashers, barbers, perukemakers and innkeepers to have accounted for the increase in permanent residents. The evidence of the transcribed probate inventories might be expected to show some such trend in the earlier years before the heyday of the Hotwell.[67] No such trend is apparent, yet when the Hotwell was in rapid decline, the population of Clifton rose from 2,205,[68] to 4,457 by the time of the 1801 census.[69]

This increase in population followed the beginnings of the development of upper Clifton after 1760. The 'rage for building' was commented on in the local press in November 1786 at the time Sion Row was being built. By 1791, *Felix Farley's Journal* commented that 'ground is actually taken for more than 3,000 houses, which will require some hundreds more artificers than are already employed'.[70] These schemes included such undertakings as Royal York and Cornwallis Crescents. In addition to building craftsmen, other workmen had been required in 1765 to construct William Champion's large dock for repairing ships on the banks of the Avon near Rownham Meads. After the Merchants' Hall bought the dock, from 1776 great schemes to enlarge the capacity were put in hand to contain 36 large ships. Furthermore, in order to minimise the great risk to the central docks area from fire due to inflammable imports such as turpentine, tar and pitch, unloaded next to piles of timber, an Act of Parliament was secured in 1776. This brought the area of Clifton from Jacob's Well Road to Rownham Passage within the City and County of Bristol and secured the maximum use of their newly acquired dock by requiring all the dangerous combustible imports to be unloaded at the Merchants' Dock.[71]

During the same period the shipping industry of Bristol expanded significantly. The total tonnage of ships and vessels in the deep sea and coasting trades belonging to Bristol 1772-1800, peaked in 1786. The actual number of ships involved had reached 358 in 1775 before the American war, but was back up to 313 again in 1786.[72] This meant a substantial demand for mariners, lightermen, caulkers, shipwrights, carpenters and sailcloth makers. Rented accommodation was available along the Hotwells Road and the decline of the spa did not noticeably set back the development of Lower Clifton as a whole. In fact from 1804-9 the construction of William Jessop's floating harbour, the excavation of the Cumberland Basin at Rownham Meads, the manufacture of lime for mortar, provided a major source of employment for the area and a spur to further development of Lower Clifton.[73]

Chapter Six

Speculators and Developers in the 18th Century

From the Civil War until the turn of the 18th century the development of Lower Clifton and the Hotwell had been undirected and piecemeal. From the Limekilns westwards to Rownham Meads along the line of the Mardyke, Love Street and the Withy Bed, the Rev. John Power, Francis Freeman and Frances Hooke had been leasing ground for building.[1] The development of the Hotwell gave a new impetus to building to provide suitable houses to let for visitors who came for the season. Dowry Mead was part of the 78-acre estate owned by the Rev. John Power, and what came to be known as Dowry Square was laid out for building soon after 1720 in the Mead. It was referred to in one deed as 'a certain Square then already agreed on, and intended to be laid out in Dowry aforesaid', and the West side was 'conveyed to Thomas Oldfield and George Tully by the said John Power'.[2]

To the north of Dowry Mead was land owned by the Merchants' Hall. Home Grounds contained nine acres, and Colliers Wood seven acres, but these had been thrown into 'closes' called Upper Ground, Lower Ground and Mead Close. By 1752 they were bounded 'on the South with Buildings erected on the said Mead, heretofore called Dowry Mead, and now Dowry Square, and on the North and West with the houses and grounds of the late Mr. Power'.[3]

The layout of the square, which was planned by George Tully, was left open to the south, and the west side was extended by Chapel Row at roughly the same date that many of the houses in Dowry Square were being erected.[4] Later the eastern arm was extended through the construction of Dowry Parade. The building of the square took place over nearly 20 years and was the work of a number of speculating builders such as Richard Matthews and Thomas Oldfield. Dowry Parade, on the other hand, was constructed by a number of builders as a uniform terrace with a wide-paved walk during 1763-4. Among these builders were Benjamin Probert, Robert Comfort and Matthew Gilbert.[5] The land belonged to the Merchants' Hall and was the old withy bed, marked 'E' on the de Wilstar map of 1746.

Dowry Square was not Bristol's first square, but the haphazard way it came together over an extended period is indicative of how difficult it was for the speculative builders to assemble enough capital to carry through such a project. During the reign of William and Mary in 1699, a square was laid out which at that time was the largest residential square in the whole of England. It was named in honour of Queen Anne after her visit in 1702, and was a carefully planned extension into the Marsh of the old medieval city. The leases granted on these properties laid down stringent and specific requirements for the materials and heights of the buildings, and cannot fail to have been influenced by the London development of the Covent Garden piazza on the Duke of Bedford's estate.[6] Just as London pattern books for furniture influenced provincial towns in the 18th century, so too did the new Italianate fashion for uniform terraces around a square. But the cost of realising such a project was beyond the financial means of building craftsmen. It appears that the Dowry Square developers leased the land, and borrowed on mortgages, to complete their houses. They also appear to have limited their involvement to a small number of properties each. Nevertheless, even in the early years of the century, Tory attorneys like Jarrit Smith, who handled the business of many wealthy clients, or Samuel Worrall, who took over the very lucrative practice of Mr. Fane in 1757, began to fill the need to channel funds and to act in the capacity of developers.[7]

The importance of attorneys as developers in enabling large-scale building enterprises to take place has been explained very clearly by J. R. Ward.[8] Such men as Jarrit Smith, Samuel Worrell, Harry Elderton, Thomas Morgan, Francis Ward and Matthew M. Coates, were all attorneys and therefore had many advantages as developers. They knew the land market from their conveyancing business. They managed trusts and house property, and their function in placing clients' investments gave them the opportunity to direct finance into building development. They purchased land, employed surveyors to draw up their plans and let it under covenants to build. They were in a key position to influence the quality and overall design of large-scale projects, and had to make large investments before a single house was built. The site had to be prepared, and the topography of the steep slopes of Clifton made this a crucial factor. The vaults and basements of Royal York Crescent, Cornwallis Crescent and Belle-Vue needed thousands of pounds before the houses could be erected. William Watts, the Redcliff plumber who had made a fortune from making lead shot, was bankrupted by the costs of the retaining wall for Windsor Terrace. Anyone looking up at Windsor Terrace from the Avon Gorge can appreciate the difficulties involved.

The attorneys who became developers also came into contact with builders through management of property and its repair and maintenance. This was important because they had to rely heavily on the principal master builder who had to oversee the work of the craftsmen to whom he sold plots. If the work was incompetent and could not be sold then the principal builder would find himself in the debtors' prison. In most cases some of his own capital was invested in the materials and if things went wrong he might lose the lot. The developers also had to ensure that their builders did not misappropriate for other developments the moneys they advanced.

From time to time in the early years of the century the Merchants' Hall had granted permission to build on its land. Thomas Goldney, who had bought Lord Folliott's house, proposed to the Hall in 1717 that he build on some of their ground and was granted a lease.[10] In 1723 James Hollidge proposed to build on the East side of Dowry Square and asked for permission.[9] In 1746 it was Charles Gregory who proposed to build, and in that year the Society decided to institute a survey of the manor by Jacob de Wilstar, which is preserved in the archives of the Merchants' Hall. As a result of this detailed set of maps the Society was able to give serious thought to building development on its property. Perhaps they were jogged into doing so on receipt of a request from Mrs. Ann Hibbs, a widow, in January 1749:

Mrs. Hibbs applys to alter the tenure of some Grounds in Clifton, late Hollidge's, from lease for 99 years determinable on lives, to Lease for 40 years renewable every 14, as on those conditions she can let part of them out for Building – the Consideration thereof referred to the Standing Committee who are empowered to agree with Mrs. Hibbs and any other person holding lands in Clifton, on such terms as they think proper.[11]

The Standing Committee considered Ann Hibbs' request for nearly a year and then decided to grant similar terms to other leaseholders. Thus began the gradual building development of Clifton: 'Leases to be granted to Alderman Coombs and Mr. Samuel Gardner on the like terms'.[12]

Ann Hibbs leased part of those two steeply rising fields, belonging to the Society, which overlooked Dowry Square, and were now called Upper Ground, Lower Ground and Mead Close. (B II on the 1746 map.) Henry Coombe leased one of the two great houses and gardens which formed part of this same holding of the late James Hollidge. Ann Hibbs now contracted to build the two splendid houses called Cornwallis House and Grove House.[13] She lived in the latter and the Hobhouse family bought Cornwallis. Later in the century the Hall looked at the estimated value to William Hibbs of Grove House (£50 per annum and to Henry Hobhouse (£75 per annum, clear of Chief Rents), and decided to make William Hibbs pay £125 for renewal of his lease in 1785.[14] Ann Hibbs also built some smaller developments, in the tenure of Robert Rice, which lay above the west side of Dowry Square. These developments created Green Street and crossed what became Hope Chapel Hill:

> the same appears to consist of three tenements, two Gardens, two Coachhouses and three stables, and to be of the yearly value of £45, besides so much of the street called Green Street as ranges before two of the said tenements, the two Coachhouses and one Stable.[15]

At about the same time, Francis Freeman, who owned 189 acres of Clifton, decided to grant building leases as well. His proposed road would take in part of the manorial waste, so even he needed the Hall's permission.[16] Richard Coombe erected a number of buildings on Mead Close, a four-acre plot, and by 1752 his houses had been bought by Tobias Middleton, William Morris, Henry Marsh, John Watkins, Thomas Morgan and William Biss.[17]

Holding land above Ann Hibbs' building development, John Deverell, the surgeon, initially complained that his view of the country from the 'Hill Close' (DV), was spoilt. He changed his mind however and decided to get in on the act by applying to the Society in 1758 for 40-year building leases, renewable every 14 years.[18] These leases related to Cecills Littlefields (7 acres), D II on the 1746 map, which were adjacent to Francis Freeman's Battons Ground (U VIII), and Littlefields (or leadfields) (U VII), and Frimmers (U VI).

Samuel Gardiner leased from the Society two acres of land to the south of Dowry Square called the Withy Bed, which in 1757 was meadow, and bounded by the road running from the Hotwell to Bristol. In 1761 he surrendered his lease, in return for another, on his undertaking to lay out £500 on a good and substantial house within three years.[19] The Rev. Alexander Daniel held a lease next to the Withy Bed and he agreed to give up half an acre for brickmaking.[20] Gardiner had received a number of leases from the Society in 1739, 1752, 1757 and 1762 in connection with the Withy Bed, and these grants are referred to in the Society's 19th-century Inventory of

Deeds as the 'lands and premises whereon Love Street, Charles Place, and the first six houses in Dowry Parade are built'.[21] At the end of the century another deed referring to the Withy Bed, speaks of

> all those 23 several messuages or tenements thereon erected, 19 whereof fronted towards a certain street called Love Street, and the other four to a certain place called the Parade, the first of which said Messuages in Love Street aforesaid adjoined to a House called or known by the name or sign of the Salutation Inn ...'[22]

In 1764 and again three years later, Richard Coombe exchanged his leases to 40-year building leases and continued to develop the ground above and to the west of Dowry Square. In October 1764 the Hall Standing Committee viewed from Ann Hibbs' house the proposed line of these buildings and defined how far they might extend without inconveniencing Mrs. Hibbs.[23] Coombe was also given permission to quarry stone from the east side of Honeypen Hill, an area which is now covered by Park Place and Richmond Hill.

In the 1760s there was a continuing need for lodgings for the fashionable visitors to the Hotwell and further building land was needed close to the Pump Room. Just above Dowry Square and continuing the line of Love Street, was land belonging to Christopher and Mary Budge.[24] In 1762 John Webb was granted a plot of land in land in Albermarle Street. It is probable that his architect was Thomas Paty, and certain that the builder was the house carpenter, James Fear. Cumberland House, no. 5 Albermarle Row, was the centre of a development carried out at the same time as nos. 2 to 8. Their fronts had to be stepped up to accommodate the rise in the ground from south to north. The result was Bristol's first red brick terrace, with freestone dressings, and a central pediment with a monogram. The houses are three stories high, with a basement and a garret storey. The land to the north of Albermarle was leased by James Fear, and the street to the south had been contracted for by Nathaniel Crook.

Another similar range of three double-fronted houses, each of three stories with a garret and basement, was erected for Thomas Boyce near Clifton Green in 1763. Boyce was a wigmaker and he invested £8,000 in the speculation, hoping the houses would meet the demand by wealthy visitors for rented accommodation. These houses were originally built of red brick and dressed with freestone, and Ison believes the fronts to be the work of Thomas Paty.[25] At the back were five stables containing 34 stalls, and 10 coach houses. Unfortunately, Thomas Boyce became bankrupt in November 1772 and the properties were sold by auction in February the next year.[26] One can only speculate that the seasonal nature of the Hotwell Spa meant that while the strain on lodging accommodation was present from April to September, Boyce was not getting sufficient return throughout the year.[27]

More of Paty's work can be seen facing Clifton Green, next to Clifton Court (The Chesterfield). In about 1765, two adjoining houses were built for Samuel Worrall on land originally belonging to John Hodges, but acquired by Worrall.[28] Prospect House has a marked similarity to the central section of Boyce's Buildings, but Beresford House was a less sophisticated construction, and has been much altered.[29] This land was originally part of that manor belonging to the Deans and Canons of Westbury.

The Rev. Alexander Daniel had in 1755 leased from the Merchants' Hall a large part of the 31 acres of Rownham Meads: 'all those 27 acres of Meadow and Pasture Ground in Rownham Mead, together with the Salutation Inn, and also one other piece [A V] and also one moiety of ⅗ths parts of one other plot'.[30]

His executor surrendered one acre (Parson's Breach, A IV), and was regranted it on a 40-year building lease on condition that he laid out £500 in building within three years.[31] The rest fortunately remained meadow with one exception until the construction by William Jessop between 1804-9 of the Floating Harbour.[32] This was the construction of a dock by William Champion in 1765, through part of this land. The Merchants' Hall agreed with Champion in 1767 to make an exchange of land to facilitate this:[33]

> All that piece of ground heretofore commonly known by the name of Parsons Breach, but which is now built upon, containing by estimation ½ an acre, ... heretofore bounded on the East with a Brickyard, on the West with Lands belonging to the Deans and Kellys, on the North with the highway leading to Rownham, and on the South with land belonging to Mr. Wickham; ... but the said premises and Boundaries thereof are all now transformed, and sundry Buildings erected and a Dock and Yard made thereon, or on some part thereof, by him, the said William Champion. And also all that one other piece of Meadow Ground lying and being in the said Mead called Rownham's Mead, containing one acre (A V) ... William Champion gives an acre and a half in Rownham Mead, late in the occupation of Alexander Daniel, Clerk, and now of John Davie, Clerk, and also one moiety of ⅗ths of parts of one other Plot or Piece of Ground lying and being in the same Mead, heretofore the land of the Deans and the Kellys.[34]

William Champion in 1767 granted a quarter part of Champion's Dock to William Bridges Champion, and in 1768 another quarter, for £2,750. He also settled on his children, William Bridges, John and Ann, an undivided half of his Docks, houses etc., but then became bankrupt in 1769.[35] The Dock had not been fully used, and had proved too shallow for some boats, so it was put up for auction. In a private capacity, some members of the Merchants' Hall made a successful bid of £2,615 for the Dock and £1,420 for the houses and ground nearby. They then offered it to the Hall which borrowed the money and accepted the offer. From then on it was known as Merchants' Dock. The Society also ensured the Dock would be fully used by obtaining an Act of Parliament compelling all vessels with tar, pitch, deals and combustibles to off-load on a wharf on the west side of the Merchants' Dock, not allowing such cargoes to off-load in the heart of the city.[36] The Society enlarged the dock to take 16 ships, and exploited the adjoining property which included a saw pit, a brickyard and kiln, and a smaller dock let to Mr. Hilhouse.

Building activity in the 18th century was inevitably influenced by the state of trade and the frequency of war. Government borrowing for war reduced the finance available in the private sector, and this was particularly true for the period of the War of American Independence, 1776-83. Even with the developments described so far, Clifton in 1780 was still essentially an area around the Green. Several larger individual houses had been built along Clifton Down Road from the isolated terrace of Boyce's Buildings to Manilla Hall. Down near the river, centred on Dowry Square, and dependent on the Hotwell, lodgings for visitors had been built: Albermarle Row,

The Parade, Chapel Row, Love Street and Avon Street. Sion Hill climbed up from St Vincent's Rocks with what Andor Gomme has described as a delightful variety of bows, bays, balconies and verandas.[37] Yet Clifton was still a village with footpaths linking the hill to the lower ground near the river, as can be seen on M. Hill's map of 1787.

With the return of peace in 1782 building activity increased in pace. This was true for Bristol as a whole, but for Clifton in particular it was dramatic. Spectacular terraces changed the shape of Clifton in the last 15 years of the century from a village into the prosperous outer suburb of a great trading city. The terraces began slowly at first and in an oddly haphazard manner so far as siting was concerned. The attorneys

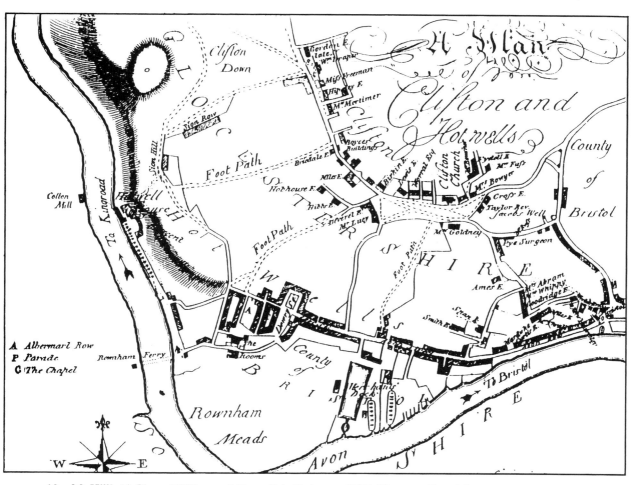

19. M. Hill's 'A Plan of Clifton and Hotwells', 11 August 1787. The compiler of the map was primarily interested in the occupancy of the main Clifton residences. Rownham Meads are literally meadows. Gloucester Row, Rodney Place, Windsor Terrace, Royal York Crescent and Cornwallis Crescent are not built. Fields like Brimley Close are not covered by The Mall, and Ferney Close still awaits Lansdown Terrace and the Royal Promenade.

Thomas Morgan and Matthew M. Coates financed the building of Sion Row, and also of Gloucester Row, on land belonging to Parsons and to John Power's heir, Mr. Beames.[38] Down by the river, on land belonging to the Merchants' Hall, Samuel Powell developed St Vincent's Parade.[39] Along the higher ground on the 12 acres of Brimley Close (P XIII) belonging to Mr. Beames, Rodney Place and The Mall were constructed. In May 1788 Sarah Farley published a letter listing the building works then proposed or actually in progress, and noted that the majority was speculative.[40] In April 1791, Sarah Farley wrote in her *Journal* that: 'So great is the spirit of building in this city and its environs that we hear ground is actually taken for more than 3,000 houses, which will require some hundreds more journeymen artificers than are already employed ...'.[41] The most glorious building phase of the Royal York Crescent, Cornwallis Crescent and Windsor Terrace was yet to come.

The guides covering this area are widely available, detailed and more than adequate. Walter Ison's work on Georgian buildings, Gomme, Jenner and Little's survey of Bristol's architecture, Patrick McGrath's study of the Merchant Venturers, and J. R. Ward's research into the financing of the building speculators, are all comprehensive. It might be thought that there is nothing more to be said, but an area that has not yet been worked over is that of the Merchant Hall's building leases. Before attempting to do this it is worth looking in some detail at the bankruptcy proceedings of one of the building speculators whose papers have survived. Normally such papers are returned to the plaintiffs, but one splendid exception exists at the Public Record Office in Chancery Lane.[42] A few relevant deeds have found their way into Bristol Archives Office, together with some bankruptcy papers,[43] but nothing to compare with the Examinations, Depositions and other Proceedings under Commission of Bankruptcy, October 22 1794, against William Bleuden, carpenter, builder, dealer and chapman, which are at Chancery Lane.

William Bleuden rose from small beginnings to contract for whole terraces and squares such as Gloucester Row (13 houses each costing £1,000), Granby Place and Hope Square (20 houses each costing £600). He was finally bankrupted by the Mariners' Path development on land released by the Rev. John Taylor in Westbury-on-Trym. All trace of this development has been removed long since. Bleuden was not an established master craftsman. J. R. Ward has discovered that in the 1760s and '70s 'about 70 per cent of the known builders on speculative developments were established master craftsmen, but in the 1780s and '90s the proportion fell to less than 30 per cent'.[44] Reputable builders were unwilling to take part in the more ambitious schemes and so developers had to sell much of their land to mere 'journeyman carpenters and working masons'.[45] Bleuden was one of these carpenters upon whom the developers came to rely. He was declared bankrupt in October 1794, Simon Oliver, merchant and Harry Elderton, Attorney-at-law, seizing his estate and effects, as the chosen assignees. This estate consisted of

> sundry Leasehold Houses and Estates in Sion Row, Hope Square and Gloucester Place in the parish of Clifton ... and sundry other property to a very large and considerable amount, and much more than sufficient to pay the just debts of the said William Bleuden at the time he was declared a Bankrupt under the said Commission, he the said William Bleuden, being indebted to sundry persons at that time in a very small and inconsiderable sum of money in the whole.[46]

This was particularly devastating to a small builder like Bleuden since he was owed a far greater sum by the chief of developers, James Lockier.

> James Lockier, a Timber Merchant and Builder in Bristol and Thomas Sims of the same City, Builder, are jointly and severally held and firmly bound unto William Bleuden of Clifton ... Builder, in the sum of £1,000.
>
> Defendant (Lockier) was a Timber Merchant and Builder in Bristol, he was some time ago declared a Bankrupt, and his debts appear to exceed £300,000.
>
> Defendant (Sims) is a Carpenter in solvent Circumstances and carrying on his trade in Bristol.[47]

The sum owed by Lockier and Sims was roughly the cost of a couple of houses in Hope Square. Harry Elderton, who was bringing the bankruptcy proceedings against Bleuden, was himself declared a bankrupt, 'and soon afterwards departed this life insolvent, without having received any part of the monies arising from the sale of the said William Bleuden's Estate and Effects'.[48]

During the bankruptcy proceedings his creditors examined Bleuden at the *White Lyon*, Broad Street, on 27 January 1795. He told them that he was born at Taunton, Somerset, the son of William Bleuden, a labouring weaver. He left home at the age of 13 and went into service with a local carpenter, William Preece, and stayed three years. When he was 16 he moved to Dundry, Somerset for six months and served Mr. Sampson for eight shillings per week. He then moved to London and for the next three years worked for different masters as a journeyman. Bleuden's next move was to Faversham, Kent, for eight months, then to Dover, where he took a boat to Exeter. In 1779 he finally settled in Bristol and worked as a journeyman carpenter for 12 shillings per week for various masters until 1782. Although he could not read or write he set up on his own account in 1782, purchasing his necessary timber on credit, and working on Thomas Morgan's developments in Clifton. About the same time he leased a piece of ground from Morgan, built a single house costing £400 and sold it to Mr. Wood for a profit. The next year he leased another piece of ground, built two houses and sold them. Over the years he prospered until he was able to contract for whole streets or squares.[49] He worked on Harry Elderton's developments as well as Morgan's, in partnership with other builders like William Jones, carpenter, John Harris, mason, and Thomas Evans.[50] He bought large quantities of timber, ashlar, and rough stone, bricks, lime and other materials.

On each development the pattern was repeated. Bleuden took land from Morgan or Elderton under covenant to build, and built some of the houses himself while selling the rest of the plots to other builders. When the houses were sold he took the profits and moved on. The developers, like Harry Elderton, 'consented to provide them, in the whole, with at least £5,000 in occasional sums ... but he never should be any more Money in advance than ⅔s of the value (of houses built on the ground)'.[51] J. R. Ward has shown how the developers obtained such capital from wealthy clients, country banks, and West Indies absentee proprietors. On the rising housing market there was the likelihood of high returns, and there seemed little risk involved.[52] Sometimes, as with the land called Brimley Close, Bleuden built the ends of the terrace:

The Cttee. viewed the ground at Clifton adjoining the Dean's field called Brimley's, proposed to be taken by Mr. Bleuden and others, who have agreed for that part of Brimley's, as mentioned in the proceedings of the Cttee. of 16th October last. Mr. Bleuden attended and was directed to prepare an elevation of the West front of the two Houses proposed to be built by him; the one at the Northward and the other at the Southward end of the said ground ... at a rent of 1d. per foot, ... and covenanting that if any Houses are built fronting to the Westward between the two now proposed then the same shall be uniform with such two houses.[53]

One of the leading developers, Harry Elderton, an attorney, had come to Bristol in the 1780s from Frome in Somerset where his brother Thomas owned a textile manufacturing business. Cloth, shirts, linen, muslin, velverett, striped and checked pieces, cambricks, serges, women's silk hose, corduroy, ribbons, threads and cottons were sent all over the country. Customers received goods in London, York, Bath, Brighton and Tavistock. As a lawyer, Harry Elderton acted for his brother in cases concerning recovery of outstanding debts.[54] After moving to Bristol Elderton was involved in developing some key sites in Clifton, such as Cornwallis Crescent, Bellevue, Hope Square and Granby Place.

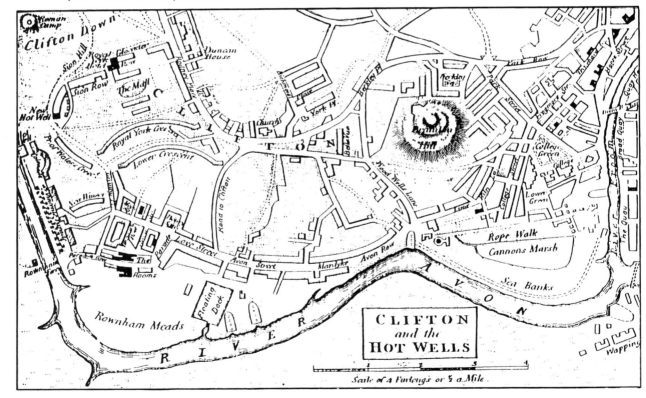

20. John Feltham's map of Clifton and the Hotwells, 1803. This map comes from his *Guide to the Watering Places*, and is not a very detailed plan. A blank space indicates the site of the Assembly Rooms behind Rodney Place and The Mall is roughly shown. Rownham Meads still remains pasture ground.

Another leading developer for whom Bleuden worked was Thomas Morgan, who had been a member of the Bristol legal fraternity for many years before becoming a developer and 'adventurer'.[55] Latimer even describes him as a 'local benefactor' for improving the amenities of Upper Clifton, and incidentally his own properties in Sion Row, by drilling a shaft down 250 ft. through the limestone to tap a spring which yielded 34,000 gallons daily. At great expense, Thomas Morgan laid supply pipes to many neighbouring houses, and supplied more distant customers by carts. He also erected a steam engine to supply the water at pressure. The water was at 70 degrees which was nearly as high as the temperature at the Hotwell, and, inevitably, a Pump Room was built, with hot baths and a Reading Room. The site is now covered by *St Vincent Rocks Hotel*. Over 300 houses were supplied from the spring, but Sion Spring never attracted visitors on the scale of the Hotwell.[56] Morgan was responsible for developing The Mall, Sion Row and Gloucester Row.

James Lockier was, undoubtedly, the most extensive of Bristol's developers. His work can be seen in various other parts of Bristol such as Portland Square and James Square, as well as in Clifton. His most spectacular undertaking of about 1790, in conjunction with a number of other builders, such as John Coles, Michael Davis, Ezekiel Evans and Richard Constant, was the Royal York Crescent.[57] His other developments in Clifton included Richmond Place and, in conjunction with Robert Jones, Davis and Husband, and Thomas Rawlings, he built Berkeley Square. Lockier's bankruptcy in May 1793 brought down all these other builders.

Lockier had been a furniture maker, and was described by Sketchley in 1775 as an 'Upholsterer, 45 Wine St'.[58] By 1780 he had become one of the leading importers in the Honduras mahogany trade, and also imported wood from Norway and from the Baltic.[59] He moved by this route into speculative building and by 1792 had 250 houses under construction.[60] However, this did not give him entry into the charmed circle of the oligarchy that ruled Bristol in the 18th century. He perhaps sought to achieve prominence by spectacular wealth since he was not likely to become a Merchant Venturer nor a member of the Common Council. Since Lockier joined the boom late when land prices were nearing their peak, his massive involvement in speculative building was achieved in a matter of months rather than years. He built a few houses himself, and his attorney, Henry Cooke, then sold plots on Lockier's behalf to other builders, under covenants to build. For example, he sold plots one, two and three in Paul Street to Jacob Davis and to Rowland Thomas in 1792.[61]

Berkeley Square was originally planned by Thomas Paty and Sons as a crescent, but the layout was changed by James Lockier and his associates, probably to get more houses on the site. Berkeley Crescent, containing six houses, may have been built in this form as a concession to those who wanted the original scheme. It is an appendage on the north end of the west side of the Square. The site formed a part of the Bullock's Park estate at the top of Park Street, below Brandon Hill.

Richmond Place appears to have been built on land belonging to the Hodges family (Z on the de Wilstar map), while Royal York Crescent lay across the former gardens, orchards and home close of the Rev. John Power's Clifton mansion, and also his Fern Close (P III and P IV on de Wilstar). Ison suggests John Eveleigh of

Bath may have surveyed and laid out the site in 1789, and that William Paty designed the Crescent. Building began in the summer of 1791, and the basements and vaults required to produce a level surface for house building and a semi-private terrace walk proved very expensive. At the west end the terrace is 20 ft. above the road. The Crescent contains 46 houses with a total of 146 bays and was originally built in brick. From the rear it is apparent that behind the common façade John Coles, Michael Davis, Ezekiel Evans and Richard Constant were allowed to vary the designs. By December 1791 £20,000 had been spent on the project and Lockier tried to raise more money by offering £100 shares in a tontine subscription to raise the £70,000 needed. It was not forthcoming, despite the eminence of those who were appointed to manage the scheme, such as the banker Joseph Harford, the politician George Daubney, Richard Vaughan and William Fry.[62] When Lockier, MacAulay and Co. were declared bankrupt in March 1793, only one quarter of the Crescent was completed. There were 34 roofless houses and several forced sales of unfixed materials took place.

Royal York Crescent was not completed until 1820, and Clifton very nearly lost the site to the War Department which purchased the property for barracks. The War Department was persuaded by public outcry to sell the houses and site it had acquired, and most of it passed into the hands of another developer, the attorney, Isaac Cooke.[63] Royal York Crescent is about 25 ft. above the Paragon, while 25 ft. below it is Lord Cornwallis' Crescent, or the Lower Crescent. This site belonged to the Merchants' Hall, who granted a 40-year building lease, renewable every 14 years, to Harry Elderton. This land had once been leased to James Hollidge and then by Ann Hibbs (B I on de Wilstar).[64] This was to be almost equal in size to Royal York Crescent, and, according to Walter Ison, 'was a conscious attempt to reproduce at Clifton the splendours of the upper and lower crescents at Bath'.[65]

Harry Elderton had the ground surveyed and then sub-let the plots to speculating builders. Avard, Lewis and Mitchell was the principal firm concerned in this develop-ment, and the architect was probably Thomas Paty. Owing to the bankruptcy of the principal builders, the scheme was never completed, and as late as 1827 the Merchants' Hall was granting leases of several unfinished houses. By this date a right of way had been established across the site, which remains there today. The west end of the crescent contains 23 houses, and the east block contains eleven. Along the south side of the crescent is a wide terrace walk, supported on vaults, and viewed from the gardens has a series of wide arches with rusticated stonework. It is faced with dressed stonework on the south side, though the north side, where the front doors are, is brick faced with stucco.

The Society kept a careful watch on the way its land in Clifton was used. They only wanted superior property and they did not want buildings crowded together. For example, Mr. Elderton 'is to produce a Certificate that the Houses are built agree-ably to his Covenant, such Certificate to be signed by a Surveyor to be named by the Hall, to intitle him (Mr. Elderton) to future Renewalls'.[66] James Lockier was informed by the Clerk to the Hall's Standing Committee 'that they do not approve of this plan; that they consider the ground as a very eligible spot and that it should be laid out for larger and better Houses and not so much crowded with Buildings'.[67] Isaac Cooke was told that the 'Front of the said intended Crescent (namely the Southward) to be Ashlar; the other Stucco ... The Society to name a Surveyor, whose Certification the lessees are to produce that the Houses are built agreeably to their Covenants, similar to those in the present Lease, or not to be intitled to renewal'.[68] James Lockier's plans for Honeypen Hill 'were produced, but the Committee declined to come to any Resolution till further discussion, and the Clerk was directed to show the Plans etc. to Mr. Paty and consult him thereon'.[69]

Where the Merchants' Hall did not own the site, as with Royal York Crescent on John Power's land, or Windsor Terrace which was also on his land, their careful monitoring could have gone wrong so easily. We owe a great debt to John Eveleigh and William Paty for producing such splendid designs for these sites. But Eveleigh's plans went adrift when Watts became bankrupt, and the site reverted, with the shells of two houses, to the ground landlords. The next developer, Isaac Cooke, then bought the site, and a much reduced scheme was cobbled together. Ison described the result as 'a pathetic travesty of the original design'.[70] When 15 of the unfinished houses in Royal York Crescent were purchased from the War Department in 1809, and another 21 in 1810, it was not pressure from the Merchants' Hall which influenced the way the scheme was completed, but an articulate and insistent public opinion which was determined to preserve the essence of Clifton as a Spa.

Harry Elderton was also the developer of Bellevue on land leased from the Merchants' Hall, first by Paul Fisher and then James Cross (H on de Wilstar's map): 'One ground with a Tenement, Gardens, extending from the Garden Turrets unto Jacob's Well, 3 acres'.[71]

A plan of the ground near Jacob's Wells, held by the late Mr. James Cross, under the Society, for three Lives, and Assigned by his Representatives to Mr. Harry Elderton, with Sections, and the Elevations of Buildings proposed to be erected thereon, in case the Society will agree to alter the Tenure thereof to a 40 year Lease renewable every 14 years, were laid before the Committee ...[72]

Harry Elderton applied again after four months to propose a second terrace on the Bellevue site to which the Hall agreed provided they saw the plans beforehand.[73]

Bellevue consists of 19 houses with a wide terrace walk facing towards Brandon Hill and gardens that slope steeply down towards Jacob's Well Road. Ison tells us that all of the houses had to be abandoned in various stages of incompletion, and that the range stood derelict for many years. It was eventually completed in 1815.[74] The houses are very similar to those in Cornwallis Crescent, and the east front is built of dressed freestone. The coachhouses were to have been built on the ground opposite to the west front, on the other side of the road, but this had to be abandoned after the financial crisis of 1793 and Elderton's subsequent bankruptcy.

Undoubtedly the best known view of Clifton is of Windsor Terrace, jutting out from rocks of the Gorge on its great retaining wall. This was built on the site of

Rownham Woods (P V on de Wilstar), which consisted of 13 acres belonging to the estate of John Power and subsequently to his heir, Mr. Beames. Part of the ground was developed by William Watts who leased it in 1790 to build Windsor Terrace.

William Watts, a plumber who lived at 126 Redcliff Street, had made a small fortune from his patent for a new process for manufacturing shot.[75] As a result of a dream, he is said to have devised a method of dropping liquid lead through a sieve from a considerable height into water. The metal formed a perfect sphere as it passed through the air and cooled and his shot tower on Redcliff Hill was a local landmark. The peculiarity of the strata of Avon Gorge cost him his fortune of £10,000. The great retaining wall to secure the foundation of the end house and the vaulting necessary to level the site, obliged him to sub-let the house plots to other builders such as Samuel Screen, who became bankrupt in November 1792.[76] Watts' original scheme, probably drawn up by John Eveleigh of Bath, since it is treated architecturally in a similar manner to his Camden Crescent, was for 20 houses and the whole crescent was to cost not less than £20,000.[77] On 1 March 1794, a bankruptcy notice was issued against Watts and his connection with the project ceased. After completing Windsor Terrace, John Drew began building the Paragon. Ten houses were built and foundations for three more constructed when Drew became bankrupt in December 1813. Isaac Cooke now leased the site to

21. Windsor Terrace, called 'New Winsor' on Feltham's map, was built on part of Rownham Woods owned by John Beames and leased to William Watts in 1790. Watts speculated the fortune he had made, patenting the process of manufacturing shot, and built the great retaining wall to secure the foundations of the end house, and the vaulting necessary to level the site. Watts sublet the plots to other builders but became bankrupt in November 1792. The architect was probably John Eveleigh of Bath and the original scheme was for 20 houses. John Drew completed 10 houses to a reduced design for the attorney Isaac Cooke.

22. Royal York Crescent was built across Fern Close and the gardens of John Beames' Clifton mansion. Ison suggests that John Eveleigh of Bath surveyed the site in 1789 and that William Paty designed the crescent of 46 houses. The ground is 20 ft. lower at the west end so the basements and vaults required to produce a level surface proved very expensive. John Lockier began building in 1791 and became bankrupt in March 1793. The attorney Isaac Cooke bought the site and the crescent was completed in 1830.

another builder named Stephen Hunter, who completed the Crescent to an altered design.[78]

Another developer who leased an extensive area from the Society was Samuel Powell. Beginning in May 1786, he leased for 40 years, renewable every 14, the ground below Rownham Wood, next to the river Avon. Here he built the Colonnade, next to the Rock House, and the unfinished range of nine houses, fronting onto a raised terrace walk, called St Vincent's Parade. On the high ground above the river he promoted the building of Prince of Wales' Crescent or Prince's Buildings.[79]

The Crescent to be extended to the utmost point practicable to admit of depth for houses above or to the Northeastward of the road now intended to be made by Mr. Powell from the top of the ground to the Hotwells ... The Houses at the bottom to be set 3 feet within the Rock House, and the Parlour floors to be on the same level ... Mr. Powell's ground to terminate at the end next the shops ... [the Colonnade][80]

> The Committee also viewed the ground taken by Mr. Powell ... and they likewise viewed the Houses building by him thereon. W. Paty attended with a Plan of the said ground and with the particulars as proposed by him for the Houses at the Top as well as for the Row of Houses at the bottom of the said ground ... Five years to be allowed Mr. Powell to compleat all the Buildings, and if not then completed, the Lessors to enter ...[81]

The housing plots for the Prince of Wales' Crescent were then sub-let to other builders in June 1789, and 14 three-storied houses in seven pairs, linked by single-storied annexes, were constructed. The central pair have a representation of the Prince of Wales' feathers and the motto 'Ich Dien' on the pediment. In 1796 the property was conveyed to William Paty, by way of mortgage. Meanwhile, down by the Avon, overlooking the fashionable Hotwell riverside walk, Powell was building nine three-storey houses, for letting, faced with freestone. The design of these houses was exactly the same as that provided by John Eveleigh for the north and south terraces flanking the Mall.[82] Powell's Colonnade, in front of the Hotwell shops was designed to meet the perceived needs of the visitors to the Spa. Latimer says that in 1760 a tradesman advertised his warehouse as being 'under the Piazzas, near the Pump Room'[83], so that some form of protected walk previously existed. Powell provided a more substantial two-storey building which has lasted to the present day. The shops also incorporated Anne Yearsley's well documented circulating library. Samuel Powell seems to have been one of the few speculators not to have been bankrupted by the financial crisis of 1793, and in concluding this chapter we shall consider why so many other builders were brought down.

In April 1793 five builders became bankrupt, and in May a further 15 followed, including Lockier, Woodward and Co. By the end of the year about one third of the builders in the Bristol area had been issued with commissions of bankruptcy.[84] Using the London Gazette, J. R. Ward has analysed the local variations in the incidence of bankruptcies in the building industry between 1790 and 1815. He has shown that where in Manchester there were 39, in Birmingham 22, at Bath 47, at Liverpool 55, at Cheltenham 11, in Bristol there were 63 bankruptcies.[85] Why should this have been so? Various explanations suggest themselves.[86] Among these are the widespread availability of credit, the relative expensiveness of the houses being built, the lack of experience of country banks in the south-west, the relative decline of Bristol's trade and the need for investors to find outlets for their funds, either in canal building or speculative building in Clifton.

Further factors, following the crash of a number of banking houses, were panic, lack of confidence and an acute shortage of money in the form of negotiable notes. The crisis was less in some places like Liverpool because of the energetic measures taken by the Common Council, the setting up of a loan office and the creation of a Negotiable Note issue scheme. Nothing like this occurred in Bristol. The collapse in Bristol was so much worse than elsewhere, it is suggested, because of the disproportion in the rate at which the housing stock was being increased, to the underlying growth of demand. Latimer tells us that five years later, in 1798, 500 houses still stood unfinished.[87]

Most of the houses involved in Clifton were large, and the speculative builders depended on credit in building them to a greater extent than they would have done

23. Cornwallis Crescent, with St Andrew's church, *c.*1825. This watercolour by Samuel Jackson shows the view from York Gardens at the top of Granby Hill. Cornwallis House is in the centre. St Andrew's has been rebuilt centre right. To the left is the detached eastern end of Royal York Crescent.

for smaller developments. There was a great deal of investment money available in the south-west, not only from the farming interest, but from the profits of the West Indies planters, many of whom were absentee and lived in the West Country. The generally agreed view seems to be that following the sudden and unexpected declaration of war with France in February 1793 there was a collapse in confidence and in the circulation.

> As country banks stopped payment the circulating medium ran short. Other banks in country and town clung to their cash and would not discount. Industry that had been so active but had relied on the resources procured by discounting bills to carry on, even to pay current wages, was brought up with a jerk.[88]

In March, Elderton told his builders 'to discharge nearly all the workmen then employed, alleging he could not advance the money to pay them, and that the times were much altered and credit very low'.[89]

The business cycle had peaked in 1792 and a downturn in activity had been made worse by the impact of international events on an overstretched credit situation. So

24.   The Paragon consists of 21 houses on the upper part of
the 13 acres of Rownham Wood, part of John Power's estate.
Having completed Windsor Terrace, Drew began building
the Paragon. Ten houses were built and the foundations of
three more constructed, when Drew became bankrupt in
December 1813. Stephen Hunter completed the crescent.

much of Clifton's building had
been speculative, that is to say,
without a known purchaser. The
finance had been channelled
through attorneys, who managed
to survive the débacle, and undis-
couraged, were to start the process
all over again. By 1805 de Wilstar's
Clifton had been radically altered:

> It appears to the Committee that
> the present Plan of the Manor of
> Clifton is very inaccurate in
> regard to Quantity, and that
> owing to the alterations of Roads
> and the great number of new
> Buildings, it is not now so dis-
> tinct and clear as it ought to be.
> It is ordered that the Clerk do
> direct Mr. White, the Surveyor,
> to prepare a new Plan ...[90]

The next century was to see
Clifton incorporated by the 1835
Act within the 'city and county' of
Bristol. As the century progressed,
while Clifton still retained its
charm, it underwent massive
building development so that by
1881 its population had risen to
28,695 and it had become simply a
suburb of a great commercial and
trading city.[91]

Chapter Seven

People on Clifton Hill 1750-1800

Among the families that came to live on Clifton Hill were some that raised themselves by means that were beginning to be challenged in their own day, from low
beginnings to considerable wealth. Thomas Elton, the father of Sir Abraham Elton,
M.P. who died in 1728 leaving a fortune of £100,000, was a market gardener in
St Phillip's out-parish. He probably collected the town refuse to improve his land
and this gave rise to the allegation that he was a scavenger. His wife, Elizabeth, was a
milkmaid.[1] John Brickdale, the father of Matthew Brickdale, M.P. for Bristol, 1768-74,
1780-90, was a woollen draper who by the time of his death, aged 89, on 25 October
1766,[2] had accumulated a fortune of £100,000.[3] This had been achieved partly
through trade in sugar from the West Indies[4] and partly through privateering in the
War of Austrian Succession.[5] He was also engaged in the slave trade.[6]

Henry Hobhouse, who bought Cornwallis House in 1764, shared the fortune of
his uncle, Isaac Hobhouse, with his brother John and his cousin Thomas Jones. Isaac
Hobhouse died on 26 February 1762-3 leaving a fortune of £70,000 which had been
made mainly through the slave trade.[7] He had acted as agent for 44 slaving ventures.[8]
The Ames family, who followed the Farrs into Clifton Wood House, came from the
villages of Evercreech and Charlton, near Shepton Mallet, Somerset. Jeremiah Ames,
sugar baker and merchant, made money through privateering in the War of Austrian
Succession 1739-48, and the Seven Years War 1756-63, and left a fortune of £70,000
in 1776.[9] The last family we shall consider is that of Sir William Draper, who built
Manilla Hall, Clifton Down. General Draper was born the son of a customs officer
and attended the Cathedral school before going to Eton. He entered the army as an
ensign in a foot regiment.[10]

Abraham Isaac Elton, grandson of Sir Abraham Elton and partner in the Old
Bank, Corn Street from 1750-77, bought Freemantle House in 1750 for £500 from
Francis Freeman. According to the deeds, the mansion and grounds were not called
Rodney Lodge until 1863. In that year the paddock and pasture land adjacent to
Freemantle House were divided into two lots and the B. Dunn map of 1769 appears
to show Mr. Freeman living in the house next down the hill. Isaac Elton married
Mary, daughter of Edward Mortimer, Esq., and lived next door but one at 19 Clifton
Hill. This area had once been meadow or pasture ground called Hollylands. Isaac
was Sheriff of Bristol in 1743, mayor in 1761 and Master of the Merchant Venturers
in 1764-5. His eldest daughter, Mary, married Michael Miller (junior), the only son
of Michael Miller who was one of the original partners in Miles' Bank (1752-85).[11] It
is already obvious that there were very close ties binding together Bristol's social élite
at this time.

While it may well be true that Thomas Elton, Sir Abraham's father, had been in
reduced circumstances, the Elton family had ancient roots in Hasles in the county of

25.   Originally called Freemantle House, Rodney Lodge was built on part of the close called Hollylands,
owned by Francis Freeman, and sold to Abraham Isaac Elton in 1750. Abraham Isaac was grandson to the
first baronet who lived in Small Street and died in 1728 leaving a vast fortune of £100,000. Abraham Isaac was
brother to Sir Abraham Elton III, and was a lawyer and town clerk of Bristol. Freemantle House passed to
E. Hopkins in 1861 and he changed its name to Rodney Lodge. His heirs sold it in 1877 to J. D. Weston and
it was sold again in 1884 to P. J. Worsley. In 1950 Worsley's two unmarried daughters sold it to the university.

Hereford. Sir Abraham Elton bought Clevedon Court in 1709 from the Digbys, Earls
of Bristol, and Whitestaunton Manor, Chard, in 1723. How had he made a fortune
and acquired a baronetcy after his apparently humble beginnings? He had been
sheriff in 1702, Master of the Merchant Venturers in 1708 and Mayor of Bristol in
1710. From 1693-4 he was Treasurer of Lewins Mead Presbyterian Meeting. He had
achieved these eminent offices through his success as a merchant and ship-owner
and good fortune in privateering during the War of the Grand Alliance 1689-97 and
the War of the Spanish Succession 1702-13.[12] Together with his sons, Isaac, Jacob
and Abraham, he was part owner of the *Alexander*, the *Ambuscade*, the *Caesar*, the
Constantine, the *Elton*, the *Jamaica*, the *Jamaica Merchant*, the *Jason*, the *Kirtlington*, the
Lion, the *Mediterranean*, the *Olive Tree*, the *Prince Eugene*, the *Prince of Hanover*, the
Severn and the *Stanhope*. All these ships were equipped as privateers and many took
part in the Africa Trade.

It was Isaac I who was listed in 1759, together with his brother Abraham, as a
member of the Company of Bristol Merchants trading to Africa.[14] It was Isaac I who
was one of the owners of the *Morning Star* involved in slave trading between Africa,

Barbados and South Carolina in 1716, 1717 and 1720. The vessel delivered 134 slaves in 1717 and 114 slaves in 1720 to Barbados. The vessel's imports into Bristol on two of the return trips consisted of 39 cwt and 20 cwt of ivory, eight tons of redwood and 155 lbs of Guinea grains.[15] This involvement by the Eltons in the slave trade originated with Sir Abraham in 1711 when he was a partner in the voyage of the *Jason Gally*. The ship traded to the Guinea coast and delivered 278 live slaves to Kingston, Jamaica.[16] It is chilling to realise that it was necessary to use the adjective 'live'. In his capacity as mayor in 1761, Isaac I played host to the Duke of York, brother of George III, when he made an official visit to the city. The duke stayed at the mayor's official residence in Queen Square and appears to have enjoyed the Eltons' company: 'After dinner to a ball at the Assembly Rooms. His Royal Highness opened the ball with Miss Elton, the Mayor's daughter ... when the minuets were over he began the country dances with Miss Elton. Supped at the Mayor's and slept there'.[17] The

26. Richard Farr's house, Clifton Wood House, c.1721. This house was built for Robert Smith, and leased, first to the Duchess of Huntingdon and then, for most of the century, to the Farr family. The doorway and much of the interior is original, but the two unsightly bows on either side of the doorway were added in the Regency period. The staircase is one of the finest in Bristol.

family would have been honoured by the visit and among those whose attendance would have been required was Isaac's second son, Isaac II.

Like his father, Isaac Elton II was a partner in Old Bank. he also became sheriff in 1765 and 1770 and again like his father he was Master of the Merchant Venturers. However, he broke with family tradition in refusing the mayoralty in 1783. As Master of the Merchant Venturers in 1773, Isaac II was in a position of leadership at a particularly prosperous, though worrying, time for Bristol's trade with the American colonies. It was the large export orders to America and healthy remittances from the colonies which made the merchants unwilling to involve themselves in politics as long as Bristol's welfare was not jeopardised. Edmund Burke wrongly attributed this attitude to fear of displeasing His Majesty's Government.[18]

As Master, Isaac II received letters from Matthew Brickdale M.P. on the American question, which appeared complacent and were to cost Brickdale his seat six months afterwards. The Whigs' charge against Brickdale in the summer was that this was one of 'the sins of commission and many of omission'. Brickdale wrote to Isaac Elton:

> Many Gentlemen I have no doubt are anxiously waiting the Event of this days delibera-tion in the House respecting America, and I am happy (to inform) them sooner than they Can learn by the Votes, what has been done in that Business ... Lord North opened the debate with a recapitulation of the late very extraordinary proceedings at Boston and as a beginning of Punishment of that Town has moved for, obtained leave to bring in, a Bill to remove the Custom House from thence, and to take away from it the privileges of an Harbour. It is intended to be followed by another to oblige the Inhabitants to make the East India Company Compensation for their loss ... I sincerely wish that some plan may be devised that will quiet the inhabitants of that part of our Dominions, and make them as usefull to us and themselves as they are Capable of ...[19]

On 23 March Brickdale wrote again to Elton to tell the merchants that the Boston Port Bill would go into effect on 1 June and that any ships arriving after that date would not be allowed to enter the harbour. Burke felt that Bristol merchants could not

> much care whether America is lost or not, till they feel the effects in their purses or in their bellies. While they can go on as usual they speculate but little as to futurity; or at least their thoughts lead them only to grumble and growl; they must feel and be pinched, and in some tender part too, before they will put themselves to any inconveniency to prevent the impending mischief.[20]

Bristol merchants, in fact, tried to beat the impending non-importation scheme by stepping up their exports in anticipation. They did not think the colonists could keep it going for longer than six months since that had been their experience on the previous occasion.

Isaac Elton II lived until 1790 and saw the 'Intollerable Acts' passed, the incidents at Lexington and Concord, the Declaration of American Independence and the war with the colonies. The Eltons were part of that closely knit structure of relationships in the ruling élite of Bristol at that time. They provided seven Masters of the Merchant Venturers out of the 13 members of the family who were freemen of the Hall in the first three-quarters of the 18th century.[21] Isaac Elton II was the last of them.

Another example of this closely knit structure of relationships is the Hobhouse family. As Bonner's *Bristol Journal* puts it, they also raised themselves from 'small beginnings, but died rich'.[22] For the early years of the 18th century some of the business papers of Isaac Hobhouse and Co. have survived in the Jefferies Collection, Vol. XIII in Bristol Central Reference Library. Isaac Hobhouse is an example of those Bristol merchants who combined the three functions of wholesaler, factor and shipowner. Some of the documents are reproduced in Latimer,[23] and some in Minchinton.[24] The account books of Henry Hobhouse, his nephew, exist for the years 1763-72, but there is a total absence of private correspondence. Fortunately, the family memories were recorded in 1927 by the Rt. Hon. Henry Hobhouse.[25]

The Hobhouse family moved to Clifton when Henry Hobhouse, whose offices in Queen Square were next to the Custom House, acquired the newly-built Cornwallis House from Mrs. Ann Hibbs. In 1757 Mrs. Hibbs had acquired a new lease of Cornwallis Grove, a large hillside building plot, from the Merchant Venturers. She then built two houses, Cornwallis House and Grove House, and chose to live in Grove House herself. Seemingly it was the Merchants' Hall which had encouraged Mrs. Hibbs and others in 1749 to let the land they held in Clifton from the Society for building development, in return for new leases.[26] In 1767 Henry Hobhouse was already protesting to the Hall about the threat to the view from his house by proposed stables which Richard Coombe wanted to build.[27] There has been some speculation as to why the plot was called Cornwallis Grove. It might stimulate further discussion to point out that the bishop of the diocese, Dr. Spencer, had married Lady Charlotte Cornwallis in 1756, the year before Mrs. Hibbs acquired the new lease. Lady Charlotte was sister to the Earl Cornwallis and niece to the previous Archbishop of Canterbury.[28]

The Hobhouse family originated in west Somerset and the adjoining parishes of Devon, where they are mentioned in the Court Rolls of the Hundred of Milverton. From 1537 until 1681 the Hobhouses appear in the parish registers of births, marriages and deaths at Holcombe Rogus (or Regis), seven miles south-west of

27. Cornwallis House has spectacular views above Cornwallis Crescent. It has no pediment, but an impressive Ionic portico, added in 1813, and was built as a speculation for Mrs. Ann Hibbs, together with Grove House, on Merchant Venturers' land. The wealthy Bristol merchant, Henry Hobhouse, bought the leasehold in 1764. He had been apprenticed in his uncle Isaac's business and had traded in slaves, tobacco, copper and sugar. He died in 1773 and Cornwallis House passed to his eldest son.

Milverton.[29] Some members of the Hobhouse family lived at Minehead from 1675 onwards. John Hobhouse held two leases from the Luttrell estate, dated 1686 and 1687. These comprised two houses and gardens on the wharf and 100 ft. of waste land behind the quay. Subsequently John was appointed Constable of Minehead in 1688 and from 1690 was one of the churchwardens.[30] He was described as 'marriner and wheelwright'. When he died in 1711 he left his wife, Anne, and four living children. His second son, Henry, was also a 'marriner' and owned his own vessel, trading between south Wales and Ireland. Apparently he died before he was forty. John's third son, Benjamin, was apprenticed to a ships' carpenter in Bridgwater, but appears to have returned to Minehead and to have lived for most of his life at 155 Quay Street. Born in the year of Monmouth's Rebellion, 1685, it was John's fourth son, Isaac, who created the family fortune.

Isaac Hobhouse did not take to seafaring occupations like the rest of the family. He seems to have been a delicate child and he never married. Isaac's sister, Joan, married Christopher Jones who lived in Bristol and who was engaged in trade. Isaac seems to have had some connection with them and when Christopher died in 1720 Isaac was one of the trustees of his property. Isaac Hobhouse had not served an apprenticeship as a merchant, nor was he the son of a freeman. Nevertheless he was admitted as a freeman on 9 December 1724 by vote of the Common Council on the nomination of the mayor. This was a privilege that the mayor could only exercise once during his year of office, so the implication is that by 1724 Isaac had achieved a position in the trade and commerce of the city such as to justify the honour. He was a member of a number of partnerships for trade.[31] The letters in the Central Reference Library from and to Hobhouse and his nephews relate to the affairs of his trading company. In 1725 the partnership included Noblet Ruddock and William Baker. Isaac's two nephews, Henry and John, joined the partnership in 1729.

The firm had agents in Jamaica, Barbados, Virginia and elsewhere, and traded with Africa. During the years to 1729, Isaac Hobhouse was the responsible agent for 11 slaving voyages,[32] while his partner, from 1712 to 1725, Noblet Ruddock the agent for 30 such ventures.[33] Their fleet of trading vessels consisted in 1724 of 10 ships. These boats usually sailed from Bristol direct to Gabon or Angola on the west coast of Africa. There they bartered for 200-300 slaves, ivory, redwood and wax. On one voyage the barter included copper, iron bars, muskets, bugles, brandy and cotton goods. The vessels then sailed to the West Indies, touching Antigua, Barbados and Jamaica to sell the slaves. They then made their way to South Carolina or Virginia to sell the other goods and to pick up a return cargo of tobacco, sugar or molasses.

As agent for these slave voyages Isaac Hobhouse supervised the selection of the outward cargo and the fitting out of the ship; he corresponded with the Master and gave detailed instructions to the Company's agents in the West Indies and the American colonies regarding the sale of the slaves and how to remit the proceeds. He was responsible at the end of the voyage for selling the return cargo, paying off the crew, finalising the accounts and then sharing out the profits.[34] Sometimes losses occurred: for example, the *Greyhound* in 1723 lost 125 slaves out of 339, together with seven members of the crew.[35] Isaac Hobhouse was only too well aware of the risks involved. He warned Captain Barry of the *Dispatch*: 'Let your care be in preserving as well as purchasing. Let the provisions be carefully looked after and boiled and given them in due season, and see the sailors don't abuse them'.[36] But the slaves were to be kept 'shackled and hand bolted' to stop them jumping over the side. The negroes were each purchased for about £5 worth of barter goods and, at this time, fetched about £19 to £30 according to their age, sex and condition. In 1730, the *Freak* made a slaving voyage when 329 slaves, sold in Barbados, grossed £6,207; £5,746 after paying dues and commissions.[37]

Between the years 1722-47 Isaac Hobhouse had acted as agent for another 44 slaving ventures and had become a very wealthy man.[38] His two nephews, the sons of Benjamin Hobhouse, joined their uncle's business in 1729 and were apprenticed for seven years. Henry became a freeman in 1736, married Jane Banister and in seven years they had five children. Isaac (b.1739) and John (b.1740) both died of smallpox in November 1742, and the youngest, another Isaac, only lived five months. Thus there survived Henry (b.1742) and Jane (b.1743), but their mother died of consumption in 1756.

The other nephew, John Hobhouse, lived at Westbury College, Westbury-on-Trym, and subsequently became Warden of the Merchant Venturers in 1756-7. The two nephews continued their uncle's business when Isaac died in 1763, leaving £70,000 to be divided between them and a third nephew, Thomas Jones.[39] The names of both John and Henry Hobhouse appear on the list of merchants trading to Africa in 1759,[40] but the ascendancy of Bristol in the slave trade was relatively short-lived. Between 1728 and 1732 slave voyages from Bristol had reached 48 each year, but from 1744 onwards Liverpool began to outpace Bristol as Britain's leading slaving port. In the years following the peace of 1748 which ended the War of Austrian Succession, fewer than 30 ships a year left Bristol on slaving voyages.[41] This would explain why in 1753 Henry Hobhouse set up in partnership with Nicholas Bloome and James Banister (Henry's brother-in-law) as sugar bakers and sugar refiners. The business premises were between Redcliffe Street and Redcliffe Baths.[42] Henry was also involved in shipping copper and tobacco as well as sugar.

Henry Hobhouse married a second time, to Mary White, on 30 March 1761. She had a considerable fortune and owned lands at Norton Hawkfield and Dundry in Somerset. Being now a wealthy man, Henry bought a new house in Clifton in 1764, Cornwallis House, which passed on his death to his eldest son. He also bought a landed estate at Norton Ferris in 1766. It consisted of 113 acres of meadowland, 223 of arable, 212 acres of down and woods and was situated on the western edge of Salisbury Plain.[43] Another new house that Henry bought was a town house in Park Street in Bristol, at number three, and this he left to his widow when he died in 1773. The next occupant of Cornwallis House was therefore Henry Hobhouse II, a lawyer, the only surviving son by his first marriage.[44]

Henry Hobhouse II married Sarah Jenkyns, but the marriage was cut tragically short. They had two children, Henry born in 1776 and Sarah born in 1777, but their mother died on 24 July 1777 at Cornwallis House. Young Henry III became a lawyer like his father. He went to Eton and Oxford and was called to the Bar in 1801. He had a successful legal career and in 1819 became Permanent Under-Secretary of State for the Home Department. He was created a Privy Councillor and a D.C.L.

A
L I S T
OF THE

Company of MERCHANTS trading to *Africa*, (established by an Act of Parliament, passed in the 23d Year of His present Majesty, intituled, *An Act for extending and improving the Trade to* Africa) distinguishing their Places of Abode.

June 1, 1759,

B R I S T O L.

ALEYN William
Atkins Michael
Ames Jeremy, *Esq;*
Aleyn Henry
Averay John
Averay Richard
Arnold William
Alker George
Brown Humphry
Brickdale John
Becher Cranfield, *Esq;*
Baugh Isaac, *Esq;*
Brackendrige John
Bright Allen
Bright Henry, *Esq;*
Berrow William
Bonbonus James
Brown Francis
Bannister James
Beaton John
Ball John
Bayly Giles, *Esq;*
Berrow John, *Esq;*
Baker Slade
Brown Richard
Bayly John
Berry Samuel
Bull John
Barnes William, *jun. Esq;*
Baugh Francis
Brodribb Isaac
Bedham Joseph
Birkbeck John
Charleton Edward
Champion William
Campbell David
Champion Joseph
Curtis John, *Esq;*
Cox Stephen
Chamberlayne Edward Pye
Clarke John
Camplin Richard
Chivers John

Cornish James
Champness Richard
Cadell Thomas
Collett John
Henry Dampier, *Esq;*
Dean Thomas, *Esq;*
Devonshire Christopher
Durbin John, *Esq;*
Dinham Robert
Daubeny George
Dickenson Caleb
Dyer William
Davis Samuel
Davis Mark
Dymock Thomas
Daltera James
Davis William
Davis Edward
Delpratt William
Davis Alexander
Davis Stephen
Daniel Francis
Durbin John, *jun.*
Dixon John
Dinwoody John
Easton Thomas
Elton Isaac, *Esq;*
Edward Thomas
Elton Abraham Isaac, *Esq.*
Ellis Henry
Eaton Thomas
Edridge Thomas
Ellis Richard
Farr Richard, *Esq;*
French Martin
Ford Alexander
Fisher Paul
Freeman John, *jun.*
Farr Thomas
Farrell Joseph
Foy Nathaniel
Farr Thomas, *jun.*
Franks Richard

Field Pitman Scandret
Gordon William
Gordon Robert, *Esq;*
Gwyn Charles
Gardner Samuel
Gressly John, *jun.*
Griffin William
Griffiths John
Gregory Joseph
George William
Hobhouse John
Hobhouse Henry
Hobhouse Isaac
Harris Thomas, *Esq;*
Harmer John
Hare Ebenezer
Hilhouse James, *Esq;*
Hale Matthew
Hutchenson William
Hunt William
Hilhouse William
Hanson Richard
Hagley Fortunatus
Hill Jeremiah
Harford Thomas
Hellier Elisha
Hawkesworth Ab. Rich.
Hall John
Holland Joseph
Houlton Robert
Iredele Francis
Jenkins Philip
Jolliffe Richard
Jenkins Richard
James William
James John
Knox Thomas, *Esq;*
King Walter
Kill Joseph
Kill Daniel
Laroche James, *Esq;*
Lougher Walter
Loscombe Joseph

Lloyd Caleb
Lloyd Edward
Lucas Robert
Lewis Joseph
Love Joseph, *Esq;*
Longdon Thomas
Meylet Richard
Martin William, *Esq;*
Meyler Richard, *jun.*
Matthew William
Munckley Samuel
Miller Michael
Mac Neale Hector
Miller William
Macartney James
Matthew James
Masters John
Martin Josiah
Nicholas Edward
Nash Stephen
Pennington Thomas
Prankard Richard
Perks John
Prothero Philip
Percival Joseph
Pollard John
Perkins Richard
Peach Samuel
Peach John
Pope Andrew
Pitman John
Powell John
Perkins Walter, *jun.*
Pennington Ferdinand
Perry Stephen
Powell William
Pyne Thomas, *jun.*
Robinson Richard
Ruscombe James
Reed James
Reed John
Rogers Corsely
Rogers Francis

[3]

Rogers Francis, *jun.*
Reeve William
Rickards Joseph
Robson Joseph
Roberts John
Rumsey James
Rigg Joseph
Reeve John
Rogers Corsley, *jun.*
Rogers Robert
Rock Thomas
Reed Edward
Rodbard William
Swymmer William, *Esq;*
Smith Robert
Sedgeley Samuel
Stevens James
Seaborne Richard

Smith Samuel, *Druggist*
Smith Morgan, *Esq;*
Smith Thomas
Smith Henry
Seede William
Stretton John
Steevenson John
Smith Samuel, *Distiller*
Smith Francis
Smith Standfast
Symmons Samuel
Saunders Hollis
Smith Samuel, *Lin. Drap.*
Stephens William
Short Walton
Stephens Will., *Lin. Drap.*
Searle Edward

Shepherd Joseph, *jun.*
Stock John
Swymmer Henry, *Esq;*
Swymmer Anthony
Tonge Henry
Tonge John
Tyndale Thomas
Trevaskes John
Thompson John
Tate John
Thornton Christopher
Teaste Sydenham, *sen.*
Teaste Sydenham, *jun.*
Tayler Josiah
Teague Joseph
Viner George
White Daniel

Whitehead Thomas
West Henry
Whatley Edward, *Esq;*
Wraxall Nathaniel
Willoughby Christopher
Weare Henry, *Esq;*
Wansey William
Wilcox Joshua
Webb Samuel
Webb Nathaniel
Weare George, *Esq;*
Wood Leighton
Willett John, *jun.*
Whatley Henry
Watts Phineas
Ward Edward
Yeamans Frederick

28. List of Bristol merchants engaged in the Africa trade, 1759. Since the opening of the Africa trade to the outports in 1698, pressure had been put on Parliament to dissolve the Royal Africa Company and this was achieved in 1750. All British traders to Africa were to be deemed a corporation styled the 'Company of Merchants trading to Africa'. All the old company's forts and trading posts were vested in the corporation and direction was in the hands of nine merchants, elected by the members in London, Bristol and Liverpool. Each city was to have three directors. The Bristol list gives the names of members (electors) as 237 in Bristol, 147 in London and 89 in Liverpool.

However the Hobhouse family moved from Cornwallis House to Hadspen House, Somerset, where Henry II died in 1854. None of the Hobhouse family served on the Bristol Common Council and Isaac I in particular seemed to shun publicity, perhaps because of an infirmity.[45] He held no office in the Merchants' Society, nor the Incorporation of the Poor, nor the Colston Society. Henry Hobhouse II became Master of the Society of Merchant Venturers in 1788,[46] but seems to have avoided becoming involved in local politics.

Among the families living on the Hill in the second half of the 18th century, in Rodney House on the opposite side of the road from the Eltons and the Mortimers, was the Brickdale family. Sketchley records that in 1775 Matthew Brickdale Esq. was living at 9 Clifton Hill.[47] Matthew Brickdale, M.P. for Bristol 1768-74, 1780-90, was a woollen draper and merchant in the High Street. His brother, John, shared the same occupation. Their father was John Brickdale, woollen draper, who by the time of his death in 1766 was a very wealthy man. According to Bonner, he was among those 'who had small beginnings, but died rich', and Brickdale's estate was valued at £100,000 at his death.[48] Like the Eltons, the Hobhouses, the Farrs, Michael Miller, Nehemiah Champion, Jeremiah Ames, Gabriel Goldney and other residents on Clifton Hill, John Brickdale senior was a partner in privateering voyages during the war of Austrian Succession, 1739-48. For example he was part owner in the *Phoenix*[49] and his ships also took part in the slave trade. Together with Isaac Hobhouse, he was a partner in the voyage of the *Loyal George* which delivered 220 slaves from Africa to Barbados in 1728/9.[50] As a merchant, his boats were engaged in importing raisins from Spain and the Mediterranean and also in importing sugar from the West Indies.[51]

Matthew Brickdale inherited part of this family fortune in 1766 and promptly invested it in winning a Parliamentary seat as a nominal Tory at the 1768 elections.[52] As a draper's apprentice in his youth, Matthew had won some notoriety by sweeping the filth of the High Street gutter under the dark and narrow roadway of St Nicholas' gate at night, so that unsuspecting pedestrians were distressed.[53] His brother, John, won notoriety in 1753 through his involvement in putting down a riot caused by the export of wheat from Bristol to Dublin in a time of scarcity. The riot extended over several days and involved up to 900 colliers and weavers in attacks on the Council House, the quay and the Bridewell. Four colliers were shot dead, 50 wounded and between 30 and 40 made prisoners.[54] There had been a disastrous harvest the previous year and the poor were in great hardship by the spring of 1753. Troops were sent from Worcester, following the mayor's request to the Government for help, but the colliers roamed around the countryside threatening vengeance and against John Brickdale in particular. A verdict of wilful murder had been returned against him, Michael Miller and others following the coroner's inquest. John Brickdale fled to London for a time to escape the wrath of the Kingswood colliers and the Government instituted proceedings in the Court of the King's Bench to quash this and other similar verdicts, and to institute pardons.

As a merchant of the City of Bristol, Matthew Brickdale was an assiduous M.P. and active in the interests of his constituents.[55] Between 1766 and 1774, opinion in the Society of Merchant Venturers hardened in support of the government's American policy, but outside the Society some Bristol merchants urged repeal of the Townshend Duties and petitioned the king. The Society, however, sent the Loyal Address of 11 March 1769 to His Majesty and this view was shared by Brickdale.[56] The dissolution of Parliament in 1774 was to lose Brickdale his seat and to precipitate the most interesting election that ever took place in Bristol. The ministry was probably trying to avert criticism of its policy which it anticipated would follow the meeting of the Continental Congress. Both the sitting M.P.s, Lord Clare and Brickdale, had made themselves unpopular outside the Society by their support for the coercive measures against Boston and Massachusetts. Both members sought to safeguard their position by electoral agreements between the local political clubs, but caucus politics was at an end in the city. A realignment of political groupings was taking place in Bristol and led to the development of an Independent Society led by two Bristol merchants, Samuel Peach and his American-born son-in-law, Henry Cruger. A meeting of Whigs, held on 5 October, unanimously supported the candidature of Henry Cruger, who advocated conciliatory measures towards the American colonists. This was in opposition to the views of Matthew Brickdale. Some wanted to go further and Richard Champion and Joseph Harford put forward the name of Edmund Burke, but at the time this did not find favour and was not pressed to a vote.[57]

In 1774 Edmund Burke was aged 45 and at the height of his powers. From 1765 to 1774 he had sat for Lord Verney's pocket borough of Wendover and was the outstanding spokesman in the Commons for reconciliation with the colonies. He was perhaps the most distinguished orator in the House and acted as agent for the Rockingham Whigs in their negotiations with other factions. When he heard that Champion and Harford's proposal had not been favourably received, Burke went to Malton, which was one of Lord Rockingham's pocket boroughs and was returned unopposed. Formal nomination of candidates in Bristol took place on 7 October 1774 when Lord Clare, Matthew Brickdale and Henry Cruger presented themselves. However, by the end of the first day's polling, Lord Clare realised that his popularity had ended and that many of his former supporters were working for Cruger. He therefore withdrew his name from the poll. This opened the possibility once more for Burke's supporters to get their candidate elected.

Burke made the journey from Malton to Bristol (270 miles) in 44½ hours and was nominated after the poll had started. In the days before the secret ballot each person's vote was declared openly and a running total could be kept for each of the 23 days of polling. At the close of poll on 2 November, the numbers were: Cruger 3,565; Burke 2,707; Brickdale 2,456; Lord Clare 283.[58] Cruger and Burke were declared elected M.P.s for Bristol, but Matthew Brickdale petitioned against the result. He contended that Burke's nomination after the poll had started was illegal and that many people had voted whose freedoms had been granted after the issue of the writ. Unfortunately for Brickdale his agents had to admit that 772 of their own votes had come from freemen admitted during the contest and the Commons decided that post-nomination was valid.[59] Nevertheless, six years later, after a poll lasting nine days, there was a very different result. The numbers were: Brickdale 2,771, Sir H. Lippincott 2,518, Cruger 1,271, Samuel Peach 788, Burke 18.[60] Burke, however, had withdrawn to save his supporters from the enormous expense of a contested election.

During the previous six years Burke had made no effort to work with Cruger, nor had he bothered to maintain a constituency organisation. From 1778-80 Burke had differed from his constituents over three important matters affecting their interest. His views on insolvent debtors and his support for a relaxation of the Irish trade laws roused much opposition. Burke's courageous support for an Act giving some relief to Catholics at the time of the Gordon riots was misrepresented in Bristol, quite unfairly, and he lost support on all three issues and was defeated at the poll. Matthew Brickdale was again a candidate for election in the spring of 1784. This was the longest and closest contest ever known in Bristol, according to Latimer and nearly 1,000 new freemen were admitted during the contest.[61] The final result was Brickdale 3,458, Cruger 3,052, Daubney 2,982, Peach 373.

Matthew Brickdale finally retired from Parliament in June 1790. He had been a common councillor since 1767 and had been asked to take the office of mayor. He tried to avoid being forced into that office in 1791 by resignation, but the council would not hear of it and elected him mayor. Brickdale would not take the oath, nor pay the fine, so the Corporation took him to court and he was forced to pay £400 as a fine and also the costs of the case. He remained a councillor until 1824, illustrating the fact that the old Corporation contained a large number of aged and very conservative members. Brickdale was councillor for 57 years, but his old rival, Cruger, was a councillor for 61 years.[62] Brickdale's son, John, was Collector for the Customs in Bristol and the old man could regularly be seen in the Long Room in the Queen Square Custom House, gossiping with the people who came in to pay their duties.[63] Among these might well have been members of the Ames family or Sir William Draper, whom we shall discuss next.

The Ames family followed the Farrs into Clifton Wood House. They had originally lived near Shepton Mallet, east Somerset, in the villages of Evercreech and Charlton. Like Isaac Hobhouse who left Minehead for Bristol to make his fortune, Jeremiah Ames is also listed by Bonner's *Bristol Journal* as one of those eminent local merchants 'who had small beginnings, but died rich'.[64] Not only did Jeremiah Ames take out Letters of Marque during the War of Austrian Succession,[65] he was also a partner with Nehemiah Champion in the voyages of the *Duke of Cumberland*, the *Duke of Marlborough*, the *Hawke* and the *Scipio*.[66] The two *Dukes* captured a number of prizes during the hostilities. In the Seven Years War, Jeremiah Ames was a partner in the *Bellona* which captured two 100-ton French merchantmen, loaded with wine and brandy, which were brought into Galway,[67] and a partner in the *Constantine* which also sent in two prizes before itself being captured by the French.[68] He was part-owner of the *Trial* which, in March 1762, sent into Falmouth a ship from St Domingo loaded with 140 tons of sugar, indigo and coffee.[69]

Jeremiah Ames, sugar baker and merchant, was elected Sheriff of Bristol in 1742 and mayor in 1759. He served as a common councillor for 34 years until his death in 1776, aged seventy.[70] Not only was he a ship owner and sugar baker, but he was also involved in the early banks of Bristol, as a partner in the Harford Bank in Corn Street from 1769 until his death. His son, Levi Ames, dry salter, continued his father's interest in banking and, on 1 February 1786, was co-founder of Ames, Cave and Co., also in Corn Street, which was styled the New Bank. He was joined, as partners, by George Daubney, Richard Bright and Joseph Harford and he maintained this connection until his death in 1820. Levi, like his father, became Sheriff of Bristol in 1771, Mayor in 1788 and served as a common councillor for 49 years.[71] The shipping interests of the family were continued through the merchant house of Elton, Ames and Co. The next generation of the Ames family moved out of Clifton Wood House, Levi II to the family roots at Charlton and George to Cote House, Westbury-on-Trym.

On the opposite side of the road from the Brickdale residence overlooking Clifton Down, was Manilla Hall. Sir William Draper was a latecomer to Clifton as he had Manilla Hall built after his victories in the Philippine Islands in 1763. He was a Bristol boy, attending the Cathedral School under the headship of the Rev. W. Bryant. Born in 1721, the son of a customs officer, he was sent to Eton and then to King's College, Cambridge, where he became a Fellow of the college. It was assumed he would make a career in the church, but he chose instead to enter the army as an ensign in a foot regiment. He fought at Culloden and in Flanders and became a colonel in the East India Company's army. Draper raised the 79th foot regiment (Queen's Own Cameron Highlanders) and distinguished himself as their commander at the siege of Fort St George in 1759. On the Green in front of Christ Church, Clifton, stands an obelisk with slate panels and also a cenotaph. These two monuments were in the grounds of Manilla Hall until 1882 when Mayor Joseph Weston bought the house and moved them out. The cenotaph consists of a raised casket, surmounted by an urn. This was set up to honour the 30 officers and 1,000 men of Draper's regiment who fell in India fighting the French. It commemorates Madras 1759, Wanderwash and Arcot 1760, Pondicherry 1761, Manilla and the Philippines.

29. 6 Dowry Square, built *c.*1725, is an oddity with a tiny frontage squeezed into the corner with two façades. Here Dr. Thomas Beddoes, reader in chemistry at Oxford 1788-92, set up his 'Pneumatic Institution' to treat diseases by inhalation. Beddoes' assistant was Humphrey Davy, the inventor of the miners' lamp, who also experimented with nitrous oxide as a means of anaesthesia. His apparatus was constructed by James Watt and partly paid for by Thomas Wedgwood.

Draper's greatest exploit was the capture of the city of Manilla in 1763. One million pounds sterling was proposed in lieu of pillage of the city, but although it was never paid in full, it must have helped Draper to get Manilla Hall built. He was knighted in 1766 and also in that year the Society of Merchant Venturers made him Conservator of Clifton Down. In this capacity he supervised the limeburners, the lead miners and the quarrymen, whose activities had so annoyed the residents of Clifton, particularly through the noxious smoke of the lime kilns. In retirement, General Draper drew the full pay of the Governor of Great Yarmouth. His first wife had been a niece of the Duke of St Albans, and after her death he married a rich American lady from New York, the daughter of Chief Justice de Lancey. She died in 1778. The next year Sir William became Lieutenant Governor of Minorca, an island which was surrendered to the Franco/Spanish fleet. He died at Bath in 1787 and there is a memorial tablet to him in Bath Abbey.[72] Manilla Hall's subsequent occupants were members of the Miles family. William Miles, a partner in Miles' Bank, Corn Street, lived in Manilla Hall at the turn of the century and was uncle to Philip John Miles, M.P. for Bristol, who lived at 8 Rodney Place.

We have investigated the history of the larger houses built on Clifton-on-the-Hill and discussed something of the background of the families that occupied them. In most cases these were merchant families of humble beginnings who, through privateering, slaving, trade, shipping and subsequently banking interests, achieved considerable wealth over two generations. They formed a close knit community with family pews in St Andrew's church and sometimes marriage ties between them. Politically they played a leadership rôle during a critical century in Bristol's history, and in the Society of Merchant Venturers they played an active part in formulating Bristol's trade policies. Almost 600 ships undertook slaving voyages from Bristol during the 18th century. Most of the families we have discussed were involved in this trade in some way, or in privateering, which was just as uncertain. Windfall profits for the few attracted much speculative investment into such ventures and it was the successful families in this lottery who were able to build the splendid mansions which make Clifton such an attractive place today.

Chapter Eight

Social and Economic Change in Clifton from 1700-1850

Sources used so productively elsewhere in historical demography, the parish registers, are seriously incomplete for St Andrew's, Clifton. The register for the years 1681-1721 is missing, but the second and third volume of the registers cover marriages from 1722-60 and a separate marriage register overlaps and covers 1754-66. Dr. Prouse, the churchwarden of St Andrew's for 27 years from 1888, only transcribed the registers up to 1681, but Bishop's Transcripts survive for 1710, 1718, 1725-6, 1728, 1731, 1746-9, 1751, 1756 and 1759-60. The registration of marriages is widely regarded as more reliable than that of baptisms or burials. The vicar of St Phillip's, Bristol, commented in 1801 that his parish contained four private burial grounds, and that 'here people bury without ceremony or register'.[1] The figures for Table IV have been taken from the separate marriage register and from the second and third volumes of the parish registers, transcribed by Mary V. Campbell. Many partners chose to get married in St Andrew's although neither of them lived in the parish. This was true in 1733 and 1734 for example, when many of the couples came from the castle precincts. Unfortunately, from August 1739 when Thomas Taylor became vicar, the names of the partners' parishes were omitted, and after 1743 the number of marriages solemnised at St Andrew's fell dramatically. Probably this was due to the vicar insisting that at least one partner should be a resident in the parish. The parishes of the couples are entered again when the marriage register of 1754-66 begins, and from then on one partner is always a Clifton resident.

The harvest of 1752 had been particularly bad and a destructive cattle disease had killed a large proportion of the local herds. By the spring of 1753 the poor of the district were in great distress and in May the Kingswood miners resorted to open violence, resulting in four deaths and 50 wounded. In 1754 attempts were made to smuggle in Irish beef, some of which succeeded. Latimer tells us that in 1756 the harvest was greatly deficient and that, owing to the war, the imports of grain were much reduced. This caused the price of wheat to rise to 80s. per quarter, causing great hardship. During the winter many families were dependent for food on relief committees and the following year the harvest failed again.[2] This may explain the low incidence of marriages in the years 1754-6.

Because the marriage licence bonds for 1762-7 give not only the occupation of the groom but also of his chosen bondsman, it provides an interesting cross section of the men who chose to get married in St Andrew's, Clifton. There is no way of knowing whether, although one partner was a Clifton resident, they continued to live in the parish after the marriage. Table V gives the occupational distribution of a sample of the 92 males. The first thing to point out about this table is that the absence of women totally distorts the size of the service trades which by the time of the 1851

Table IV

Marriages in Clifton, 1722-66

Year	Nos. of Marr.		Both resid.	1 partner resid.	Neither
1722	23		12	0	11
1723	23		4	5	14
1724	215		6	10	
1725	29		3	3	23
1726	53		7	6	40
1727	43		3	7	33
1728	48		2	3	43
1729	40		5	6	29
1730	36		15	3	18
1731	36	J. Hodges	3	4	29
1732	27	vicar	10	3	14
1733	56		10	2	44
1734	41		8	2	31
1735	61		8	3	50
1736	41		8	2	31
1737	38		9	1	28
1738	40		9	2	29
1739	43	T. Taylor	3	0	40
1740	52	vicar	–	–	–
1741	62		–	–	–
1742	88		–	–	–
1743	56		–	–	–
1744	25		–	–	–
1745	29		–	–	–
1746	29		–	–	–
1747	21		–	–	–
1748	30		–	–	–
1749	27		–	–	–
1750	19		–	–	–
1751	21		–	–	–
1752	16		–	–	–
1753	22		–	–	–
1754	8		5	3	0
1755	15		9	6	0
1756	9		7	2	0
1757	20		12	8	0
1758	20		14	6	0
1759	14		7	7	0
1760	26		19	7	0
1761	17		11	6	0
1762	18	J. Taylor	12	6	0
1763	32	vicar	23	9	0
1764	18		16	2	0
1765	25		14	11	0
1766	15		9	6	0

Table V

Occupational distribution in the Marriage Licence Bonds for 1762-7, sample 92 males

Gentry and the Professions 14 males (15·21 per cent)		**Food and Drink Trades** 10 males (10·86 per cent)	
Accountant	1	Butcher	1
Clergy	3	Malter	1
Esquires	2	Poulterer	1
Gentlemen	5	Victuallers	6
Merchants	2	Wine Merchant	1
Surgeon	1		
		Service Trades 7 males (7·6 per cent)	
		Coachman	3
Farming 12 males (13·04 per cent)		Farrier	1
Yeomen	12	Key Porter	1
		Perukemakers	2
Shipping Trades 19 males (25 per cent)		**Clothing Trades** 7 males, (7·6 per cent)	
Anchorsmith	1	Clothier	1
Mariners	11	Cordwainers	4
Shipwrights	6	Linen Drapers	2
Waterman	1	Tailors	4
		Miscellaneous 6 males (7·1 per cent)	
Building Trades 10 males (10·86 per cent)		Hooper	1
Carpenters	5	Miner	1
Glassmaker	1	Pewterer	1
Glazier	1	Upholsterer	1
Painter	1	Watchmaker	1
Tyler and Plasterers	2	Whitesmith	1

census had, out of a random sample of 709, come to represent the largest sector (47.24 per cent). Another interesting comparison concerns the farming community represented by 12 yeomen in this table or 13.04 per cent. By 1851 the farming trades had been reduced to the level of 2.1 per cent of a random sample of 709 people and the category of yeoman has simply disappeared. There are more mariners in this small sample of 92 males in the mid-18th century than in the much larger sample of 709 in the middle of the century (7 males). Could the fact that St Andrew was the patron saint of seamen have drawn them to the church? The relative proportion of gentry and professions is larger in terms of percentage in the mid-18th century Clifton (15.21 per cent) than it became by 1851 (13.1 per cent).

Using Mary Campbell's transcripts of the St Andrew's registers from 1764-1812, we can deduce figures for burials and baptisms (see Table VI).

One can assemble enough sources to show the main direction of demographic change between 1700 and 1851. John Moore has added to our available information by using estimates based on ecclesiastical returns of 1768 and 1784 in the B.R.O., which sought to discover the prevalence of nonconformity. By using appropriate multipliers he has turned these returns into population estimates. The evidence shows that the trend of Clifton's population is markedly different from that of surrounding areas (see Table VII).

Moore shows that the population of most parishes experienced a slight fall or stagnated in the first 30 years of the 18th century. It began to grow again by 1770 and then almost doubled in the last three decades of the century. It may have fallen slightly after 1800 during the last years of the Napoleonic War and it mirrors what we know of Bristol's economic life. The early years of the century were years of rapid growth in the West India trade, but then Bristol's pre-eminence gave way to that of rival ports like Liverpool. A period of comparative stability followed, marked by a series of wars such as those of 1756-63, and in 1778-83. A resumption of our trading with America and a growth in industrial activity followed but was much reduced by the Napoleonic Wars. Clifton's population on the other hand, having 'increased by three quarters in the first half of the seventeenth century, trebled in the second half of that century, trebled again by 1770, and trebled again by 1801'.[13]

Table VI
Burials and baptisms, 1764-1812,
St Andrew's parish registers.

Year	Burials	Baptisms	Year	Burials	Baptisms
1764	66	34	1789	31	61
1765	53	44	1790	39	67
1766	36	33	1791	46	61
1767	63	36	1792	40	82
1768	52	30	1793	35	69
1769	49	41	1794	48	64
1770	49	40	1795	48	58
1771	59	35	1796	61	71
1772	53	39	1797	36	71
1773	44	47	1798	57	58
1774	68	48	1799	50	63
1775	60	45	1800	57	86
1776	45	47	1801	47	52
1777	27	55	1802	40	66
1778	51	52	1803	57	43
1779	40	59	1804	43	78
1780	53	48	1805	46	52
1781	59	53	1806	69	77
1782	55	53	1807	65	66
1783	34	68	1808	51	78
1784	46	60	1809	48	84
1785	31	62	1810	61	79
1786	51	45	1811	69	61
			1812	83	58

The figures for burials and baptisms above do not suggest that natural causes such as rising birth rates or falling death rates provide the explanation. The rise in Clifton's population must have been the result of population mobility into the area. The industrial development of Lower Clifton after 1638 and the growth in popularity, first of the Hotwells area and later of Upper Clifton, have been covered in other chapters.

The church of St Andrew's which was the centre of all this activity was quite small, and furnished with proprietory pews. It had been found necessary in 1654 partially to rebuild it, although the size remained the same. In 1716 the north aisle was added and in 1768 a south aisle was built to accommodate the increasing number of worshippers. It was a 'society' church and among the pewholders were members of

Table VII

Population of Clifton 1700-1851

1712	450[3]
1766	1,540[4]
1770	1,365[5]
1784	2,205[6]
1801	4,457[7]
1811	6,981[8]
1821	8,811[9]
1831	12,032[10]
1841	14,177[11]
1851	17,634[12]

the Elton, Goldney and Hobhouse families, and Sir William Draper. Within 50 years, however, it was decided to build an entirely new church, slightly to the north of the existing one. The new church was begun in 1816 and completed in 1822. As can be seen from the watercolour and pencil sketches made at the time, the two churches stood side by side until the new church was ready. The sketches show the original churchyard as a field, with a church path and a right of way through the middle of it.[14]

In the 19th century it became even more a place for the élite of Clifton to be seen on Sunday. Mary Campbell has drawn attention to the views of a widely-travelled visitor to the church in September 1843:

> Clifton church, though a parish church, and a church capable of accommodating a large number, is not to any extent the church of the parishioners, the rich and the non-resident occupy the reserved seats, and those few that are nominally free are filled by servants ... it is not a church of the poor man; he has no business there in that atmosphere of eau de cologne and bouquet de la Reine ... the poor ought not to be kept out their own parish church – from the pews by the rich and from the free seats by their powdered footmen.[15]

30.   In 1654 the old Clifton church had to be rebuilt. In 1716 a north aisle was added, and in 1768 a south aisle, but it still remained a small church. This pencil sketch (12½ × 7¾ in.), drawn in September 1822, shows the larger new building before the old church was removed.

To conclude this review of the parish registers of St Andrew's, some indication of the home parishes of the people from outside Bristol is necessary. The marriage licence bonds from 1661-1700 reveal that the vast majority of partners came from Somerset or Gloucestershire. Occasionally one came from London or Ireland, from Yarmouth or from Hullavington, Wiltshire, but usually they came from Marshfield, Slimbridge, Stoke Gifford, Almondsbury, Northwick, Westbury on Severn, Hawksbury or Rownham. Partners from Somerset came from Nailsea, Chew Magna, Weare, Glastonbury or Wraxall. Compared with the geographical origins of Bristol apprentices these parishes do not seem far distant.[16] Perhaps the requirements of courting were a constraint on distance in this period. Attention has been drawn already to the 12 yeoman farmers mentioned either as the groom or bondsman in the marriage licence

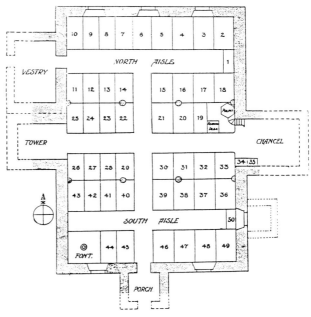

31. St Andrew's, 1654-1822. The seating arrangements consisted of family box pews with lockable doors. In 1768, when the south aisle was added, 15 families subscribed 25 guineas each for the ownership of private pews. Members of the Goldney, Elton and Hobhouse families were among the pew holders. Gradually the church raised funds to buy up these proprietory pews and by 1922 only four private pews remained.

bonds 1762-7. We turn now to consider the pressures of change as population growth necessitated greater agricultural efficiency locally.

We shall find that whereas the trend in the surrounding area towards the end of the 18th and the beginning of the 19th centuries was towards an increase in farm size, Clifton bucks the trend. Here land use moves away from grazing and pastoral farming towards building leases and market gardens. By the Tithe Act of 1836 (6 and 7 Wm.IV c.71) almost all tithes in kind were commuted by fixed rent charges and for this purpose a large scale map of each parish was made and the award for each plot of land was drawn up.[17] These maps, which are the diocesan copies, can be viewed in the B.R.O.[18] The Tithe Apportionment for Clifton in 1844 shows the 740 acres that were used or cultivated as being:

Pasture	282 acres
Common	250 acres
Gardens	30 acres
Nurseries	26 acres
Buildings and Gardens	150 acres
Quarries	2 acres

32. This view from Sea Banks was painted by Pocock more than once. It shows the large glass-house at the bottom of Jacob's Wells Road and Limekiln Lane. On the hill can be seen St Andrew's church and Thomas Goldney's colonnaded rotunda and tower, built in 1764, to house a steam engine to pump water to the grotto and fountains in his garden. The large house to the right is Clifton Hill House. The frigate being rowed up the Avon to the left needed five boats, 20 oarsmen and five steersmen.

While there were still landowners such as Francis Adams with 80 acres, George Rooke Farnall with 117 acres, John Hurle with 24 acres and Thomas Goldney with 24, these men were not farmers in any sense. The seven remaining agricultural holdings in Clifton in 1844, held by tenant farmers, were between 12 and 29 acres. William Hain, for example, still farmed Road Close, The Pen, Whiteladies Paddock and Eight Acre field (19 acres). Joseph Hemsley farmed Nutts Five Acres, the East Four Acres, the Three Acres West Ground and the Four Acres West Ground. Other farmers included John Carter, Robert Whaits, Richard Stevenson and Walter Wilkins. For surrounding areas, however, Moore has found that in Westbury and Stoke Bishop a minority of large farmers (six), held between 100 and 300 acres each. The majority of farmers had less than 80 acres and many of the smaller holdings were either market gardens or large houses with their grounds. He found that Shirehampton had four farms over 100 acres, but most were between 11 and 70 acres.

The Henbury Tithe Apportionment, 1841, shows the existence of a large number of small tenant farmers with a wide range of holdings. Most farmed between 20 and 80 acres, though one farmed 91 and two farmed over 100 acres. In size, therefore, the Clifton farms were not typical of the Vale of South Gloucestershire generally. They were dairy farms and most of their holdings were simply pasture. In this respect they probably differed from dairy farms in the rest of south Gloucestershire where convertible husbandry was practised and where arable and pastoral farming were flexibly linked. Moore has drawn attention to the view of J. M. Tucker, a surveyor of the tithes of corn and hay in the hamlet of Ham in the parish of Berkeley which belonged to the dean and chapter of Bristol. Tucker pinpoints the close link between the two kinds of farming in the Vale in August 1831:

> ... on an average a farm of 180 acres of grass lands would have only 10 acres. All the farms in this Tithing are Dairy Farms and on Farms of this kind there are a great many pigs fattened and a great many potatoes are grown for that purpose to be used in the Autumn, Winter and early Spring when whey from the dairy is scarce the quantity of potatoes consumed by the family and workmen on a Dairy Farm is much greater than on a Corn Farm.[19]

It is not only the St Andrew's registers that are fragmentary. It is probably equally true that every historical source for 18th-century Bristol is less than comprehensive, so research has tended to be particular. We know much about Bristol's Quakers, or about the merchant community, and, indeed, about Bristol's slave traders, but we still need to know what was happening to the whole population and not just significant groups. It is for this reason that the local historian turns with relief to the census returns of 1841 and 1851 which are a goldmine of information for the first half of the 19th century. The first decennial enumeration was in 1801. Numerous returns had been collected in the past, generally by church authorities or the privy council, prompted by the need to know how many households were receiving the Sacraments, or whether or not depopulation really was occurring. No reliable general statistics were available before 1801. The 1841 census provided the first detailed and complete list of all the inhabitants in an area, but the 1851 census greatly improved on this. It gives the place of birth of each person, the relationship between each person and the 'Head of Household' and more detailed information under the heading 'Occupation' than was provided in 1841.

The census of 1851, like every other kind of information, has its limitations. It describes but does not explain. To know the average number of persons per household is in itself to know little of housing conditions. Above the Hotwell Road, in the area known as Mardyke, cottages climb up to Clifton Wood. They looked picturesque but an inspector described them in 1850 as containing

> all the worst features of these hillside houses, having crowded damp back premises, privies draining upon the houses, a deficiency of drinking water, and a perpetual oozing into the house from the wet rock behind it. There are ash-heaps and deposits of house refuse in every corner. There is much disease here.[20]

To eliminate errors due to poor sampling or bias, I used random numbers tables. This was a time-consuming procedure but the figures that emerged are the result of random sampling (See Table VIII). Fourteen houses in the sample were uninhabited at the time of the 1851 census, including the Hotwell House and three houses in the

Table VIII

Households, 232 houses in random sample from the Census of 1851 for Clifton

No. of occupants in each house	No. of such houses
1	1
2	6
3	20
4	29
5	31
6	28
7	19
8	14
9	10
10	18
11	7
12	4
13	10
14	6
15	4
16	5
18	1
20	2
22	1
23	1
26	2
46	1

Colonnade. Overcrowding is a relative term, but multiple occupancy in the houses along the Hotwell Road, or in Green Street or Love Street or Jacob's Well Road created the conditions which spread the epidemic diseases.

Out of the population of Clifton in 1851, 18.8 per cent were under nine, 17.87 per cent were aged between 10-19, 19.5 per cent were 20-29, 16.9 per cent were 30-39, 11 per cent were 40-49, 7 per cent 50-59, 5 per cent were 60-69, 2.63 per cent were 70-79 and only 0.64 were over 80.

Out of the 17,634 inhabitants 36 per cent were under 20, 73 per cent were under 40 and those over 60 amounted to 8.39 per cent. This reveals a very limited expectation of life and as S. R. Woods points out in his survey of Shirehampton, epidemics came and went. In 1849 cholera in Gloucestershire killed 1,465 people, but in 1850 only 15.[21] The absence of modern drugs for the treatment of chest conditions among the elderly is also a relevant factor. With a population of 17,634 divided in proportion to take the table above, there would have been 7,008 males and 10,626 females resident in Clifton. Clearly the younger men chose to reside in areas of the city that were less expensive and the large number of opportunities for young females in the service industries attracted them to the area. The census records against many children the occupation 'scholar', in some cases up to 17 years of age. There was no evidence of child labour between the ages of five and nine, but from the age of 13 there were many errand boys. Of the male age group 10-14, 20.4 per cent were in work.

Of those aged over 70 in the sample (38 men and 54 women), only two of the men were paupers and nine were still working: James Pickard at 72 was still working as a cabinet maker; William Davis at 84 was still employed as a gardener; Francis Evans at 72 employed five men in his farrier's yard; and Samuel Lydden was still making sails at 85. Six of the women in the sample aged over 70 were receiving poor relief. Mary Davey at 86, Catherine Firth at 75 and Daphne Hunt at 70 were all widows. Of the others over 70, 16 are listed as 'Heads of Household', although this means in most cases living in multiple occupancy houses as subtenants. The rest either lived with their relatives or as lodgers.

Clifton by 1851 was no longer in any sense an agricultural community. It had expanded as a spa in the 18th century and this had encouraged many service industries to develop, which by 1851 provided more occupations than anything else. The

Table IX

Examples of household structures compared with Royal York Crescent, 1851

Nos. of occupants	Street No.	Household Structure
14	9 Love St	3 households. (1 with 4 sons, 2 dau. and mother of 68).
24	8 Love St	7 households. (M + W, 2 sisters in law and 1 cousin) M + W, 1 dau. 1 son-in-law, + 1 grandaughter), (Widow with son and dau), (1 widower), (M + W, 2 sons and dau).
46	6 South Green St	9 households. (M + W) (M + W, 3 sons, 2 dau) (M + W, 2 sons) (Widow, 2 sons) (M + W, 3 sons, 1 dau.) (Woman, 3 sons, 2 dau.) (M + W, 3 sons, 3 dau., 1 other woman) (Woman, 4 dau.) (M + W, 1 son, 1 dau.).
22	5 South Green St	6 households. (M + W, 2 lodgers) (Man, 1 son) (M + W, 4 dau., 1 son) (Man, 1 son) (M + W, 1 son, 1 dau., 1 mother), (Widow, 1 son).
26	2 Power St	9 households. (M + W, 4 sons) (Woman) (M + W, 1 son) (M + W, 2 sons) (M + W) (M + W) (M + W, 1 dau.) (M + W, 1 son, Mother-in-law) (Single man).
20	2 South Green St	4 households. (M + W, 1 granddaughter) (Man, 1 son, 2 dau.) (M + W, 2 sons, 2 dau.) (M + W, 2 sons, 3 dau.).
13	Clifton Wood House	1 household. (Widower, sister-in-law, 4 dau., 7 servants).
16	Merchants' Road	4 households. (M + W, 3 sons, 1 dau) (M + W, 3 sons, 1 dau) (M + W, 3 sons) (M + W, 1 son) (M + W).
14	18 Berkeley Place	3 households (M + W, brother, sister-in- law, 1 son, 3 lodgers) (Man, brother, sister) (M + W, 1 son).
13	3 Granby Place	2 households. (M + W, 1 son, 1 dau., 2 visitors, lodger and 3 sisters, 1 nephew, 1 niece).
15	29 Royal York Crescent	3 households. (M + W, 3 dau., 2 servants) (M + W, 2 servants) (M + 1 dau., 1 visitor, 1 servant).
13	25 Royal York Crescent Home of Sir J. Douglas, Lt. Gen., Army.	1 household. (M + W, 2 sons, 4 dau., 5 servants).
14	39 Royal York Crescent	1 household. (Man + 3 dau., 1 grandson, 1 granddaughter, tutor, butler, 6 servants).
24	16 Royal York Crescent Home of Dr. J. F. Bernard	1 household. (M + W, 2 sons, 6 dau., 5 nephews, 1 niece, 2 governesses, 6 servants).
14	14 Royal York Crescent	1 household. (1 76 yr. old spinster and 5 servants, 5 visitors with their 3 servants).
11	30 Royal York Crescent	3 households. (M + W, 1 dau., 4 servants) (1 widow and servant) (widow and servant)

Table X

Age Structure of Population in Clifton, random survey of 2,808, Census 1851

Ages	Males	Females
0 – 9	253	276
10 – 19	222	280
20 – 29	181	369
30 – 391	62	312
40 – 49	131	182
50 – 59	76	128
60 – 69	53	93
70 – 79	30	44
over 80	8	10

1,116 males   1,692 females

existence of a large professional and wealthy community of fund holders and landed proprietors, living in large houses in great crescents, drew young women from all over the United Kingdom to work as housemaids, laundresses and cooks. Dressmakers in the clothing trades were kept busy by the wives and daughters of this wealthy class, as were the ironers, milliners and silk mercers.

The proximity of Clifton to the docks and the shipbuilding is apparent and several trades connected with the sea are represented in the sample. Clifton by 1851 had become the desirable residential suburb of a great city offering a highly diversified variety of crafts and minor industries to its residents. The size of the category of miscellaneous occupations (11.42 per cent) is remarkable (see Table XII).

The area proved very attractive to young women in their late teens and early twenties. Their influx accounts in part for the marked disproportion of the sexes in the population structure.

Born in the city of Bristol	Born in Gloucestershire	Born Elsewhere
37 (16·15%)	39 (17·03%)	153 (66·81%)

The female servants came from as far away as Scotland and Ireland in a very few cases, but many more came from Somerset, Wiltshire, Devon, Dorset and South Wales. Lincoln, Liverpool, Chester, Manchester, Leeds and Beverley all sent young women to Clifton. From Ellesmere in Shropshire, Northwick in Cheshire, Spratton in Northants., Cheadle in Staffs. and Gateshead in Durham, they made their way down to Bristol to work in service.

Table XI

Occupational structure of Clifton in 1851, sample of 709 (using random numbers table)

Gentry and Professions	13·1 per cent
Service Industries	47·24 per cent
Shipping Trades	8·18 per cent
Clothing Trades	9·59 per cent
Food and Distribution	5·59 per cent
Building Trades	2·96 per cent
Farming and Horticulture	2·11 per cent
Miscellaneous	11·42 per cent

Of those born in Gloucestershire, most came from south of the line Frampton on Severn – Stroud – Cirencester. There had always been some population mobility down the Severn trade route from Worcester as evidenced by apprentices since Elizabeth I's time. By 1851 this mobility on the part of young women is a striking aspect of the census, but probably still has more to do with job opportunities than with the impact of the 'Hungry Forties' on agricultural areas or with intended emigration from the port.

Table XII

Occupations of Clifton residents, 1851, random sample of 709

Gentry and Professions (13·1 per cent)

Fundholders and Landed Proprietors	34
Clergy	8
Annuitants (Male)	2
Annuitants (Female)	10
Merchants	6
Solicitors	9
Physicians	4
Accountants	6
Joint Stock Bankers	2
Dentist	1
Attorneys	2
Army Officers	6
Graduate	1
Architect	1
Sculptor	1

Service Industries (47·24 per cent)

Housemaids	232
Lady's or parlour maids	8
Nurses	11
Hotel porters	9
Laundresses	14
Butlers	2
Coachmen	3
Kitchen maids	1
Cooks	9
Grooms	1
Liverymen	1
Ironers	1
Gardeners	6
Charwomen	4
Footmen	4
Needlewomen	4
Lodging house keepers	14
Errand boys	10
Chiropodist	1

Shipping Trades (8·18 per cent)

Mariners	7
Marine engineers	5
Shipwrights	5
Ships' Carpenters	16
Steam Packet labourers	2
Sailmakers	1
Boatman	1
Dock labourers	2
Watermen	2

Clothing Trades (9·59 per cent)

Dressmakers	33
Linen drapers	4
Milliners	4
Silk mercer's Shop	8
Haberdashers	3
Shoe and Boot makers, and Cordwainers	12
Saddle makers	2

Clothier	1
Tailors	6
Tailoresses	2
Lace mender	1

Food and Distribution (5·35 per cent)

Victuallers	5
Pork butchers	2
Corn factors	5
Brewer	1
Beer sellers	5
Baker	1
Miller	1
Grocers	2
Dairy keeper	1
Tea dealer	1
Bar maid	1
Coal merchant	1
Publicans	3

Building Trades (2·96 per cent)

Masons	6
Builder	1
Cabinet makers	4
Painters	4
Plasterers	3
Stone polisher	1
Joiner	1
Glass cutter	1

Farming and Horticulture (2·11 per cent)

Farm labourers	3
Farmers' wives	2
Stablemen	4
Ostler	1
Stockman	1
Haymakers	3
Nurseryman	1

Miscellaneous (11·42 per cent)

Governess	8
Schoolmistress	5
Schoolmaster	1
Proprietor of a school	2
Post master	2
Fly driver	1
Excise surveyor	1
Searcher in H.M. Customs	1
Tutor	2
Miniature portrait painter	1
Pigeon fancier	1
Stationers and Booksellers	3
Pupil teachers	2
Student at Baptist College	1
Clerks	10
Chemist	1
Drawing master	1

33.   The new Hotwell House and pump rooms, 1822-67. In 1820 the Merchant Venturers decided to try to increase their income from the Hotwell by erecting a new pump room, four veined marble baths and a marble fountain. It opened in 1822 but failed to make money. The merchants disposed of it to the Corporation when it was decided to improve navigation on the Avon by removing Hotwell Point, and to permit construction of the new Bridge Valley Road. The Pump Room and other buildings were destroyed in 1867.

Shirehampton was the smallest and most northern of the three tythings into which Westbury-on-Trym was divided in 1851. It covered 1,300 acres but the population only numbered 632, compared with Clifton's 17,634. S. R. Woods found the age profile to be not dissimilar; roughly 40 per cent were under 20 (36 per cent in Clifton), and a little more than 10 per cent were over 60 (8.39 per cent in Clifton). Shirehampton also had a remarkable excess of females over males, particularly in the 20-29 age group. Shirehampton however was an agricultural area, though the building of the docks at Avonmouth and Portishead must have altered the pattern of employment. Agricultural labourers formed the largest group of male workers (48 out of 171 employed men), but they must have found work outside Shirehampton since the census showed that local farmers only employed 17 of them. Female domestic servants formed by far the largest group of workers, – 58 out of 148 women employed.

Of the total population of Shirehampton, Woods found that 'very roughly one third ... was born in Shirehampton (229), one third in other parts of Gloucestershire

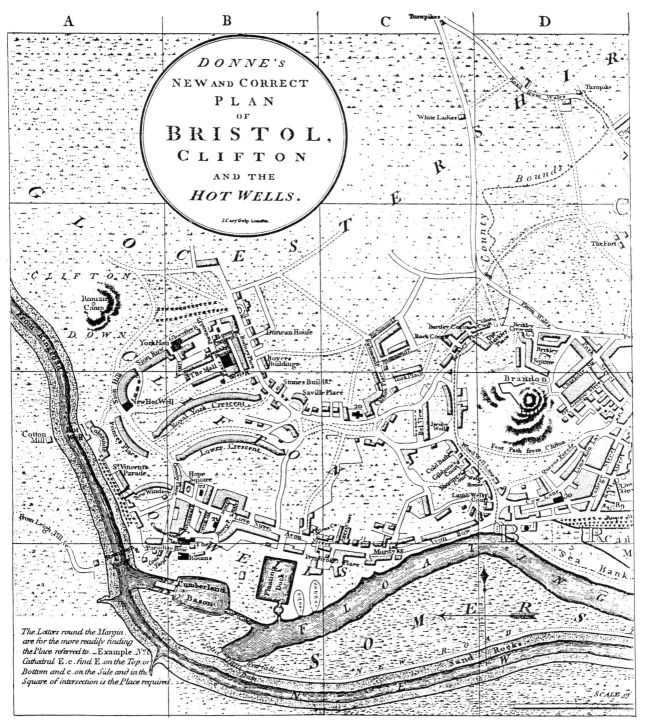

34. Benjamin Donne's 1821 issue of 'A New and Correct Plan of Bristol and the Hotwells, Clifton'. Published originally in 1800 by B. Donne (junior) and engraved by J. Cary of London (scale 6 in. to the mile), this map illustrates how slowly building in Clifton progressed. The main terraces are in position and Brimley Close is now covered by The Mall, Assembly Rooms and Rodney Place. However, Ferney Close is still behind Boyce's Buildings and from there onwards is pastureland.

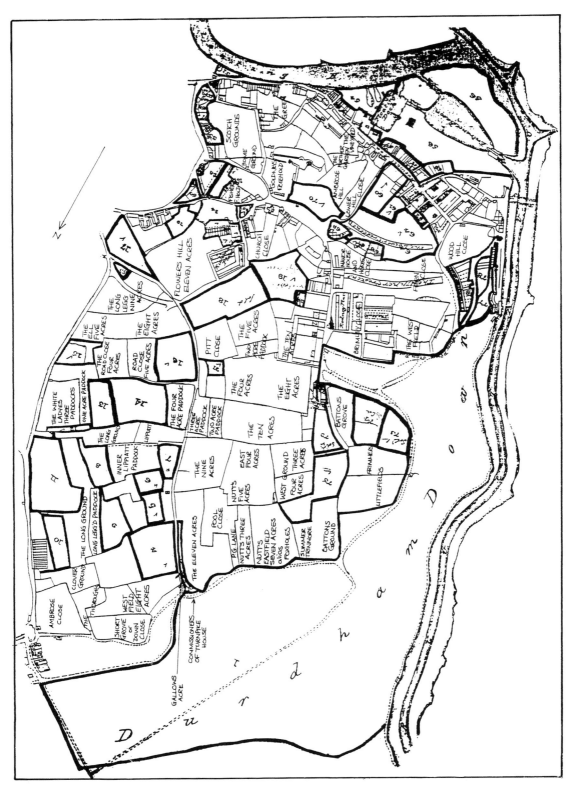

35. Map of Clifton in the 1820s, with field names added. The Merchants' property is outlined in heavy black (green in the original). The plan is in the Society's Schedule of Deeds 2, and is a loose sheet. Rodney Place and The Mall are shown as built on Brimley Close, but not the Assembly Rooms. The sites of Upper and Lower Crescents are shown, but not Windsor Terrace. No. 19 (Ferney Close) was to become Victoria Square; no. 18 (Broadmoor and Larridge) are shown as sold (to Samuel Hemming); and no. 17 was Honeypen Hill field.

36. *Clifton from Rownham Meadows, c.*1800. This watercolour shows the view across Rownham Meads, now the Cumberland Basin. On the hill can be seen Goldney's tower, the line of mature yew trees in the garden, Goldney House, Prospect House and Beresford House, and Clifton Court (now the Chesterfield). On the right-hand side ships are berthed in Merchants' Dock. In the foreground, the large building on the left, the Assembly Room, is flanked by Paradise Row and Dowry Parade. The Assembly Room was used as a school until its demolition in 1963 to permit the construction of the Cumberland Basin flyover.

(207) and one third in counties other than Gloucestershire (183)[22] For the nearby tything of Stoke Bishop in 1841, 1,572 were born in Gloucestershire and 1,079 born out of Gloucestershire, which suggests considerable population mobility.

Clifton in 1851 had been total transformed in the century since de Wilstar's survey of 1746. It had evolved from a village community, with a thriving spa at one corner,

Table XIII
Number of servants per household, Census 1851

A random sample of 709 revealed 130 households with servants	
More than 5 servants	2·30 per cent
5 servants	1·53 per cent
4 servants	4·61 per cent
3 servants	12·30 per cent
2 servants	26·15 per cent
1 servant	53·07 per cent

to the most desirable residential suburb of the city. The census of 1851 confirms, enumerates and identifies the extent of that transformation. The subsequent censuses show the continuation of that process:

1851	1861	1871	1881	1891	1901
17,634	21,375	26,364	28,694	29,345	27,761

The Growth of Clifton as a Residential Suburb in the First Half of the 19th Century

William White completed the up-to-date plan of Clifton for the Merchants' Hall in 1806. A copy of this survey, together with the accompanying reference book describing the fields, their relative acreages and the names of tenants, has survived in the Society's archives. As the pace of building quickened, this survey was, in its turn, replaced by John Marmont's in 1837,[1] by which date Clifton had been incorporated within the 'city and county' of Bristol. Perhaps the most massive and far-reaching change that had occurred in Clifton between the drawing of these two maps was the excavation through Rownham Meads of the new Cumberland Basin and entrance lock, converting two miles of water from Temple Meads station to the Hotwells into a floating harbour. The landowners involved were William Jeffreys, Francis Adams and John Beames, but the pressure for the project came from the Merchants' Hall who had formed a committee in the autumn of 1791 to bring about some action.[2]

Various schemes to overcome the inconvenience of the twice daily ebbing of the water in the Avon and Frome had been proposed in the 18th century.[3] Ships had increased in size, the wharves were now inadequate and the port of Liverpool was

37. Cumberland Basin from Rownham Hill, *c*.1825. This watercolour by Samuel Jackson shows the new locks in what had been Rownham Meads, and to the right of the picture is the New Cut which changed the course of the tidal river. Entry from the Avon into the Cumberland Basin involved a very sharp turn into one of the two locks. In the background is the junction lock into the Floating Harbour. On the right is Clift House, previously the site of Mr. Warren's two glasshouses.

38. The construction of the Cumberland Basin (1804-9) totally altered the appearance of Rownham Meads. The picture, c.1862, shows Jessop's North Entrance lock and Brunel's lock (built 1844-9 to replace Jessop's South Entrance lock). This lock has now been sealed by a concrete wall. At high tide the ferry boat was secured by a cable. At low tide several small boats were placed across the stream with gangplanks laid across them.

expanding rapidly at Bristol's expense. From 1804-9 the excavation of the Cumberland Basin and the new bed for the Avon from St Phillip's Marsh to Rownham, together with the construction of new quay walls and locks, provided work for more than 1,000 men at a time when the great speculative housing boom in Clifton temporarily had ended.

In January 1809 the Avon was diverted into its new channel and a great celebratory dinner was held on 1 May in a field opposite Mardyke. Two oxen were roasted whole and six hundredweight of plum pudding was prepared for 1,000 of the workmen who had been involved. A whole gallon of strong beer was provided for each man. Inevitably, with so much liquor, a fight broke out between the Irish and the English labourers which ended in arrests and a memorable occasion.[4]

The population of Clifton expanded steadily during the 19th century from 4,457 in 1801 to 27,761 in 1901.[5] This involved sporadic bursts of housebuilding throughout the century with problems of an adequate water supply, proper sewers, drainage and new roads. Clifton landowners were able to benefit from the rising land values by leasing land for building development and by charging ground rents. They were also able to determine the way in which the area was developed and this chapter will be concerned with a detailed examination of their contribution. The de Wilstar survey of 1746 had revealed that besides the Merchants' Society there were other landowners in Clifton such as John Power, Francis Freeman and John Hodges. Let us look at what happened to each of these three estates in turn.

The Rev. John Power was a cleric in East Hampstead, Berkshire, who died on 18 May 1746. He was the nephew of Ayliffe Greene of Clifton whose will of 17 October 1690 required that to inherit the entire estate, 'his nephew John Power, Clerk, should not intermarry with a daughter-in-law of one, Mr. Evans of Oxford.' If he were to marry her, then 'immediately after such marriage the Estate so limited to him ... should cease and be void, and in such case the said Testator gave the said premises to John Ellys and the heirs of his body ...'.[6] John Power did not marry the lady in question, but Sarah, by whom he had two daughters. She died in January 1765.

39. *The Overfall Dam near the Floating Dock and Cumberland Basin*, watercolour by T. L. S. Rowbotham, 1827. On the right, on the slope below the Paragon, is Hope chapel, 1786. When Brunel was consulted about the problem of silting, he increased the flow of water through the floating harbour by means of a culvert under the Overfall Dam. It was thenceforth called the Underfall. Between the ship's masts Windsor Terrace juts out on the rocky precipice of the gorge.

Ayliffe Greene had bought part of William Whittington's estate on 14 October 1668. It had included, among various other closes, the 11 acres of Brimley Close, the 13 acres of Clifton Manor House and the 11-acre close of pasture adjoining it called the West Ground. It also included 'the Wood and woodie ground called Rownham's Wood', the 'two acres of pasture more in the fields called the Littlefield',[7] and 'a certain Close called Dowrie'.[8] This estate was devised in John Power's will of 26 March 1743 to his grandson, John Beames, after the trustees had sold certain closes to provide for Sarah's natural life and that of his daughter, Mary Hawkins. The *King David* public house he left to his other grandchildren, George, Sarah and Mary Beames.

Royal York Crescent, Windsor Terrace and the Paragon were already being built on John Beames' land in the 1780s and 1790s. By 1788-9 he was selling parts of Brimley Close, on mortgages of £2,000 and £500 for building plots. It was noted:

> part of the said Ground called Brimley' which was then staked out and intended to be granted to Wm. Bleuden and Thomas Baker for building on ... to the intent and purpose that the said John Hughes, Surgeon and Apothecary, and Proctor Anderson, Gent., their heirs and assigns, should for ever thenceforth yearly receive and take one yearly rent of £121.10.0 to be charged upon and issuing and payable out of said premises thereby granted and released.[9]

Robert Bayley was another speculator who bought land for building in Brimley on 22 and 23 December 1788. He secured a 427-ft. frontage of the turnpike road which formed the boundary of Brimley Close and divided it into nine plots 50 × 175 ft. He bought this land in December, just before John Beames' death in 1789, through a five part indenture which again involved John Hughes and John Proctor Anderson, attorney, as well as John Beames, Henry Dupont, Gent. and James Hughes, Gent. The estate of John Power was being sold to wealthy merchants like Henry Dupont, vintner, or John Hughes, surgeon, who in turn sold to Bayley for substantial ground rents.

To get to his land Robert Bayley had to pay a substantial yearly ground rent himself to the Merchants' Society, for the right of 'free ingress, egress and regress over the said waste ground'. On the 427-ft. frontage Robert Bayley set Joseph Fussell to work in 1789 constructing Rodney Place. Robert Bayley had also bought land behind the Rodney Place development and had contracted 'that he would, before 29 Sept. 1791, lay out £5,000 at least in building twelve or more good and substantial Dwelling Houses in manner therein mentioned'. He conveyed this land to Thomas Coates in 1791, 'to the intent that he said Bayley, his heirs and assigns should for ever yearly receive one clear annual sum or yearly rent charge of £160 to be issuing out of the said plot of ground'.[10]

Brimley Close was also the site of The Mall, designed by the Bath architect, John Eveleigh.[11] In the year 1791:

> Samuel Powell and Thomas Morgan had laid out part of the said piece of Ground conveyed as aforesaid to the said Thomas Coates in trust for them ... for the purpose of erecting thereon a double row of Houses with an Acre or Pleasure Ground to be inclosed in front thereof called Clifton Mall'.[12]

Thirteen plots of 25 × 80 ft. were laid out on each side and builders, for example John Pike, William Horn and Thomas Ball, borrowing £700 on the security of each house erected, proceeded to construct The Mall. Thomas Morgan and M. M. Coates provided the weekly sums that enabled the whole project to go ahead. Subsequently, both sides of the Mall were extended as New Mall, now called West Mall, with another 21 houses and Caledonia Place with another 31 houses. The architects were James Foster and William Okeley, and building took place between the years 1841 and 1845. In the meantime the builders faced the market crash of 1793.

The crash bankrupted John Pike and Thomas Pike along with the rest. The Bankruptcy Commissioners in December 1793,

> in further execution of their Commission ... did order, bargain and sell unto the said John Jayne, his Heirs and Assigns ... [everything that Thomas Pike and John Pike] ... had been any way seized or possessed of or interested in ... In trust for the Benefit and Advantage of all and every the Creditors ...

John Jayne put all these houses up for auction on 23 December at the *York Hotel* at Clifton. Matthew Mills Coates attended the sale and bid on the joint account of Thomas Morgan and himself as co-partners, under the firm of Morgan and Coates. These houses they subsequently sold with mortgages at £800, with ground rents of £2 14s. per annum from 1795 to 1807.[13] It has been suggested that Eveleigh's original design of 13 houses on each side, facing one another, were two sides of a square, and that the Assembly Rooms were intended to look out on to it.[14] In the event the fourth side was never filled in.

The building of the Assembly Rooms across the east end of The Mall, on Brimley Close, started in the early months of 1806. Felix Farley reported on 17 May 1806 that two plans had been submitted to the gentry of Clifton and that Francis Howard Greenway's had been chosen. It is an imposing building and served as a hotel as well as assembly rooms while Clifton still prospered as a resort. Wholly built in dressed freestone, the central block has six plain shafted columns based on a low basement of rusticated arches. In 1818 it was adapted to form the Clifton Club.[15] In October, gentlemen who wanted to establish a club where they could play billiards and cards were invited to subscribe £50 each. There were to be 20 subscribers initially to raise the £1,000 necessary to fit out the accommodation. The names of those first 20 who subscribed reveal the élite of Clifton society at the time. They included Admiral Nichols, Admiral Sotheby, Gabriel Goldney, James Elton, George Ames, Sir Richard Vaughan, Levi Ames, Charles and Samuel Harford, Philip John Miles, Lt. Col. Coke and Lt. Col. Huddleston. Later in the century, in 1856, the whole right-hand wing had its basement and ground floor converted into shop fronts by J. H. Hirst, and in 1894 E. H. Edwards converted the centre block ground floor, with a series of heavy Italianate windows.

In exactly the same way that Morgan and Coates, attorneys, bought up the unoccupied houses of The Mall after the crash of 1793, so too did Isaac Cooke, attorney, buy the unfinished houses of Windsor Terrace for £2,000 in 1807. Through his management of clients' estates he had ready access to mortgages. In 1808, he and his mortgagees leased numbers 1,3,6,7,8,9 and 10 to John Drew, a builder of Dial House, Clifton. Drew finished the terrace to a much reduced design and in 1811 mortgaged them back to Isaac Cooke in order to finance the building of the Paragon.[16]

Following the bankruptcies of James Lockier, John Coles, Michael Davis, Ezekiel Evans and Richard Constant in May 1793, the derelict buildings of Royal York Crescent were put up for public auction. Isaac Cooke bought Lot 1 and one of the conditions of the sale was that the purchaser should have custody of all the original title deeds for the whole crescent: 'and whereas the said Isaac Cooke became the purchaser of Lot 1 at the said Auction, and the Title Deeds referred to by the said Condition ... have been delivered to him and are now in his custody ...'.[17]

Cooke and his mortgagees again gave John Drew the task of completing some of these houses, but the last gaps in the crescent were not closed until about 1820.[18]

Francis Freeman's estate of 189 acres was another of those described on de Wilstar's map of 1746. The way in which it was acquired and the manner in which it passed to the Adams family have been described in Appendix I.

Over the years since October 1705 the Merchants' Hall had leased the fields adjoining Fearney Close, called Broadmoors and Larridge.[19] In 1835, on that part of Broadmoors fronting the north side of Fearney Close, Samuel Hemming built Lansdown Place. This remarkable terrace, designed by Foster and Son, initiated the plan of the big terraces which followed. As Gomme, Jenner and Little have explained, 'there are no pediments, no columns, only pilasters', but 'the continuous first floor balcony is for the first time intrinsic in the design'. Both the end houses of the terraces are stepped forward, as is the central house. Samuel Hemming was very pleased with the result and boasted to the Merchants: 'My Property at Lansdown Place, Clifton (the finest Row of Buildings erected I think I am justified in saying), in your neighbourhood, and built in the best and most substantial manner'.[20]

Another estate described by de Wilstar in 1746 was that owned by John Hodges. Anthony Hodges had purchased the land in December 1608 from the young sons of William Clark and Frances Brooke.[21] The estate included the old Manor House and Church Close (5 acres), Shortgrove (12 acres), Causeway Close (3 acres) and Three Acre Paddock. The estate passed from Anthony to his eldest son John Hodges and then to his grandson, Hazelgrove Hodges. Hazelgrove's heir was his daughter Elizabeth Ann Manley and she also inherited land from her uncle, John's younger brother, Stephen. Her daughters inherited in equal shares. The eldest sister, who lived in Bath, was also called Elizabeth Ann, and she sold her undivided third of Shortgrove on 7 February 1777.[22] His son, also Samuel Worrall, moved to Bristol to join the very successful law firm of Thomas Fane in Small Street. When Thomas Fane became heir to the earldom of Westmorland, resigning from the law practice and from being Clerk to the Society of Merchant Venturers, Samuel Worrall succeeded to both positions. He made a fortune and bought the splendid Queen Anne building, Church House, in 1776 from the Hodges family. As an attorney he became involved in speculative building in the 1770s. The Bishop of Bristol in 1770 obtained an Act of Parliament enabling him to lease his 'park', adjoining the palace, for speculative building and the dean and chapter obtained similar powers with regard to White's Garden. Worrall gained a 90-year building lease and let out the land in building plots in what became College Street, one of the main red light areas in the city.[23] He died in 1804.

His son, Samuel Worrall III, was also a lawyer and became town clerk of Bristol. He died unmarried in 1873. His brother, General Henry Worrall, had died the previous year, leaving four daughters, of whom the unmarried Sophia began selling land in the area of Blackboy Hill in the 1870s. These sales were made to James Bigwood between Belgrave Road and Worrall Road, to John R. Shorland, builder, of four acres along Worrall Road, below Anglesea Place, and to John Davies, builder, of ground in Pembroke Road.[24]

Having completed our survey of the way in which three important estates were devised, we turn now to the continuing development of Clifton. In the early stages of development, drainage in Clifton made full use of the tidal Avon. Culverts were constructed to convey surface water from the street while sewage was dealt with quite successfully through 'ash pits'.[25] As the population grew, however, and the construction of the floating harbour cut off most of the old city's waterways from the cleansing action of the tides, the high ground of Clifton became an even more desirable place of residence. The Frome, now sealed off from the tides, became virtually stagnant, and Clifton, despite its elegance, had its problems. The majority of the 'good quality' houses drained into cesspools and Victoria Square, which belonged to the Merchants, was planned from the beginning with adequate drainage. However, the Hotwells was particularly unfortunate, being too low to drain freely at all states of the tide and being loaded with water and sewage from the upper levels in addition to its own.

The Hotwells area also suffered from a shortage of clean water. In 1850 in the Hotwells district there were 56 courts, only four of which were supplied by a water company, and 995 houses in streets, of which only 220 were supplied by a water company.[26] On the hill 304 houses were reasonably supplied from Sion Spring, water being pumped up by the steam engine, and another 100 from Richmond Spring.[27] Nearly all the houses in Richmond Terrace drained into cesspools and the same was true at Clifton Park, Cambridge Place and Burlington Place. John Latimer wrote in the 19th century:

> The Whiteladies Road has an open gutter, down which the house drainage runs into a side ditch, and is most offensive. Above Whiteladies Gate, in the bottom of the valley, several open sewers meet, and their contents are generally complained of. In a field in front of West Clifton Terrace [now the site of Alma Road] the sewage (from the Blackboy district and West Park) escapes over a large space. Hampton Terrace suffers materially from an old ditch, in which the sewage is collected. From thence it finds its way to the Froom [sic] ... At the back of Park Place is a peculiarly filthy crossroad and a market garden, the stench of which is much complained of.[28]

The Merchants' building scheme for Cornwallis Crescent had been halted with the bankruptcy of Harry Elderton in 1796 and his death quite soon afterwards.[29] The property reverted to the Hall as the ground landlord and in June 1796 the Merchants granted Henry Worrall a 40-year building lease to complete the eastward end within 14 years. On the same date they granted Henry Brooke a similar lease of all the remaining property on which 33 houses had been started. He had to promise to complete 15 of the houses within 14 years. By assignment from Worrall, Henry Brooke was given the task of completing the whole crescent of 40 houses. By March 1821 he had to have completed 16 houses, roads and pavements and to have finished the crescent by March 1835.[30] He did not comply with the first date, but was allowed by the Society to continue. Although he died in 1829, Cornwallis Crescent was finished by the agreed date despite problems over the right of way through the property which had been established in the meantime.[31] The Society had, reasonably enough, suggested an archway under one of the houses as a way round the difficulty, but Brooke had objected and was allowed to leave a gap.[32]

Henry Brooke had also been involved in completing the Polygon on a piece of ground at the top of Green Street. By leases of 1821 and 1823 renewable every 14 years, Brooke was granted building permission and sublet the task to George Jones, builder, who finished the crescent in May 1826.[33]

Permission was sought from the Society in 1810 to begin building on Honeypen Hill fields and the promoter promised to lay out £3,000 in building.[34] They were required to submit plans but none were forthcoming. Nevertheless in 1822 Messrs. Bowsher asked again for a 40-year lease and again were told to submit plans of the proposed buildings.[35] In the event Honeypen Hill fields were leased to Benjamin Tucker who sublet 21 out of the 32 plots and reported 12 of them near completion in 1825.[36] In 1829 Tucker reported to the Hall that he had completed all 32 houses with the exception of five in Park Place which would be finished within a year.[37] Building had also been in progress at York Place and Clifton Place. In 1805 the lease of the ground on which York Buildings stood became renewable and an application was made by Isaac Cooke for Messrs. Langston, Howgood and Co., but no lease could be made at that time as the property was then involved in a Chancery suit.[38]

In 1828 freehold land behind King's Parade, near Blackboy Hill, was put up for sale. On the 1746 map these fields were KII, Clover Ground, KIII, the Long Ground, and KIV, Road Close, described by de Wilstar as Mr. Keen's freehold. In 1828 they belonged to the estate of Mr. Thornhill and the 15 acres were bought by William Hurle for development.[39] The Hurle family added to this estate the field called Longcroft (UXXVI on de Wilstar) which in 1746 was called the Long Legg'd Paddock, which John Hurle purchased from Francis Adams III in 1839.[40]

The Merchants also owned three fields, comprising 11 acres, leased to Mr. Deverell, called Cecills Littfields, 'bounded on the North with a ground called Battens Ground, on the East with the Downs, on the West with Mr. Freeman's Littfield, and on the South with the Highway under St Vincent's Rocks'.[41] In December 1818 their tenant John Deverell wanted to change to a building lease but found the Hall wanted to buy out his interest, and a price of £2,800 was negotiated. In 1824 the Hall asked Mr. Brigden to plan the fields for building development and when he did so they rejected his ideas on the grounds that the principal rooms were on too small a scale.[42] The eight lots were then put up for private tender and in November 1825 'it was recommended that the Tenements to be erected on the eight Lots should be intitled Camp Place or Camp Buildings'.[43]

40. *View of Granby Hill, Clifton* by Lt. Colonel William Booth, 1822. To the left can be seen Cornwallis Crescent and just above it Prospect House and Beresford House, whilst at the end of the crescent is Goldney House. In the centre is Dowry Parade, with the Merchants' Dock behind. Cumberland Basin was still relatively new, having been cut into Rownham Meads 1804-9. This hill was for many years the only route to Clifton from the Hotwell and was notoriously difficult for horse and carriage. By the prominent blank white wall of Rutland House at the corner of Granby Hill and Hope Chapel Hill, a sledge is being used.

The name lasted perhaps for a decade, but evidence suggests that the more picturesque name was reasserting itself by 1839:

> Mr. Pinney applied for permission to plant some Trees on that part of the Society's Plot of Ground behind his Dwelling House at Clifton, as at present he's open and uninclosed against the Road laid out for the use of the Houses in Camp or Litfield Place.[44]

Ten plots faced the Promenade and four plots faced the rear. Behind this development Francis Adams was starting building on Frimmer's (5 acres, U VI) and on Littlefields (5 acres, U VII).

In 1835 Francis Adams' trustees, Robert Casberd and John Lowe, sold to the Bristol and Clifton Zoological Society, at a ground rent of £800 per annum, two Closes called Summer Trinmore and the Ten Acres, known as Foxholes. The leading

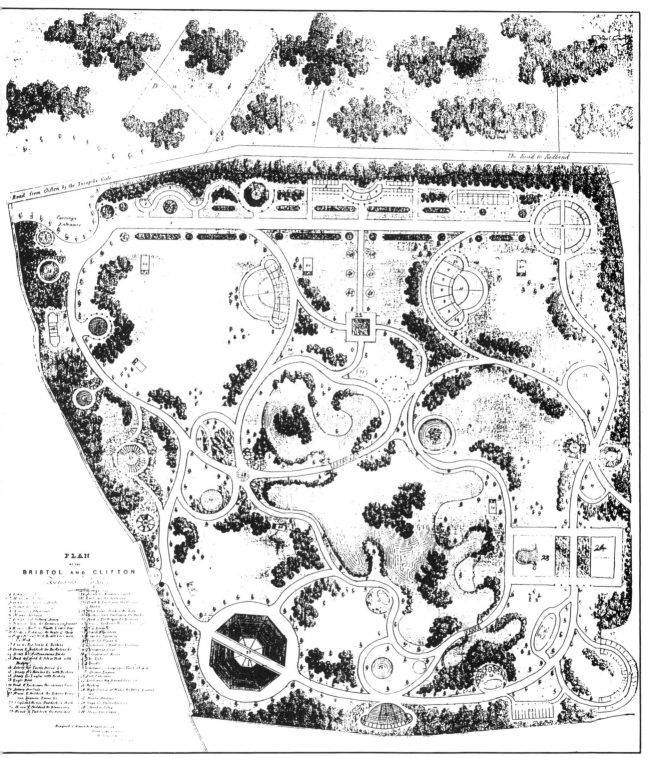

41. R. John Forrest's original plan of the Bristol and Clifton Zoological Garden. Forrest was an eminent landscape gardener from Acton, London. The 12-acre site comprising Summer Trinmore and Foxholes was purchased in 1835 from Francis Freeman II by the 220 original shareholders. The site of the old lime kiln (11) halfway along the main walk from the carriage entrance became the bear pit, with six monkey poles (49) on either side of the approach walk. The elephant house (23) and the rhinoceros house (24) were in the bottom right-hand corner.

spirit in the project to set up a zoo was Dr. Henry Riley, a physician at the B.R.I. He was born in Clifton in 1797 and was notable as the first doctor in the West Country to use the stethoscope. Riley was also an enthusiast for anatomical dissection and was fined £6 when caught in the act of raiding a grave in the Brislington cemetery. He had a large collection of fossils, some of which came from the stone workings on the Downs, especially from Upper Belgrave Road.[45]

The zoo came into being in September 1835, supported by 220 proprietors who purchased the 500 shares at £25 each. Among the original subscribers were I. K. Brunel, W. D. and H. O. Wills, Joseph, Robert and Zephania Fry, Sir John Smyth, John Harford, William Goldney, George and Abraham Hilhouse, Dr. John Beddoe, His Grace the Duke of Beaufort, George Braikenridge, George Daubney and Thomas Tyndall.[46] This was not the first attempt to found a zoo in Bristol, as John Miller, vice-president of the Society of Florists, planted eight acres of ground at Arnos Vale early in 1835, but the site was not thought to be as suitable as Clifton Down. Dr. Riley did not live long after the zoo was founded and died at Slough in 1848.[47]

The site consisted of 12 acres of Francis Adams' land with a limekiln which was to become the site of the bear pit and the aquarium. An eminent landscape gardener from Acton, London, named Richard Forrest, planned the zoological gardens so well that they largely remain unchanged today, as his original drawings show. The weekly wage bill was £5 16s. 6d.: the beastkeeper received £1 plus cottage and coal; the deputy keeper £1 2s. 6d.; the two underkeepers 18s. 0d. each; two labourers 12s. 0d. each; and a gamekeeper 14s. 0d.[48]

Immediately below and adjacent to the zoo was pasture ground belonging to Francis Adams (U XV, Nutts Five Acres and XII, Pool Close). To the east of this was land which in 1746 was known as The Nine Acres (XXVI) and had belonged to the apothecary D. Ross, but which in 1861 belonged to Mr. Haynes. To the south, below the Close, was land which had been Adams' but which was now owned by Dr. Black. The original purchase for Clifton College was 'Adams' land' in October 1860, which covered nearly 10 acres and lay between Worcester Terrace and the zoo. In March 1861 the solicitors for Clifton College Company Ltd. bought three acres of Haynes' land at £1,250 an acre. The two and three-quarter acres of Dr. Black's land adjoining the southern portion of Pool Close was leased and eventually bought in June 1862.[49]

The Clifton College Company Ltd. was founded as a result of a meeting in April 1860 of Bristol professional and businessmen after two previous attempts to found a public school in Bristol for the sons of the prosperous middle classes had failed. Shares to the value of £10,000 were sold, a site chosen and a headmaster appointed. By 1861 building was in full swing on the site.[50] Of Clifton at this time John Addington Symonds wrote, 'There were few buildings then between the Parish church and Durdham Downs. The suburb which has grown up round the College was a tract of fields, at the end of which lay the Zoological Gardens'.[51]

There were no houses and no roads where Guthrie Road, College Road, Percival Road, Albert Road and Northcote Road now are, and no houses in Pembroke Road. W. Chamberlain was present with his parents at the school's opening and wrote:

We Redland boys walked over the fields every day to the College. In those days the fields extended from Redland right across to Clifton Promenade. When you came to what is now Pembroke Road, at the end of Beaufort Road, there was a wicket-gate, and you went through that and crossed on to what was then called Gallows Acre Lane ... The Lane was so narrow that two vehicles could not pass each other. There were green hedges either side. Having crossed over you went through another wicket-gate, and went over the fields where Emmanuel Church and the College now stand.[52]

Charles F. Hansom was chosen as architect and instructed to prepare plans of one wing of the school buildings and a headmaster's house. The stone had to be brought from Bath and the first buildings were opened on 30 September 1862. The chapel, with its detached spire, was completed in 1866 and various sympathetic additions to the buildings were made throughout the century, and indeed up to the 1920s, on this site.[53]

Directly south of Clifton College fields, and built on John Beames' land, is Worcester Terrace. Clifton was still attracting the most distinguished Victorian architects although the sites were less spec-

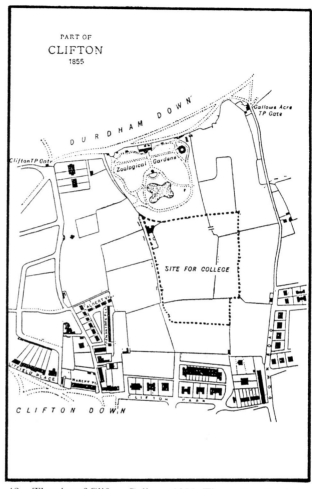

42. The site of Clifton College, 1855. The pasture land immediately below Summer Trinmore and Foxholes (which were now the zoological gardens), comprised Nutts Five Acres and Pool Close belonging to Francis Adams, and, to the east, the Nine Acres, which belonged to the apothecary Mr. Ross. The original purchase by the Clifton College Company Ltd. in October 1860 was 'Adam's land', which covered 10 acres. Between this and Worcester Terrace lay three acres of Haynes' land which was purchased in March 1861.

tacular than those developed in the late 18th century. Charles Underwood was the architect of Worcester Terrace and it was completed in 1853. Within a stone's throw below this terrace was Vyvyan Terrace, a magnificent Regency building. It was built on ground belonging to George Rooke Farnall of Durley Park, Ringwood, Southampton, and covered 'part of two pieces or parcels of Ground called respectively the Little Field or the Four Acres, and Hollylands, and together with other

43. Vyvyan Terrace was conceived in the form of a palace by the architect Richard Pope. Building may have commenced in 1842 and some houses were occupied in 1844. The land consisted of several closes called Four Acres, Hollylands, etc., which had been purchased by George R. Farnall of Durley Park, Southampton, in November 1842, from William E. LeBlanc. The palace has an Ionic colonnade of eight columns in the centre, with two more each on the flanks.

lands called or known by the name of Clifton Park'.[54] The architect of the terrace was Richard S. Pope and he conceived this palace with an Ionic colonnade of eight columns in the central portion, partly repeated with two more each on the flanks. The houses were to be of the value of £800 at the least and a ground rent of £8 per annum on each house was payable to George Farnall, his heirs and assigns, for ever. Several of the houses up to no. 9 were already occupied by October 1844. George R. Farnall had bought the land two years previously from William Elliott LeBlanc and building may have begun in 1842.[55]

Another splendid terrace was built on the south-west side of the Merchants' ground of Ferney Close (Victoria Square). The original plans of James Foster and Sons date from 1837 but as we shall see it took more than 15 years to complete the Royal Promenade. As its name implies, it was conceived as much as a palace as a terrace. Foster and Wood, the successors to James Foster, were the architects.[56] The Merchants' interest in Ferney Close as building ground was aroused in 1837 by an application from their tenant for three lives, Abraham G. Harford Battersby, to purchase the land, but the Hall would not part with it.[57] Battersby was followed as tenant by John Lunell who had the idea not only to build on Ferney Close, but to set up a permanent market and construct a road right through the Close.[58] The Merchants were next faced with the situation where Lunell announced his intention of selling his leasehold land in nine lots fronting each side of the pathway across the field.[59] Having advertised his interest as lessee for sale Lunell could not do much about it when the Merchants authorised their treasurer to buy him out for £1,100.[60] This enabled the Society to contemplate building on Ferney Close themselves and to draw up plans.

Facing the Merchants' ground was the recently completed Lansdown Place and the Hall naturally thought of incorporating that terrace as one side of their proposed Square. They therefore ordered their clerk to approach Samuel Hemming with the suggestion that, in compensation for leaving the ground open in front of Lansdown, his tenants should pay the Hall a ground rent of not less than £3 per annum on each house. Since no reply was received from Samuel Hemming by March

44. Victoria Square, 1846-74. Originally Ferney Close and owned by the Merchant Venturers, plans for the Royal Promenade (south-west side) were drawn up in 1837 by James Foster. It took three different builders to get the square completed by 1874. The photograph shows the north-east side, Lansdown Place, built by S. Hemming in 1835.

1845, the Hall decided to construct their Square as if Lansdown Place were not there and to mark out the land for building a square.[61]

This provoked a response from Hemming's solicitor offering £750 to keep the frontage of Lansdown open, but the Merchants, thinking of the ground rents they would have to forego, would not agree to less than £1,000.[62] As they saw it:

> they had originally offered to sacrifice for the benefit of Lansdown Place upwards of £80 per annum in Ground Rents and to have given them in addition not only the benefit of the first Cost (upwards of £2,000), of laying out a Square of the most ornamental description, but of that of its subsequent maintenance. This liberal offer has been declined.[63]

Hemming was in touch with what was going on, although he later pleaded ignorance through being in Londonderry for two years. His solicitors, Savery, Clark and Sons, reported to Robert Osborne, clerk to the sub-committee on the proposed buildings on Ferney Close, that 'Mr. Hemming has again consulted his Friends and his London Solicitor, and has now sent to us to say that he cannot submit to the terms on which the Soc. of Merchants propose not to injure his Houses at Lansdown Place by building immediately opposite to them'.[64] In January 1846 Hemming realised he had no option left and appealed to the Merchants' 'best feelings'.[65] However, the Hall's patience had become exhausted and they now demanded Hemming should pay £1,500, of which £350 was the cost of drawing up plans which were now wasted. The supply of water to Hemming's houses was to be from the Society's waterworks at three per cent on the annual value of each house. He was to join his houses to the Society's main sewer at £1 per annum for each house and to fill in his cesspool. Although Hemming accepted these terms he had to be taken to court to get the money.[66]

Having had plans drawn up, the Society now contracted with a builder to erect houses on one side, in accordance with their specifications. By August 1847 the builder, William B. Reed, had completed six houses at a right angle to Lansdown Place along the side which finishes with the Pharmacy Arch through to Boyce's Avenue. This represented a very considerable outlay of money for a speculative builder, particularly since none had yet been sold. Reed therefore asked the Society for a loan of £5,000 on the security of the houses erected and five others which were well advanced. He got his loan at five per cent per annum.[67] This was a pattern which was repeated with three different builders before the square was finished. The next year the Society agreed to lend him £6,000 at five per cent,[68] and in December of the following year another £2,000 to complete the terrace.[69] William Bateman Reed strongly opposed the request of the City Council to drive a road through the centre of Victoria Square and in this he received the total support of the Hall who also rejected the idea.[70] Eventually, by 1855, all 14 houses and Albert Lodge were sold, bringing in ground rents to the Society of £217 10s. 0d.[71]

A proposal to build a large hotel on either of the other two sides of the square was welcomed by the Hall until the inhabitants of Victoria Square protested vehemently and John Paull's scheme had to be abandoned.[72] The need to make repeated loans to builders while construction took place cooled the Society's enthusiasm for building for several years, but in 1863 they received an offer by John Yalland to build Victoria Square West to the splendid designs of Foster and Wood 'provided he could receive pecuniary assistance from the Society, he himself being prepared to complete two houses out of his own funds'.[73] The Society agreed to lease to him 'the Society's Ground on the West side of Victoria Square for the erection thereon of 12 houses in conformity generally with the elevation now submitted to this Committee ... and on Ground Rents of not less in the aggregate than £144 p.a. ...'.[74] By June 1866 Yalland had erected six houses of the terrace, but could not sell any of them and asked to be relieved of his contract.[75] This the Merchants refused to do and advanced him some more money.[76] However, the committee asked the Master to write to the builder, George Gay, to see if he was interested in building part of the terrace.

Meanwhile another builder, John Davies, had contracted with the Merchants' Hall to erect four detached houses on the south-east side of the square, designed by James Adam Clark. Davies guaranteed to have the roofs on by Christmas 1869 and to finish them by Michaelmas 1870. The ground rents were to be £15 per annum on each house. The Society also agreed to advance money to the builder as the work progressed, up to two-thirds of the cost.[77] Their terms grew harsher as time passed and it paid off. Mr. Davies was 'to proceed with the houses on certain fixed times being agreed for completion, the failure of any one time being a forfeiture of the whole, unless consequent upon a delay arising otherwise than from the default of the Builder'.[78] John Davies offered in August 1870 to complete the five remaining houses of the terrace on the west side of the square.[79] Although declined in August, the offer was accepted in October and he was to get advances of £1,200 on the centre houses and £1,600 on the end house. The ground rent would be £12 per annum on each house, starting in June 1872,[80] but it was not until March 1874 that the last five houses were finished.[81]

While the Merchants were engaged in building on Ferney Close, Francis Adams, who lived at Cotswold Grange, Cheltenham, was selling building plots on his land in several parts of Clifton. One such sale, on 3 February 1838, was of a piece of land formerly called Lower Welch Leases, on which the Victoria Rooms were built.[82] The ground rent payable under the grant to A. G. H. Battersby was £50 per annum. Charles Dyer was the architect of this impressive structure with its Corinthian portico and building took place between the years 1839 and 1841.

45.   The Royal Promenade, Victoria Square, 1853. Built on the north-west side of Ferney Close on the Merchants' land, this palatial building, consisting of 15 houses, was designed by William Bateman Read. The middle pediment bears the royal coat of arms.

The Victoria Rooms was the centre for one of the two exclusive 'sets' that cohabited in Clifton in the 1850s and '60s. The *Bristol Times* rebuked the community 'composed entirely of traders or sons of traders' who were ashamed of the means by which they had acquired their wealth and were ridiculously 'turning up their noses at each other'. When Charles Vaughan died in October 1850 the office of master of the ceremonies at the balls in Clifton became extinct. Within two or three years of his death rival coteries emerged, one of which held its balls in the large room at The Mall, the other in the Victoria Rooms. So bitter were the feelings aroused that the balls had to be discontinued for some years and some families left the district.[83]

The Victoria Rooms was one of the first buildings in Bristol to be fitted with electric lighting. It was also famous for its organ which had three separate keyboards intended to be played by three separate organists. Along with most of Dyer's interior, it was destroyed in the great fire of 1934. About 1911 the original two sphinxes on the forecourt were removed and an ornamental Baroque fountain designed by Edwin Rickards, and the statue of Edward VII, put in their place. The new interior of the mid-1930s was the work of Gordon Hake and E. H. Button, and included a sprung dance floor and a fine stage. It was subsequently purchased for the university students' union.

Another of Francis Adams' projects involved a six-acre field called Littlefields and a five-acre field known as Frimmers (U VII and U VI). An agreement was worked out with the Merchants' Hall who had the adjoining land and the recommendations of Foster and Okeley for laying out the promenade along the frontage of the Downs in building lots which continued Camp Place, were put into effect.[84] Exchanges of ground took place and a splendid progression of large residences were built along the promenade. These included Camp House, Sundon House, Avonside, Crofton House (which became Trafalgar House), Felixstowe, Avondale (which became Fern House), Aukland and down to Elmdale House, built for Alderman Thomas Proctor.[85] This last house was designed by George and Henry Goodwin *c.*1867 and was presented to the Corporation of Bristol in 1874 for use as the Mansion House.[86]

The Merchants' Hall did a number of land deals with Francis Adams in 1858-9 involving Adams' property in Regent Street in particular, the site of what had been Carter's Brewery, and two pieces of the Merchants' ground adjoining Gallows Acre Lane. Carter's Brewery was bought for £3,500 reduced by £1,500 for the Gallows Acre ground sold to Adams.[87] Along this hauling way the Society constructed Merchants' Road through to Victoria Square in June 1866.[88]

The Merchant Venturers were the instigators during the 19th century of two other major projects. These were a clean water supply for Bristol and the competition for the suspension bridge across the Avon Gorge. We have already mentioned Matthew Mills Coates' water supply to 400 houses from Sion Spring. The Richmond and Buckingham Springs supplied about a hundred houses near Richmond Terrace and the Jacob's Wells spring supplied a few families near College Green. Hitherto, the Merchants' Society's main source of income had been the Wharfage Lease, which was surrendered to the city in 1861. The Hall anticipated replacing this lost income with that from a waterworks scheme, but the sources of water open to them were totally insufficient to supply the whole of Bristol.

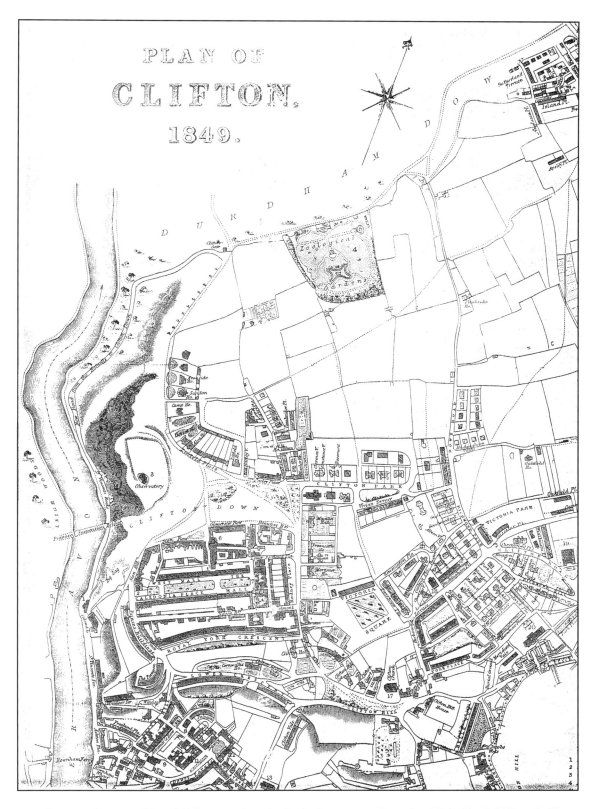

46.   George Ashmead's 'Plan of Clifton, 1849', scale nine inches to one mile, and published by J. Chilcott in *New Guide to Clifton*. It was engraved by S. Hall. The zoological gardens, King's Parade on Whiteladies Road, and Vyvyan Terrace are now in place. There is no building on either side of Gallows Acres Lane, no Bridge Valley Road, and no Clifton College.

Of the schemes put before Parliament it was that proposed by the Bristol Water-works Company which received the royal assent on 16 July 1846. In order to buy off opposition while the Bill was before Parliament, the proprietors of the chief springs in Clifton were paid as follows: the Merchants' Society for the riverside springs, £18,000; Mr. Coates for Sion House spring, £13,500; Mr. W. Hamley for Buckingham spring, £2,196; Mr. J. Coombe for Richmond spring, £4,950 and for Whiteladies spring, £400. The Bristol Waterworks Company then used the springs at Barrow Gurney, Harptree Combe and Chewton Mendip to feed the Barrow reservoir.[89] They also constructed three service reservoirs to maintain a constant supply throughout the city. One was on Bedminster Down, one on Durdham Down and the third, the Victoria reservoir, was constructed behind the Parade Ground in Whiteladies Road. From here the water was driven up to Durdham Down by pumps.[90] It was Patrick McGrath's judgement that 'What is difficult to understand is how the Society in the course of the battle could be prepared to commit itself to supplying water to the whole of Bristol. If it had been allowed to do so, the result would almost certainly have been bankruptcy'.[91]

The plan for a bridge across the gorge was promoted as a result of a legacy of £1,000 which had been left in 1753 by a Bristol merchant, William Vick. By his will, Vick required his money should be allowed to grow by the accumulation of interest until it reached £10,000. It should then be used to construct a bridge across the gorge. By 1829 the fund had reached £8,000 and the Merchants' Society were encouraged to go ahead with the scheme sooner rather than later because of the successful completion of the Menai Suspension Bridge by Telford. Rather than masonry arches, a suspension bridge seemed to offer a much more economical method of construction, so the Society went ahead with a competition to be judged by Thomas Telford. Of the 22 designs submitted in 1829 Telford faulted the lot. Based on his experience at Menai he believed that lateral wind resistance made 600 ft. the maximum span for a safe suspension bridge. Brunel's designs varied from 870 ft. to 916 ft. Telford was asked to submit a design of his own but his plan involved the construction of piers from the foot of the gorge to narrow the central span and this increased the cost to the point where it had to be rejected by the Society.

In a second competition held in October 1830, Brunel reduced his projected span to 630 ft. but incorporated a large abutment on the Leigh Woods side. This was the plan which was accepted and which the visitor can recognise today. The first sod was cut on 21 July 1831 but progress was slow and stopped altogether for four years following the riots of 1831. It was not until 1840 that the two piers were completed. In 1843 it was announced that £40,000, including the Vick legacy, had been spent and that another £30,000 would be required. The ironwork was sold to the West Cornwall Railway Company in February 1853 for the Royal Albert Bridge over the Tamar and nothing remained of the project 'save two unsightly piers which deformed the landscape'.[92]

For 17 years the scheme was in abeyance but in the spring of 1860 Brunel's Hungerford Suspension Bridge in London, and nearly the same span as that proposed at Clifton, was about to be replaced by Charing Cross railway bridge. Sir John Hawkshaw and W. H. Barlow, two well known engineers, arranged to purchase

47. *Mr. William Armstrong's design for a chain bridge across the River Avon from St Vincent's Rock to Leigh Downs*, drawn by William West, lithographed by R. Martin, and published by J. Rees (bookseller), 53 Wine Street, Bristol in 1830.

48. *Design for a suspension bridge across the River Avon*, drawn on stone by H. Harris from a design by C. H. Capper (engineer), Birmingham, and printed at his lithographic establishment, Union Passage, Birmingham.

49. *Mr. T. Telford's design for the Suspension Bridge across the River Avon*, Wright and Bagnall, Bristol.

50. *Proposed plan for the suspension bridge across the River Avon*, by William Hill of Bristol, and published by Wright and Bagnall, Bristol.

51. *Gateway of Clifton Suspension Bridge*, designed by I. Brunel Junr. and printed by C. Hullmandel.

both of the chains in London and the piers at Clifton and then put their scheme before the public. The chance to construct the bridge at a cheap rate appealed to the shareholders of the proposed new company and £35,000 was raised, exclusive of borrowing powers.

The design of Hawkshaw and Barlow was a simplified version of Brunel's design. The main chains on each side were increased from two to three, but the piers were to remain essentially unadorned. In 1836, when construction of the piers had begun again, an iron bar was suspended across the gorge, with a basket for moving materials hanging below. Brunel and a boy had crossed first, followed by many others so that the trustees were able to charge 5s. for the trip there and back. The formal opening of the bridge was on 8 December 1864 as a memorial to Brunel.

The year 1864 is a very convenient year to conclude this chapter. It marks the beginning of the second great speculative development of Clifton of the late '60s, associated with the names of James Shorland, John Clare and George Gay. These building developments on either side of Gallows Acre Lane were instigated by Francis Adams and Dr. Ross on the left-hand side, and by the Merchants' Society on the right-hand side in Great Lippiatt, Northfield and the Inner Lippiatt Paddocks. The two other arteries besides Pembroke Road were College Road and Whiteladies

52. This print shows Brunel's bridge as built, without Egyptian ornamentation. The large stone abutment rising out of the rocks on the western, or Leigh Woods, side of the gorge enabled Brunel to reduce the bridge span to 630 ft. The abutment cost the Committee £14,000 and stands as a memorial to Telford's prejudices. The Portishead railway, the 'Port and Pier', was constructed 1868-70. It remained isolated and confined to the gorge by failure to link it to the main lines. Financially it was unsuccessful, and remained largely a scenic railway line.

Road. The 1860s were characterised by a new type of detached or semi-detached house as the speculations advanced towards the Downs. These new architect-designed villas were in the Italianate style. They used well-defined quoins, string courses and more costly stone, while some of the architects preferred to use ashlar to face their buildings. William H. Hawtin in Cambridge Park and James Adam Clark in the four detached houses in Victoria Square used ashlar.[93]

This chapter has continually drawn attention to the ground rents which the Merchants imposed on all the land they leased for building. These formed an important part of the Society's income, amounting to 'upwards of £2,000 a year' by 1872.[94] Of this sum about £1,250 was 'secured chiefly upon houses of modern erection, in those parts of Clifton in which it is desirable that the Society should continue for the present to preserve an interest'.[95] Despite the problems the Society had suffered in the first part of the century in financing builders and in finding purchasers for their houses, the Merchants now embarked, at the same time as Francis Adams, on a massive building development which was clearly designed to raise their ground rent income and which completed building development up to the Downs.

Chapter Ten

Clifton since 1860

Francis Adams III was given the freedom by private Act of Parliament, under Adam's Estate Act 1852, to exercise the right to sell much of what had been the Freeman estates. Land sales had already taken place to raise £8,000 as dowries for his sisters, Charlotte and Mary Shute Anne. Provided he got the approval of the Court of Chancery, Francis Adams could even grant building leases on Mary Shute Anne's property, since she had been declared insane in 1851.

After the sale in 1835 of Summer Trinmore and Ten Acres to the Bristol and Clifton Zoological Society and the sale in 1860 of nearly 10 acres of pasture land, known as Nutts Five Acres and Pool Close, to Clifton College Company Ltd., Francis Adams now began to lease land with ground rents, for building development, along-side the zoo and to the north and east of Clifton College land. These developments constituted Northcote Road, The Avenue, Pembroke Road, Downfield Road and Downfield Road East.[1] Another development on Francis Adams' lands around Clifton College resulted in Canynge Road, Albert Road, Percival Road, College Fields, Cecil Road, College Road and Clifton Park Road. Builders such as James Rowe Shorland, John Clare, John Edmond Davies, George Gay, John Thorn, William Hain (Junior) and Richard Cosslett were building grand semi-detached houses and small villas in an Italianate style, both on the Adams' developments and on those of the Merchants' Society.

Whereas for the Merchants it is possible to document from the Hall Books and Deeds each of these developments and the ground rents raised thereby, such records are not known to have survived for Francis Adams. It is all the more fortuitous that the maps of his estates were donated to the Bristol Record Office. The Merchants' Society has an astonishing collection of maps some of which show alternative plans for their developments off Pembroke Road, or for Victoria Square.

In developing The Seven Acres the Merchants kept clear of grand projects such as those which had required them to finance builders to get Victoria Square completed. On the Society's land, agreements leasing land to builders on The Seven Acres began in October 1864 and continued until 1865-6.[2] Leases to William Hain (Junior) and to Richard Cosslett in the same field were made in April and May 1865.[3] At the other end of Pembroke Road Francis Pritchard began building on Gallows Acre in 1864.[4] In Great Lippiatts the Society leased land to John Grant and to William Hain (Junior) and building commenced next to All Saints' church at the junction of Alma Vale and Pembroke Road.[5]

The eminent London architect, George E. Street, was the creator of All Saints' church on land in Great Lippiatts conveyed to the Ecclesiastical Commissioners in 1864. Street was to plan the magnificent nave and western façade of Bristol Cathedral in 1867, in sympathy with Abbot Knowles' medieval choir. Here, in the context of the much smaller All Saints' church, Street produced a gem of church building. It was

53. All Saints' church, Pembroke Road, *c.*1872. The architect was George Edmund Street and the church was consecrated in 1868. It was one of the gems of Victorian church building but was gutted in the Second World War. Although the walls were still standing it was demolished and rebuilt to a contemporary design in 1967.

consecrated in 1868 and completed in 1872. Although gutted in World War Two the walls were left standing but, nevertheless and regrettably, later demolished. The new church, of contemporary design, was built in 1967 and the architect was Robert Potter. It retains the base of Street's tower and has rubble walls of the same red sandstone as was used for the old church.[6]

New roads leading off Pembroke Road were named in 1868 as Beaufort Road, Miles' Road and All Saints Road,[7] and builders such as John Thorn and William Hain (Junior) began building in Miles' Road.[8] Land was also leased to Samuel Worrall in Alma Road 'offering a Ground Rent equal to £90 a year an acre'.[9] The Society was not entirely able to avoid financing builders. As early as 1870 the Merchants were advancing money to Richard Cosslett on the security of houses already erected and about to be sold in Apsley Road.[10] His developments at Hanbury Road involved the quite separate scheme of Eaton Crescent, or Hanbury Road South, which was extended to include 15 houses. No 19th-century local builder could finance extended building development on this scale without the Society's support. In 1878 the Society decided to build a number of first-class villas between Hanbury Road and Oakfield Road.[11] The first eight lots were leased to Messrs. Studley and Baker and the first house sales were in 1881.[12]

54. Blackboy Hill before 1874. This inn was demolished in 1874, but the property on the extreme right is still there today, indicating where the old coaching inn stood, in the middle of the widest part of the end of Whiteladies Road.

The pace of development in some roads was such that it attracted the notice of *The Builder*, though not altogether with advantage.[13]

> New buildings are being carried up in Clifton with marvellous rapidity; in some cases indeed with so much rapidity that they do not get strength enough in their progress to remain up ... Walkers in Clyde Road, Woolcott Park, on the 1st of this month, saw a pair of what are called semi-detached villas partly roofed in, with bow-windows and every-thing pretty, but when they passed next morning they found in their place only a heap of dusty rubbish ... the workmanship is very bad. Moreover the bow-window of one house adjoined the bow-window of the next, and they ran so closely to the party wall that there was probably but little strength at the junction to carry the bressummer which supported the wall above. As to the party wall itself, it did not run through on the upper floors, but appears to have butted against the half-brick partition wall that goes from side to side through the two houses ...

It is hardly surprising that some jerry-building occurred. That there was not more in Clifton is due in large measure to the standard insisted upon by the Merchants' Society and to civic concern. Another aspect of this concern resulted in mains sewers being laid in Clifton High Level from June 1855 to July 1857 totalling 11 miles, and from June 1858 to June 1859 another three miles of sewers were constructed in Clifton Low Level (Hotwells). The Avon remained the chief receptacle, but at least it saved the effluent from the city pouring into the Frome and the harbour itself.

Dr. Kay's figures for 1841 had revealed the appalling disparity between the life expectation in Clifton-on-the-Hill compared with the Hotwell area. The rate of mortality was more than double that of Upper Clifton, although the difference in population was only 600 (6,720 in Upper Clifton and 7,314 in Lower Clifton).[14] From 1838 to 1843 the total number of deaths which occurred in Upper Clifton was 639 and that in Lower Clifton 1,248.[15] Improvements in water supply and in sewage disposal brought about an immediate benefit in quality of life.

Another development taking place in Clifton at this time concerned the campaign for the education of women and girls. In the early 1870s the Association for Promoting the Higher Education of Women held classes for instruction in Languages and Physical Sciences and masters from the Grammar School provided most of the teaching. Lecturers gave papers on history and literature, and a separate reading room for such students was set aside in the Bristol Public Library. At another level, genteel private academies sprang up to offer an education to fee-paying pupils and the 1843 Directory lists some 20 of these academies in Clifton for both boys and girls.

In 1871 a boys' school was set up 'for a limited number of high class boys who would not use the garden as a playground', at 1 Beaufort Road.[16] The Merchants' Society gave its approval to the establishment of a Young Ladies' Academy at 2 Apsley Road in 1876 'provided the neighbours did not object'.[17] At 53 Oakfield Road the widow of the former headmaster of All Saints' School, Clifton, Mrs. Walter Smith, offered a rather different institution for difficult girls. For £100 a year and slightly

55. Blackboy Hill, 1885. The *King's Arms* is still on the same spot, but nothing else remains. There is a double row of railings, and a road sweeper outside the clock shop. A single row of railings and a raised footpath still exists round the corner in Worrall Road.

more for girls over 20, Mrs. Smith offered to thrash the daughters of parents who did not feel able to do it themselves. Her method was to strap girls over a table, after stripping them down to a dressing gown put on backwards and to give them six strokes of the birch on either side.[18]

Manilla Hall, which had been built for Sir William Draper and subsequently possessed by the Gordon and Miles families, also became a school. In 1882 Sir J. D. Weston, who had bought the Hall, sold part of the grounds for building sites and the next year sold Manilla Hall to some nuns, the Dames de la Mere de Dieu, a French Roman Catholic sisterhood. They ordered the removal of the obelisk and cenotaph erected by Sir William Draper, but, due to the efforts of Dr. Beddoe and a private subscription, these were saved from destruction and re-erected on Clifton Down near their original site.[19]

Another of the 20 or so schools in Clifton was run, until 1855, from the Avon Gorge end of Royal York Crescent, in numbers one to three. Mrs. Rogers had kept a ladies' boarding school in Berkeley Square and Charlotte Street since 1819 and, because of its success, moved to Royal York Crescent with her four daughters, Sarah, Hannah, Lucy and Mary. Their success continued. From 1832 the daughters took over the running of the school. One of the pupils in 1837 was the 11-year-old red-head Eugenie de Montijo and her sister Paca, later Duchess of Alba. Eugenie eventually became Empress of France.[20] The school closed in 1855 and the sisters moved next door to number four. Eventually numbers one, two and three received the 1978 Civic Trust Award for their sensitive conversion to flats.[21]

There were a number of charity schools, orphanages and training schools for servants. For instance, behind the Mardyke in 1812 the Clifton Wood Industrial Training School for Boys was opened. It was not until Forster's Education Act of 1870 that a basic free education was available for poor children and in that year the Long Room at Hotwells, where in 1743 the Earl of Jersey had entertained 150 to breakfast, became Clifton National School.[22]

By the 1860s several excellent girls schools had been established in England. The North London Collegiate School had been founded in 1850, the Cheltenham Ladies' College in 1853, and the G.P.D.S.T. (Girls' Public Day School Trust) dates from 1872. Clifton High School was a pioneer girls' school which was planned in 1876. The headmaster of Clifton College, Dr. J. Percival and Lt. Colonel Arnold C. Pears, called together a committee to form a company to start the school. Clifton High School was incorporated as a Proprietory Company in November 1877 and the school opened in 65 Pembroke Road with 67 girls of all ages. The mother of one of the form-mistresses bought 77 Pembroke Road and this offered a pre-school and a home to the staff that needed one.[23]

In 1879 the school moved into its present buildings in a large house with an acre of ground at the west end of Worcester Avenue. The owner who had built it had decided not to live in it, probably because, with 365 windows, it was too large. It was prepared for 160 girls, with the idea that numbers would rise to 250.[24] By 1920 all the houses in Worcester Avenue had been bought and were in use, and the name of the road was changed to School Green. The school numbers passed 400 in 1924 and a new wing, designed by Sir George Oatley, was opened in 1927.[25]

56. Aerial view of the zoological gardens and Clifton College, looking to the south-east across Summer Trinmore and Foxholes to Nutts Five Acres, Pool Close and East Four Acres. To the immediate left is Northcote Road, while along the left-hand side of College Close are the rear gardens of Pembroke Road. On the right-hand side is College Road.

Numbers still continued to rise and more buildings were needed. In 1933 the riding school opposite the Clifton Park Road entrance was purchased by the school council and the new site was linked to the main building by a tunnel under the road. A gymnasium was built on the site but half the ground was deliberately left vacant for a swimming bath which was eventually opened in 1967. More houses in the area were acquired and in 1936 the school purchased an estate at Stoke Bishop called The Grove, where seven hard tennis courts and three hockey pitches were constructed. Meanwhile, numbers rose steadily, reaching 583 in 1945, 669 in 1955 and 726 in 1962.[62]

With the inauguration of the university in 1909, several of Clifton's finest buildings were purchased to become halls of residence. Paul Fisher's Clifton Hill House, which had been the home of John Addington Symonds and that of his son of the same name, was bought in 1909 as the university's first hall of residence for women. John Addington Symonds junior was an early supporter of the university college, and of the Committee for the Higher Education of Women. The decision to buy it was taken across the road at Goldney House, then the home of Lewis Fry. Soon Richmond House and Rivers Cottage joined it as annexes.

Harry and George Wills continued to add to the very generous gift of £100,000 made by their father H. O. Wills at the Colston dinner in 1908. Harry Wills bought the Tyndall's Park estate, with the Royal Fort, from the trustee of the Tyndall family during the First World War. He then gave £200,000 to build the physics laboratory there which bears his name. After the war he bought the Downside estate, flanking Durdham Down, on which his brother George built Wills Hall. Harry Wills also bequeathed a large sum which defrayed the cost of building Manor Hall.[27] This hall of residence for women students was designed by Sir George Oatley and opened in 1932. It was built in the grounds of Clifton Manor on what had once been John Beames' land.

Sir George Wills bought Goldney House and lived there until his death, when it was inherited by his daughter Mrs. Eberle. Perched on an escarpment overlooking the city, this magnificent estate passed to the university on her death. Goldney became another women's hall.[28] In 1919 Harry Wills bought the old Imperial Hotel adjoining Clifton Down station and gave it to the university, as Canynge Hall, for a men's hall of residence. The Imperial Hotel had been built too close to the railway line and, unfortunately, it was also too close to a major dairy. In Don Carlton's words, 'a combination of early morning trains and milk bottles proved too much for hotel guests and students alike'.[29] Canynge Hall therefore became the university's public health department, and subsequently the Department of Epidemiology and Community Medicine. Harry Wills also gave Mortimer House in 1922 to the university as a hall of residence for men. P. J. Worsley, one of the founders of the university college and of the university, had lived in Rodney Lodge. He bequeathed this to the university and it has housed residential short courses.

Linking the high ground of Clifton and its wide variety of shops to the low ground of the Hotwells in the 1890s was the Hydraulic Lift Clifton Rock Railway. The entrance can still be seen on the Portway, next to the Colonnade. The people of Hotwells used it like a bus and it cost 1½d. up and 1d. down. Plans for the passenger lift were submitted to the Merchants' Society by Mr. Kinkaid in 1889,[30] and by Messrs. Broad and Pottow in 1890,[31] but these were rejected. Another scheme submitted by George Newnes, M.P., in 1890, and altered slightly in 1891, received the Merchants' approval; it involved building an underground inclined lift connecting the Hotwell Road with Sion Hill, and erecting a pump room and lift in the garden of No. 15 Prince's Buildings.[32] It proved to be immensely popular and avoided the walk up the zig-zag of Granby Hill, but was eventually closed in 1934.

The period of speculative building from the 1860s to '80s shows an evolution from the Georgian styles to a variety of Victorian building. The area was rich in natural building materials and these were imaginatively used by the local builders. However, there was one area of the parish of Clifton which developed in a very different way from the rest. This was the area of limekilns and quarries that lay behind Blackboy Hill. Here are the cottages of the early Industrial Revolution. In 1841, when an appeal for funds for the building of St John's church was made, the area was described as spiritually destitute and inhabited by the poorest class of labourers.[33]

57. The Clifton Rocks Railway, 1893. Sir George Newnes' Rocks Railway opened on 11 March 1893. It had taken two years to build and cost £30,000. The tunnel is 500 ft. long and has a gradient steeper than one in two. There were four pairs of rails and the carriages consisted of an 18-seat saloon body fitted to a base which incorporated a water tank. Each pair of cars was connected by steel cables, the weight of the descending car pulling up the other car. The 500-ft. journey took 40 seconds, and the interior of the tunnel was lit by gas lights.

58. Dismantling the track of the Rocks Railway, 1934. In 1905 it cost 2d. to ascend, but if a ticket was bought from the Hotwells tram conductor the cost was 1d. The Bristol Tramways and Carriage Co. bought the Rocks Railway on 29 November 1912 for £1,500 but finally closed it in 1934. This is the only known view of all four of the cars together.

The Worrall family was closely connected with the area, and their name was commemorated around 1880 in the terrace of houses demolished for St John's school in Worrall Road. Samuel Worrall II, when a clerk to the Merchants' Hall, in 1763 proposed development on land that is now the Quarry Steps area in a 12-acre field called Shortgrove.[34] This land had lain open to common on Durdham Down for many years. He managed to acquire Short Grove himself in 1790 and left it to his son and grandson in his will, dated 26 October 1803.[35] Samuel Worrall III sold six acres in 1815 to the builder Andrew Pope. Samuel Worrall IV's niece, Sophia, subsequently sold the remaining six acres of Shortgrove as building plots to James Bigwood, James R. Shorland, John Jackson and John Davies, while imposing sizeable ground rents on the properties.[36]

This land, which was legally Samuel Worrall's, had provoked a furore in 1859 when he enclosed two large pieces of common land which had been popularly believed to be part of Clifton Down. Despite much indignation by the city council, the utmost the public could claim was a footpath over the ground. The furore helped to cause the Act of Parliament of 1861 whereby the public acquired the right of perpetual enjoyment of 230 acres of Clifton Down and of 212 acres of Durdham Down. The Merchants' Society did not give up their rights, however, over the turf or the minerals of Clifton Down, but were willing for the public freely to enjoy the open space.[37]

The Georgian cottages, 42 to 54 Worrall Road, were once called Caroline Row, hence the survival of the name Caroline Cottage for no. 46. No. 26b is called Short Grove, commemorating the name of the field. Highland Square, off Worrall Road, was the site of two limekilns in 1826, while on the left are the quarry steps that gave the area its name and the remains of the quarries that once provided its livelihood. In 1845 Bennett the limeburner had built Bennett's Row and Tedder, the builder, had erected Tedder's Buildings, yet as late as 1885 the Directories do not recognise their existence.[38] In the centre of the cottages is the Mission and Reading Room of 1870.

On the lower ground, the old Hotwell House, which had been built about 1696 and which overhung the river, was removed in 1822. This was done to permit the construction of Bridge Valley Road. The Hotwell had been leased at a very low rent for most of the 18th century, but the Merchants' Society still believed it had potential. In 1816 the Hall received a paper, written by Dr. Andrew Carrick, which suggested how to revive the popularity of the Hotwell and also that a new road from the Hotwell House to the Downs was needed. The Merchants were convinced and decided to act. A new pump room with a suite of four veined marble baths was built by H. H. Seward of London. The decline in popularity of the spring continued, however, and in June 1867 the Society was glad of the chance to dispose of the property to the Corporation when it decided to remove Hotwell Point. This was an inconvenient prominence on the right bank of the river which impeded navigation. Therefore the new pump room was closed and demolished.[39]

After World War One the Merchants' falling income from ground rents in the Hotwells area caused them to sell some of their property in St Vincent's Place, the Colonnade, Brunswick Place, Charles Place and Elliott's Buildings. By these means the Hall realised about £2,500 which it was able to invest, but it nevertheless continued its policy of developing land by granting building leases and creating new ground rents in the Hotwells area. Christina Terrace, Sandford Road, Oldfield Road and Britannia Buildings were created in this way at the beginning of of the 20th century.[40]

Another area of nine acres in Hotwells, which included the Merchants' Dock and the Cattle Pens, was also considered for development in the 20th century. The Cattle Pens were leased to the Corporation at a rent of £275 per annum at the start of the century, and at £1,200 per annum from 1961-5. The Merchants' Dock had been leased to Heber Denty and Co., and Osborn and Wallis Ltd. had leased the Coal Yard, but the Society arranged for these leases to expire in 1965. In 1963 Osborn and Wallis offered £75,000 for the Coal Yard and the Merchants' Dock, to which the Hall agreed. Then, in 1964, Osborn and Wallis bought the rest of the Docks property for £61,000, at auction.[41]

The builder and contractor, Joseph William King, who in 1865 had a yard next to the Artillery Ground on Whiteladies Road, had become an architect and surveyor by 1875. In 1878 he built the Royal Bazaar and Winter Gardens in Boyce's Avenue, Clifton and King's Road was named after him. The Arcade, which was built on two

Hotwell Rd., Bristol. 737.

59. Hotwell Road, c.1900. Lower Clifton became an industrialised area in the 17th century with shipping trades, a brickyard, a glasshouse, the Limekiln Dock and numerous limeburners. The Hotwell Road was widened in 1849, and is pictured here c.1900 looking west. From Dowry Square to Anchor Road there were, by 1901, 53 different trades: 23 pubs, 10 butchers, three fishmongers, 12 greengrocers, 10 bakers, five tailors, six tobacconists, three drapers, two hairdressers, six grocers and two chemists.

floors, included shops and tea rooms, and the Gardens covered 20,000 square ft., where the modern shops in front now stand. This splendid arcade, thought to be the only one in the country preserved in its original condition, had cost King £10,000 to build. It closed at the end of the year and became a furniture depository for Knee Brothers. This has preserved the arcade over the years and it is now in the process of being restored.[42]

Another historic building in Clifton which has just been completely restored is the Dispensary in Dowry Square which was set up by Thomas Whippie in 1812. It was opened to provide medical care for the community, in particular with midwifery services and layettes. It survived until 1948 when the National Health Service was set up, and the funds of the Dispensary are now administered by Bristol Municipal Charities. The Clifton Dispensary has now been turned into offices.

Susan Winkworth campaigned in the same area for better housing for the poor. She bought several large houses in Dowry Square and let them as flats at low rents and lived there herself to supervise the residents. So good were the results that she obtained a lease in 1875 from the Merchants' Society to build Jacob's Well Tenements, opposite Brandon Hill. These were designed by the London architect Elijah Hoole, and were virtually Bristol's first apartment block, consisting of three blocks of tenements forming an open-ended quadrangle. There were 80 flats, each provided with a balcony and water closet. Gas was laid on at the stairs and balconies, but not in the rooms. In the 1880s the rents were 5s. 6d. a week for four rooms or 1s. 3d. for a single room. Sculleries, cupboards, range ovens and communal dust chutes were provided. The tenements were demolished in the 1950s.[43]

Another shopping mall in Clifton village was the great department store of J. Cordeux and Sons. In the 1870s the store occupied all the houses on the site of the present Lex Garage showrooms and stretched round to the Post Office. Today's auction rooms were their warehouse. The firm sold furnishings, toys, drapery and underclothes. Upstairs was a tea-room and a large workroom where 400 staff made up clothes to order. In 1909 the firm moved to the Royal Parade in Queens Road.[44]

One of the features of Clifton village is Pharmacy Arch at Boyce's Avenue, which has an iron gate across it. The arch links Victoria Square to Boyce's Buildings and was built by William Mathias, one of the more eccentric inhabitants, who owned the adjacent houses in Boyces Buildings. He refused to allow anything on wheels, including bicycles or prams, a right of way through. He repeatedly built walls to prevent access, but these were knocked down again as often as he built them. In August 1861 Mathias was taken to court after slightly pushing a lady who had lifted a pram over his iron gate. The lady was wearing a wide crinoline at the time of the incident and this rendered the whole event even more bizarre. The court action was really brought by the Corporation and the jury could not agree, so, on this occasion, Mathias went free. After years of disputes of a similar character and reduced from affluence to poverty, he was imprisoned for six months at the age of 92 for contempt of the Court of Chancery.[45]

The 19th century was the great age of railways and there was a widely supported scheme in 1861 to extend a trunk line from Temple Meads into the city and to Clifton. The line would have crossed over Temple and Redcliff Streets to Queen

Square and a branch line would have extended to Brandon Hill. The scheme was supported by the Mayor, the Master of the Merchants' Society and the President of the Chamber of Commerce and the Great Western board promised to subscribe half of the £250,000 capital needed. The scheme was also backed by a petition signed by 5,000 ratepayers. Yet the Bristol and Clifton Railway Co. Bill was opposed so vehemently at Westminster that the Parliamentary Committee refused to approve the preamble of the Bill and the Great Western board withdrew its offer. The battle for the Avon Metro has a local precedent.[46]

Some tramways were allowed, however, and the first tramcars began ferrying passengers in August 1875 from Perry Road to Redland. The Bristol Tramway Company extended its track to the Hotwells in June 1880, but proposals to lay rails from the Victoria Rooms to Victoria Square, or from the Victoria Rooms to the Suspension Bridge, met so much local opposition in 1878 that the scheme had to be withdrawn. In 1887 the company applied for Parliamentary powers to substitute steam power for horses. In 1896 there were great schemes to electrify the tramways. The power was to be supplied by overhead wires, but the Corporation insisted on its sole right to supply the electric power and the scheme failed. In 1898 the opposition of the council was finally overcome by 34 votes against 30 and the Private Parliamentary Bill received Royal Assent.[47]

The Whiteladies Road line extended to the Downs in 1899, and on 22 December 1900 the entire electric system was brought into operation, the track covering about thirty miles. Honeypen Hill was an extensive quarry, belonging to the Merchants' Society and at one time leased to Paul Fisher. It is now covered by Park Place and Richmond Hill. In 1834, the Rev. Francis Edgeworth, who officiated at St Joseph's, Trenchard Street, the only Roman Catholic place of worship in the city, was persuaded to buy a field lying to the east of Honeypen Hill. On this field he planned to erect an enormous church in the classical style. The Catholic Emancipation Act had been passed in 1829 and the Vicar Apostolic of the western district, Bishop Peter Augustine Baines, dreamed of a huge basilica overlooking Bristol. Henry Edmund Goodridge was appointed to design the church and the foundation stone was laid in October 1834.[48] Unfortunately two or three landslips occurred and work was interrupted. There was considerable dispute with the Merchants' Society about whether this subsidence was the result of quarrying and blasting or was due to a sudden thaw.[49]

Father Edgeworth, the local priest who had taken responsibility for the project, was declared bankrupt and fled to Belgium in 1845, dying in 1850. What remained were the walls and six huge columns at only a quarter of their intended height. The unfinished building was advertised for sale by auction in June 1844.[50] In 1847 Bishop Ullathorne, the new Vicar Apostolic, bought the land and building from the mortgagees for £2,500. He decided that in view of the instability of the foundations he would construct a lightweight timber structure, built on shipping principles. Charles Hansom was the architect appointed to design the building and the church was designated a pro-cathedral by Pope Pius IX after his revival of the English episcopate in 1850. The structure was enhanced by the same architect in 1870 when some extensions were built to the east. Now the building stands empty and boarded up. The new Roman Catholic Cathedral of SS Peter and Paul, in Pembroke Road, designed by Sir Percy Thomas and Son, is probably the first cathedral in the world to be designed for the new liturgical requirements set out by the second Vatican Council in 1964. From 850 to 1,000 worshippers can be seated within 45 ft. of the High Altar and can feel themselves intimately involved in the celebration of the Mass.

While the increasing facilities of the city on the doorstep and the opening of Clifton College and of Clifton High School helped to attract and retain wealthy middle-class residents, the impact of the 1870 Education Act and diminution in family size after World War One caused a marked reduction in the number of servants. Many Clifton houses were converted into flats and bedsitters. Between the wars Clifton remained very quiet and respectable, but the owners or absentee land-lords struggled to bring in enough income to convert the grand villas into flats or to keep the houses in good repair. World War Two brought about a traumatic change. Many big houses were sold for a few hundred pounds. Royal York Crescent, Cornwallis Crescent, The Mall and Caledonia Place were divided into cheap flats at very low rents and Clifton became a place where students came for cheap lodgings.

In the 1960s property developers renovated the terraces to their former glory and the flats became expensive instead of cheap ones. The whole area has seen something of a renaissance. The rise in property prices and the popular appreciation of the solid virtues of Georgian and Victorian buildings, has once again led to many houses being bought for owner occupation. A new community awareness has arisen and the activities of local residents' societies have steadily improved amenities. Bristol, however, has more cars in proportion to its population than any other city in the British Isles and Clifton seems to have more than its fair share. The blight of double parking is utterly spoiling the charm and gracefulness of the squares and the frontages of the terraces.

Some things appear hardly to have changed. The visitor to Bristol who climbs to the top of the Observatory Tower, in the middle of Clifton Camp, would not be aware that it has only recently been restored. The Merchants' Society sold it in 1977 and after two years of neglect it is once more an attractive piece of Clifton's heritage. The original windmill for grinding snuff burnt down in a strong gale in 1778, when the sails were driven round so fast that the wooden pivots caught fire: barely two years after its original construction it was destroyed. The Merchants' Hall approved William West's plans in 1828 for rebuilding the ruined windmill as an observatory. West was an amateur scientist and artist of the British school, and he installed a telescope on top of the tower at first. He later added to the astronomical instruments a camera obscura which reflected images from outside onto a large shallow white saucer in a darkened room. West was originally given a seven-year lease at 5s. a year, but this was changed to a 21-year lease at 10s. a year.[51] While digging the foundations of his building, West found that it was possible to make a lateral shaft into the 'Giant's Cave' some 90 ft. below in the face of St Vincent's Rocks. In 1837, after two years of tunnelling, at a cost of £1,300, he completed a 200 ft. long passage to what was reputed to have been a hermit's cell in the Middle Ages. Although West died in 1861, his descendants continued to live in the observatory until 1943.[52]

60. Gloucester Row, shown here *c.*1900, was built by William Bleuden *c.*1793-4, on the margin of Brimley Close which was inherited by John Beames from his uncle, the Rev. John Power. The 13 houses originally cost £1,000 each. Bleuden was a journeyman carpenter who went bankrupt in October 1794, although he was owed a far larger sum by James Lockier. The *Clifton Down Hotel* behind the trees opened in 1879.

Many eminent people, in addition to the leading merchant families we have considered, have found Clifton a delightful place to live, but they have found mention elsewhere.[53] Among them would be included Hannah More (1745-1833) in 4 Windsor Terrace, Dr. Thomas Beddoes at 3 Rodney Place and with Humphry Davy at their Pneumatic Institute at 6 Dowry Square. Walter Savage Landor lived at Penrose Cottage, the Rev. Sidney Smith (1771-1845) at 8 Gloucester Row, Thomas Macaulay (1800-1859) at 16 Caledonia Place and John, Lord Lawrence (1811-1879) and Sir Henry Lawrence (1806-1857), defender of Lucknow, at 2 BelleVue. John Addington Symonds (1840-1893) lived in Clifton Hill House until his marriage to Joan North, when he settled for 14 years in Victoria Square. Mrs. Thrale, the darling of Dr. Johnson's London, died at 36 Royal York Crescent and at no. 25 lived Sir Abraham Roberts, father of Field-Marshal Lord Roberts.[54] These people lived at a time when social life in Clifton and the Hotwells had become neatly stratified and each stratum had its own entertainments.

Clifton and the Hotwells were spared the destruction suffered by the Castle area of the old city in the autumn of 1940 and spring of 1941. St Andrew's church was largely destroyed and on 2 December 1940 bombs slightly damaged 30-36 Cornwallis Crescent. Eighteen houses in Royal York Crescent suffered damage on 6 December, nos. 12a, 13 and 14 seriously. On 3 January 1941, 12-15 Berkeley Square were

61.   The Clifton Grand Spa Hydro, *c.*1909. A final effort to re-establish the Hotwell Spa was made at the end of the 19th century. In 1890 Sir George Newnes, publisher, applied to the Merchant Venturers for permission to build a cliff railway to link Hotwell Road tramway terminal with Sion Hill. The Society agreed, provided Newnes built a hydropathic institution and pump room. The hotel was opened in 1898 and the pump room beside it in 1894. The hotel became the *Avon Gorge Hotel*, and the pump room became a cinema in 1920.

sufficiently damaged for them to be demolished. Dowry Parade suffered slight damage from the raid of 2 December 1940 as did three houses in Chapel Row.

When the war began there was a shortage of bomb-proof shelters, so it was understandable that people should turn to the railway tunnel on the Portway, under Bridge Valley Road, and to the top end of the Clifton Rocks Railway. Some people used caves such as the one below Windsor Terrace. The tunnel on the Portway was 525 ft. long and had belonged to the old Port and Pier Railway. A committee of local inhabitants prepared the tunnel for occupation in November 1940 and through the bombing 1,500 people spent the night there, though it is said 3,000 people struggled at times for a place inside. Lighting was by candles and oil lamps, and toilet facilities were very primitive. The Medical Officer believed it was insanitary and the City Engineer said it was unsafe, so the city authorities planned to evict the night occupants. Eventually on 24 January 1941 all except 200 were moved out peacefully and proper bunks, sanitation and ventilation were provided.

Since the war the university has been reponsible for rehabilitating for student use an area of decaying late Georgian property behind Queen's Road. The university also built in 1965 a new Students' Union building in Queen's Road containing a 33-metre indoor swimming pool, a small theatre, a hall for 700, several bars and many meeting rooms. The architects were Alec French and Partners, and their design has proved a great success. A central Union building was a necessity since some halls of residence, such as Wills, Churchill, Hiatt Baker and Badock, are two miles from the academic buildings. Within Clifton new residential blocks were built by the university at Goldney House in 1969. Blocks of three and four storeys were constructed comprising self-contained flats for six students, yet hidden from Goldney House by the avenue of mature trees and the slope of the terrace.

The Merchant Venturers' Hall, next to their almshouses in Kings Street, was finally destroyed by enemy action in the raid of 14 May 1941. It had been hit on 2 December 1940 by high explosive bombs and extensively damaged. A bomb had gone through the vestibule to the strong room containing the charters, archives, plate and silver, but the following morning when an oxy-acetelyne torch burnt through the twisted steel door, the priceless records and plate had survived undamaged. The Hall was hit again on 16 March 1941. This time hundreds of pieces of china, porcelain and glass, carvings, mantelpieces and coat of arms were saved and removed. When the war ended the Merchants bought Fern House, The Promenade, Clifton, and moved in on 1 November 1945. In January 1949 they bought Auckland House next door, and set about converting the drawing rooms of the two houses into one. Similarly, at the back they created a large banqueting hall. A new central staircase and landing united the two houses.

The hall is the administrative centre for the very large charitable funds for which the Society is trustee. It is also the repository for the priceless archives and treasures which the Society has acquired over four centuries. In 1958 the deeds, charters and other records were brought to the new Hall from the city repository in the tunnel under Clifton Down. The decision to microfilm the Hall Books, now available in the Bristol Reference Library, was taken in 1969. Many of the functions which the Merchant Venturers performed until the 19th century are now carried out by the Bristol Chamber of Trade. The Merchants' acquisition of the manor of Clifton proved an extremely profitable investment, and through property development they have left their mark on Bristol. Bristolians especially have reason to be grateful for the preservation of the Downs

Clifton is an important suburb of Bristol. Its historic spa, its architectural charm and the awesome splendour of the Avon Gorge have made it widely known and loved. The aim of this book has been to give a balanced view of its development, but, in addition, to make available to readers a wide range of source material, with which its fascinating history may be explored still further.

Appendix 1

The Purchase by Edward Freeman of One Quarter of the Manor of Clifton in July 1698

Hugh Brook of Lower Court, Long Ashton, divided the Manor of Clifton between his four daughters, Elizabeth, Alice, Susan and Frances in February 1586.[1] Frances married William Clarke of Barrow Minchin, Somerset and in December 1608, Edward, Thomas, Nicholas and Christopher Clarke, their sons, sold their quarter share of Hugh Brook's estate for £369 to Anthony Hodges of Clifton.[2] Anthony Hodges also held by Copy of Court Roll for two lives, his own and William's, his eldest son, a large part of the ecclesiastical Manor of Clifton. Anthony Hodges' younger son, John, also held 12 acres of the smaller Manor by Copy of Court Roll. At the time of the 1625 Survey Anthony was about sixty, William about twenty-three and John nineteen.[3]

William Hodges inherited the quarter share of Hugh Brooke's estate and by Indenture of Enfeoffment on 18 April 1657 when his daughter Elizabeth married John Lambe, he settled the estate on her and Lambe and on their heirs and assigns. On Elizabeth's death he further secured the estate by another indenture. However, on 30 May 1677, 28 Chs. II, John Lambe sold the estate to John Tyndale of Bitton, Gloucestershire with a mortgage from John Wimpenny, in trust for Stephen Stringer, his heirs and assigns. This mortgage contained a proviso or condition which was not kept and so the estate legally was vested in John Wimpenny, in trust for Stephen Stringer.[4]

On 30 July 1698, Edward Freeman bought the quarter share of the manor of Clifton from Stephen Stringer for £2,075, using his own resources and the dowry of Ann Astley, his wife. Ann was one of the daughters of John Astley of Worcester, now dead. Francis Freeman inherited the estate from his uncle Edward.[5] De Wilstar's map describes Freeman's land as amounting to 189 acres, but 12 years later it consisted of '15 messuages, 10 cottages, 25 gardens, 10 orchards, 50 acres of land, 140 acres of meadow, 60 acres of pasture, 5 acres of wood with the appurtenances in the parish of Clifton aforesaid'.[6] Francis Freeman and his wife Mary had two daughters, Catherine and Frances, who were co-heiresses of the family estates. Catherine married Onesiphorus Paul Esq., later Sir Onesiphorus Paul and Frances married Shute Adams.

On Francis Freeman's death, Dame Catherine Paul and Frances Adams inherited the manors of Brosely and Norton Malreward, which together with the coal mines were valued at £12,735 0s. 2d., and the quarter share of the manor of Clifton and some land in Westbury-on-Trym which together were valued at £11,219 16s. 4d. By an indenture enrolled in Chancery on 3 November 1758, Sir Onesiphorus Paul took the Norton Malreward and Brosely estates, and Shute Adams the Clifton estates. A cash settlement of £757 11s. 11d. was paid to Shute Adams to offset the imbalance.[7]

Shute Adams and Frances had three children, a son Francis and two daughters, Mary Shute Adams and Catherine. On Shute Adams' death his widow, by indenture of 4 July 1767, devised a series of provisions for her two daughters which amounted to half the value of the estate. Within 12 months of her death, Francis would have to pay each of his sisters £3,000, or in the case of the death of one before the age of 21 or day of marriage, £6,000 to the survivor of them. On 25 October 1771 the widow changed her mind and by indenture divided the whole estate between her two daughters. Francis was not mentioned. Frances

> did grant, limit, direct and appoint, the said several moieties or half parts of all and singular the said parts and shares of said manors and said messuages, lands, tenements, rents and hereditaments ... to the use of said Mary Shute Adams and Catherine Adams, her daughters, for 500 years to commence from the death of said Frances Adams ...

She died in January 1775.

In September 1786, shortly before her marriage to William Manley of the Middle Temple, London, Catherine placed her half share in trust to the Rev. Dr. John Casberd of Bristol and John Manley of Middle Temple, her brother-in-law. Mary S. Adams had married John Manley on 9 December 1777, and being a lawyer he was careful of her interests. On his mother's death, Francis, the son, had filed a Bill in Chancery in Easter Term 1777 against his two sisters and against their trustees, John Freeman, Junior and George Wilkins, praying that the indenture of 4 July 1767 might be established, that he might be declared entitled to the estates and that he might have the title deeds.

The case went to the King's Bench on 22 November 1777 and their Lordships decided that Frances had exceeded her powers, and that her power ought to prevail only on her daughters for life. The disposition of the inheritance to their children, Frances' grand-children, was void, however, so 'the son of said Frances Adams took an estate tail therein, subject to the estate for life to his sisters, who should be considered tenants for life'. A further agreement was made, though, within the family. John Manley and Mary Shute, his wife, and William Manley and Catherine, his wife, contracted in writing with Francis Adams for the absolute sale to him of their respective estates for life at £5,000 to each of the sisters, to be paid on 24 June 1801. Before the day arrived Mary Shute Manley had died, but John Manley was legally entitled to her share. Francis Adams pledged the revenues of the estates in order to pay the sums involved.

Francis Adams I had died in July 1805. By his will he devised certain premises in Dowry Square to provide for his wife, Mary Anne, for her life. She was buried on 9 January 1835, aged seventy-one. After her death these premises passed to his son, Francis Adams, to whom the whole of the rest of the estate had been bequeathed. By his will he had also devised all the Norton Malreward estates and all his lands in the City of London, in trust, to his brother-in-law William Manley, and his friend Robert Casberd, to provide his wife with an annuity for life of £900.[8] Francis Adams II was a very wealthy young man when, on 12 January 1808, he married Mary Shute Manley, one of the daughters of John Manley. As her dower, John Manley paid £3,000. Francis Adams II settled the estate, in trust, on his friend Robert Casberd of The Temple, London and John Lowe of Inner Temple, to the use of Francis II for life, with a proviso allowing him to grant 21-year and 99-year building leases.[9] After his decease a yearly rent charge of £800 was to be paid to his wife Mary Shute Manley.

Francis II and Mary Shute Manley had three children, Francis III, Mary Anne Adams and Charlotte Sophia Adams. Francis II died on 7 June 1844. His son, Francis III had married Maria Doveton on 27 August 1835, his parents having devised the estate by way of marriage settlement on Casberd and Lowe to the use of Francis II and Mary Shute during their life, and then to Francis III and Maria Doveton. The estate had been diminished by 12 acres which had been sold in 1835 to the Bristol and Clifton Zoological Society.[10] These comprised part of Summer Trinmore and part of Ten Acres, *alias* Fox Holes. The marriage was blessed with seven children.

By deed poll dated 8 May 1839 Francis Adams II had directed that £4,000 should be the share of Charlotte Sophia out of the sum of £8,000 set aside in August 1835 for her and her sister Mary Shute Anne. This was a dowry for Charlotte who married Alfred Matson, merchant, on 16 May 1839. Charlotte and her husband did not have any children, however, while Mary Shute Anne was declared insane on 9 June 1851. Francis III was given the responsibility for administering her estate, but he could not grant building leases for her property without the approval of the Court of Chancery. By the Adams' Estate Act of 1852 Francis III was free to exercise the powers of sale, exchange and sale in Fee Farm and these he used extensively in the course of the 19th century.[11]

Note

Since 1535 the Statute of Enrolments had required bargains and sales of freehold property to be by indenture and enrolled in one of the courts. Such sales could then be taxed. To get round the property inheritance tax, lawyers developed the Lease and Release. The owner could lease the land to a purchaser for a sum of money. This created a 'use' in favour of the purchaser (which under the Statute of Uses, 1535, provided that the person to whom the use was raised was to be the owner at law and hold the legal estate). If before the expiry of the year's lease, the owner released his reversion to the purchaser, the conveyance was complete, without any tax. The Release was usually dated the next day.[12]

Appendix 2

Thomas Goldney and the Voyage round the World 1708-11

Among the Chancery Proceedings in the Public Record Office, are seven boxes relating to the voyage of the *Duke* and *Dutchess* from Bristol, 1707-11.[1] Exhibits produced in court were normally returned to the plaintiff but, in the case of Creagh versus Rogers, the issue was the distribution of the prize money after the privateering voyage. The court had required the ships' rolls, listing the ships' companies, their pay and their agreed proportion of the booty. It had also required the account books kept throughout the voyage, kept by William Bath and Carleton Vanbrugh, the company's agents on board. These accounts recorded the barter goods exchanged at each port of call and the various goods purchased for the voyage. The court required the orders and instructions to Captain Woodes Rogers, the agreements between the owners and the officers, the seamen and the landsmen and the council minutes of all the meetings on board during the voyage.

Most of all, the court wished to see the lists of the nine public sales, starting on 27 February 1711/12 at the Marine Coffee House, Birchin Lane in Cornhill, London, of part of the cargoes of the *Duke* and *Dutchess* which had been seized. The items included negroes who had been captured, pearls and rings, necklaces, gold chains, ingots of gold and silver, pieces of eight, coffee, tea, indico (*sic*), cinnament (*sic*), cloths, sergges (*sic*), Colchester bays, Norwich stuffs, silks and other fabrics. These allotments of goods were 'sold by the candle' – merchants waited for the candle to burn down and out, and the last bid at that time bought the goods. The Chancery boxes also contained the claims by the officers and seamen, widows and orphans, against the division of the proceeds by the owners. Thomas Goldney was one of the owners of these ships and held 36 shares costing £3,726, which made him the largest shareholder of the enterprise.[2]

Having assembled all this evidence, the Court of Chancery might have returned all these exhibits to the plaintiff at the end of the case. This does not seem to have been thought appropriate here. Two of the captains involved retained their ship's journals. Captain Woodes Rogers used his to write *Cruising Voyage round the World* in 1712, and Edward Cooke, second captain of the *Dutchess*, wrote *The Voyage to the South Seas*, also in 1712. In the Chancery Masters' Exhibits however can be found John Parker's *Log for the* Duke *and* Dutchess' *Council Meetings*, 1708-11, recording all the officers and Master's decisions and discussions, captured prizes, contents, sales of slaves, etc. There is also Captain Courtney's committee book for the *Dutchess*, recording the same sort of information. The court retained this remarkable collection of documents, and it was deposited in the Public Record Office where it has remained. Nobody logically would go to the Chancery exhibits to look for ships' logs or sales of captured prizes and the author found them by serendipity, while researching into Clifton bankruptcies. The last time these bundles were disturbed was in 1933.[3]

Captain William Dampier had tried in 1704 to capture one of the Manila – Acapulco treasure ships, but the prize had proved too strong for him and his voyage had been unsuccessful. He never gave up hoping to make another attempt and prevailed on a number of Bristol merchants to fit out an expedition. In 1708 Captain Woodes Rogers was also looking for backers for a privateering voyage to the South Seas. Twelve Bristol merchants, of whom Thomas Goldney was one, were willing to put up the money.[4]

> ... Our grand design Being to seek out one or bothe the Ships belonging to Acapulco in South America ... If you are so fortunate to come up with her you are to attack and use all possible means to take her, which we doubt not of through your Bravery, especially promoted by the vast Treasure you may expect to share for your reward.[5]

Thomas Goldney's summation of his claim on the proceeds has survived,[6] but he did not get all he asked for and eventually received £6,826. It had been a great gamble. In his dedication to the owners of his book, Captain Woodes Rogers recognised the merchants 'who had the Courage to adventure your Estate on an Undertaking, which, to Men less discerning, seemed impracticable'.[7]

Also lying in a dusty box in the Public Record Office, London, is a five-page testament of the Scots mariner, Alexander Selkirk, written in 1712. This was discovered by C. D. Lee.[8] Selkirk's depositions were made in July 1712, one month after the appearance in print of Captain Edward Cooke's *A Voyage to the South Sea*, containing the first published account of Selkirk's experiences on Juan Fernandez, which gave rise to the story about Robinson Crusoe. C. D. Lee argues that Selkirk was the foremastman of the *Cinque Ports*, not the Master, and that he had played a leading part in the mutiny against Captain Stradling in February 1704. Woodes Rogers accepted in 1708 that Selkirk had been Master, since Captain William Dampier recommended him.

> He had been on the Island four Years and four Months, being left there by Capt. Stradling in the *Cinque Ports*; his Name was Alexander Selkirk, a Scotchman, who had been Master of the *Cinque Ports*, a ship that came here last with Captain Dampier, who told me that this was the best Man in her, so I immediately agreed with him to be a Mate on board our Ship.[9]

Selkirk had stayed there voluntarily because he said the ship was full of holes and unseaworthy. That the *Cinque Ports* subsequently foundered suggests that he had been right. Having served for a year as Mate on the *Duke* and while anchored at Porto Seguro, near Cape St Lucas, waiting for the second treasure ship to arrive, Selkirk was promoted to Master on board the *Batchelor*, under Captain Thomas Dover. This boat had formerly been the treasure ship named the *Nuestra Senora de la Incarnacion Disenganio* (450 tons), and Selkirk brought it back to London where it formed part of the sales.

Among the many other prizes taken by the *Duke* and *Dutchess* was the Spanish ship, the *Havre de Grace*, 260 tons, which was fitted out as a privateer and renamed the *Marquis*. It was put under the command of Edward Cooke but proved unsuitable and was subsequently sold at Batavia in June 1710.[10]

> Att a Committee held on board the *Dutchess* at sea, off the island Gorgona [their base for the next two months], August 8th 1707. Memorandum: The *Marquis*, not answering our expectations but proves Cranke and sails heavy, we now advise Capt. Cooke to heave the *Dutchess'* 2 old heavy guns overboard and 20 boxes of snuff, with 2 spare topmasts, and bring his ship more by the stern, stowing everything as low as possible in the ship to indevor to make her swifter, and if he finds any more necessary for the benefit of the ship, we desire him to do it.
>
> Witness our hands,
> Woodes Rogers, Stephen Courtney, Edw. Cook, Robert Fry, Wm. Stratten, Wm. Ballet, John Connely, George Milbourne, Lancelot Appleby.[11]

The owners were quite specific in their orders and instructions to Captain Woodes Rogers, including the taking of hostages, the use of fireships, the remitting of plunder to England

and the need to guard against embezzlement.[12] Between 1708 and December 1709 the *Duke* and *Dutchess* seized 20 ships and barques, including the Manila to Acapulco treasure ship, the *Nuestra Senora de la Incarnacion*, 450 tons, with 193 passengers on board.[13] Captain Edward Cooke listed the cargoes and treasure which was captured and recorded by the company's agents on board. These lists form the basis for the nine sales in London in February 1711/12.[14]

The two Manila – Acapulco ships referred to were Spanish ships engaged in trade across the Pacific to the Philippines. Woodes Rogers states that in his time Acapulco was

> rather like a poor Village of Fishermen, than fit to be the chief mart of the South Sea, and Port for China. The Houses are mean, built of Wood, Mud and Straw ... It has nothing good but the Harbour ... that except when the two ships come yearly from Manilla to Acapulco, they have little Commerce in this Sea.

He was told by prisoners that 'the Manila ship did often return from Acapulco with 10 Millions of Dollars' each in a voyage and that the captain 'whom they call general, seldom got less than 150 or 200,000 pieces of eight'.[15]

After their long voyage the *Duke*, *Dutchess* and the *Batchelor* dropped anchors in the Texel on 23 July 1711, having sailed from the Cape in the company of six East India Company's ships and 16 Dutch ships. Stephen Creagh, previously part owner of two privateers, the *Seahorse* and the *Betty*, had thought it was worth touting in Holland as an agent to represent the interests of the crews of the *Duke* and *Dutchess* against the owners. He persuaded 209 of the men to sign a paper appointing him their agent and agreeing to a commission of five per cent of the eventual settlement. Woodes Rogers would have nothing to do with him and appointed as his agents Ward and Campbell. Creagh then lodged a complaint in the Court of Chancery, dated 11 January 1711/12, heard before the Rt. Hon. Simon Harcourt, the Lord Chancellor, citing the owners and captains with irregular practices and charging Woodes Rogers with fraud against the owners.

The Chancellor ordered the goods on board the *Duke* and *Dutchess* to be sold as soon as possible and the proceeds to be divided into thirds, the owners to get two thirds and the crews one third. Not all the goods were sold during the nine public sales at the Marine Coffee House in Cornhill. Some were sold privately from 11 February 1711/12 until December 1713. The owners had appointed six of their number to look after their interests at the sales and during the protracted Chancery proceedings. Their extravagance during their stay in London provoked Thomas Goldney into great fury. In a letter which has survived he accused them of negligence, non-attendance, greed in the allowances they awarded themselves, and weakness in handing over £6,000 to the East India Company together with a bribe of £161 'for soliciting them to accept it'.

The Governors of the East India Company believed the *Duke* and *Dutchess* had illegally traded in European goods while circumnavigating the globe and crossing the Indian Ocean, which was an area over which the Company claimed exclusive rights. The boats were seized as soon as they reached London despite protests by the owners to the Queen and to the Attorney-General. The seizures were entered in the Court of the Exchequer and proceedings were begun in the Committee of Law Suits. The Governors did not believe the protestations of the crews:

> We also further make Oath, That we went out as Private Men of War and not as trading ships, And no sort of Merchandise was shipped on board said ships to trade withall; And that we have not been in any place or places or Islands in the East Indies more than what has been above expressed. And that we drove no trade or made any purchase at Bouton or Batavia or any part of the East Indies more than for Necessarys and Provisions ...[16]

Signed by all the Men in Every ship, except Charles May, Edward Dismore and Stephen Lattin.

On 18 March 1711/12 the Governors agreed to waive their claim to ships and cargo in return for a payment of £6,000 to the Company and a bribe of £161 5s. to an unknown person. This was not the only attempted claim against the owners of the *Duke* and *Dutchess* after the completion of the voyage.

Among the Master's Exhibits is the list of the costs which the owners were required to pay from their two-thirds share. The items amounted in total to £49,584 12s. 6d.

It was nearly three years before the final stages of the account could be completed and before the crews could be paid. Woodes Rogers was himself declared a bankrupt while the Chancery proceedings were still undecided, although this was partly due to his wife's debts incurred while he was at sea. She had had to leave their house in Queen Square and live with her three children at her father's house in St Michael's Park. While the Chancery suit was still before the Court 33 of the crews took their grievances to the House of Lords on 17 June

	£	s.	d.
Owners' share of law expenses	254	0	7
Part of plunder money	219	16	9
Mistake in plunder money account	36	0	10
Wages in lieu of shares	12,262	1	5
Interest on £9,000 borrowed in 1711	264	0	0
Paid three shares to Ballett	126	18	0
Ten shares to Thomas Dover, M. D			
agreed July 22 1708	423	0	0
East India Company	6,161	5	0
Several disbursements	874	2	6
Part of sailors' account	2,575	6	3
Profit and loss on sales	219	6	7
Lost by Giles Batchelor	17	15	0
Part of Holland account	1,552	10	0
Provisions in Holland	8,720	8	1
Outsetts of *Duke* and *Dutchess*	13,188	12	0
Money to owners at two per cent on £134,473 6s. 1d	2,689	9	6
	49,584	12	6

1714, and again on 31 August 1715, claiming they were 'perishing from Want of Bread, and daily thrown into Gaols, or in danger of being so'. In this matter clearly they had a case, but it was not the owners who were at fault.

At the end of the Orders and Instructions to Captain Woodes Rogers are the signatures of the five principal owners – John Bacheler, James Hollidge, Chris. Shuter, Tho. Goldney and Franc. Rogers. Their last instruction to him is worth quoting:

And Further, itt is our Request, and we do require itt of you, your Officers and Men, that an entire Amity, Respect and Agreement, be with the utmost Industry and Methods conserved and promoted with your Consort, the *Duchesse*; And whatsoever Necessarys, as Provisions, Stores, Ammunition or men they want, You are to spare them from on board your ship with all Readiness; And in everything to behave yourselves one toward another as a kind Duke regarding his beloved Duchesse.[17]

Appendix 3

Society of Merchant Venturers Archives
Box 7 Bundle 2, Part 1

William Whittington to Isaac Morgan. Indenture 24 and 26 October 1688. Lease and Release, being a Conveyance of three-quarters of the Manors of Clifton, except such parts thereof as had been lately sold to Ayliffe Green by the said William Whittington.

... between William Whittington of Ivythorne in the County of Somerset, Esq., son and heir to John Whittington Esq., deceased, of the one part, And Isaac Morgan of the City of Bristoll, Esq., of the other part, Witnesseth, that the said William Whittington for and in consideration of the sume of Ten shillings of lawfull money of England, unto him in hand paid by the said Isaac Morgan ... Hath granted, bargained and sold ... All those the three parts of the Lordshipp or Mannor of Clifton ... the whole in four parts to be divided, late in the tenure of John Whittington Esq., deceased, father of the said William Whittington, and now of the said William Whittington, his tenants or assignes, And also all houses, Cottages, edifices, buildings, Barnes, stables, Dove-houses, orchards, gardens, farmes and Lands, tenements, meadows, feedings, seasons, pastures, Commons, Wastes and Waste grounds, libertys, franchises, Rents, Reversions, Services, Royalties, priviledges, Jurisdictions and appurtenances of, or belonging to, the said Lordshipp or Mannor or appendant or appurtenant thereunto ...

... And all the woods, underwoods, hedgerows and trees, and the ground and soyle of the same ... Pooles and ponds, Waters, Watercourses, fishings, fowlings, furze, heath, Mines, Quarries, Lymekilns, Court Leet, and view of Frankpledge, wayned and estrayed goods and chattells of felons, and fugitives fines ... advowsons and patronages of Churches, ways, paths, easements, Commons, proffits, Comodities and appurtenances whatsoever to the said three parts of the Lordshipp or Mannor ... except and allways reserved out of this present bargain and sale ...

All that Messuage, farm and tenement with all Lands thereunto belonging, heretofore in the tenure or occupation of Richard Yeamans Esq., deceased, And now or late in the tenure or occupation of Ayliff Greene, Gent., And the Wood and Woodie ground called Rownams Wood, And the Messuage or dwelling house now in the occupation of John Gayner, lately erected and built upon part of the said Wood or Woody ground, And a cottge and one other plott of ground lying and being att the lower end of the said wood or Woody ground, And two acres of ground now in the occupation of John Harvey, And two acres of pasture now in the occupation of John Hodges, Esq., And two acres of pasture more in the fields called the Littlefield.

All which said excepted Lands and premises are lately sold by the said William Whittington unto the said Ayliff Greene, To have and to hold ... for ever.

Appendix 4

Society of Merchant Venturers Archives
Abstract of Leases, 1665-1715, folio 7, no. 13, Re. Anthony Hodges

John Young of Clifton, Gent., Andrew Whittington of the same, Gent., and Margaret his wife [Young's daughter] demise to Anthony Hodges of Clifton, Gent., William Hodges, John Hodges, his children, three parts in foure to be divided of a messuage or tenement and appurtenances, with a rick yard, and 74 acres of land, meadow and pasture to the same belonging, (viz) the Home Close adjoining to the house, by estimation 5 acres, 7 acres of meadow lying together in Rownham's Mead called the Seven Acres, a pasture ground called Lydfield, by estimation 9 acres and a halfe, a pasture ground called Trinmore, by estimation 6 acres, a pasture ground called Causeway Close, by estimation 3 acres, a parcell of pasture ground by estimation one acre and a halfe lying att a place called the Great Poole in a close of pasture inclosed out of the Northfield of Clifton, and 4 acres and a halfe of arable Land in the said Northfield. Parcell of a peece of ground called Six Acres, a close of arable land called the Shortgrove Close, by estimation 4 acres.

And all those woody grounds lying at a place called Shortgrove, by estimation 12 acres, all situate in Clifton parish and then in the holding of John Satchfield, Yeoman, and Margaret his wife, who were then seized in the whole for terme of their lives, But the reversion of the said three parts to Anthony Hodges (dead) for life, the remainder to the said William Hodges for life (dead), the remainder to the said John Hodges (dyed 1 January 1688) for life, and the remainder to the said Margaret Hodges for life (dyed 26 August 1699), rent £30 payable half yearly by equall portions att Michaelmas and Ladyday, and doeing suite of Court twice a yeare on Summons, and paying on the death of Anthony overliving Satchfield and his wife the best beast for a herriott, and the like on the rest.

Also the said Lessors grant to the said Lessees in redemption of the said Satchfield, his ferme which he had therein, determinable on the death of one Mary Watts, one whole close of pasture ground in Clifton aforesaid called the Nine Acres, by estimation 10 acres, Paid in remainder part of the other rent therefore £10 att the same feasts, by equall portions.

The Lessees covenant to repaire, taking competent and sufficient Houseboote, fireboote, and plowboote to be spent on the premises, not ploeing waste, If rent behind 12 days and not distress Lessees to forfeit £3-£4 for a paine. Lessees covenant to pay the rent and herriotts. The consideration was £340 paid as a ffine. Note this deed is not executed with livery and seizin.

The Freeman and Adams Families

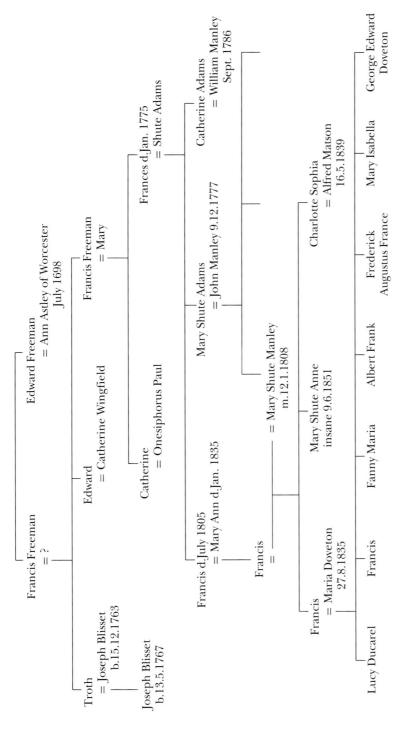

Sources
U.B. Deeds Rodney Lodge and Duncan House re. *Hollylands* Francis Freeman and Sir Thomas Daniels 15.2.1750
S.M.V. Box A Bundle no. 2. 3 Nov. 1758, Abstract of Title of Francis Adams. Indenture enrolled in Chancery, between Onesiphorus Paul and Catherine,
Shute Adams and Frances, Joseph Blisset and John Taylor.
S.M.V. Box A Bundle no. 2 1850, Abstract of Title no. 2. Marriage settlement between Francis Adams and Mary Shute Manley.
B.R.O. 21782 Box VI 104-5 Francis Adams and Francis Adams Junior to John Hurle, 9 May 1839. Abstract of title to a close of land called Longcroft in the
parish of Clifton.
Bristol Central Reference Library B.31723 Adams Estate Act, 15 and 16 Vict. Cap. 8 1852, p.164 for the children of Maria Doveton and Francis Adams.

The Champion Family

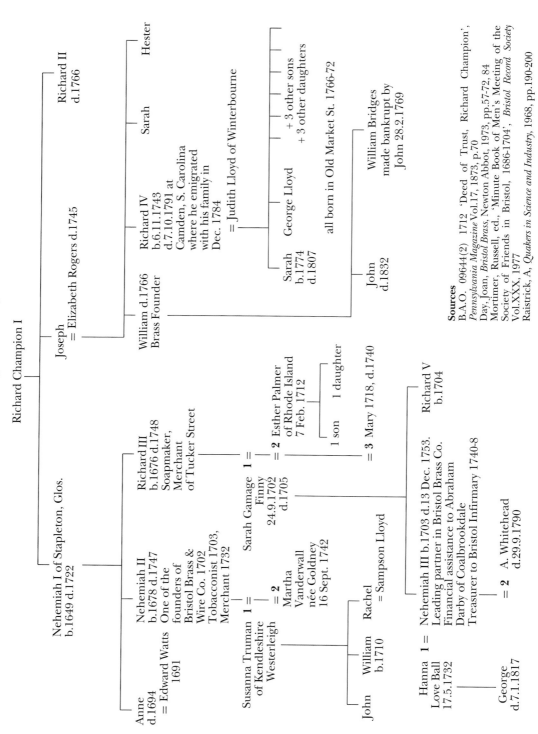

Sources

B.A.O. 09644(2) 1712 'Deed of Trust, Richard Champion', *Pennsylvania Magazine* Vol.17, 1873, p.70
Day, Joan, *Bristol Brass*, Newton Abbot, 1973, pp.57-72, 84
Mortimer, Russell, ed., 'Minute Book of Men's Meeting of the Society of Friends in Bristol, 1686-1704', *Bristol Record Society* Vol.XXX, 1977
Raistrick, A, *Quakers in Science and Industry*, 1968, pp.190-200

The Hobhouse Family

John Hobhouse d.1711 = Anne Madox of Norton-in-Gower, Glam.
b.1640 d.1720

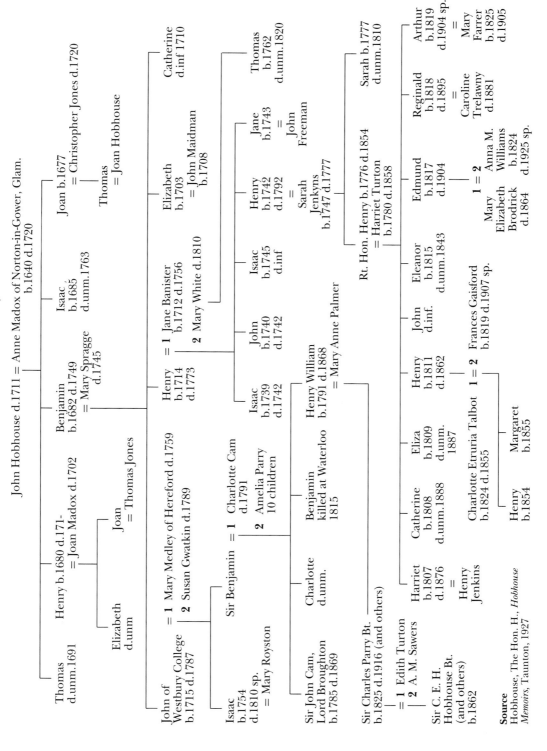

Source
Hobhouse, The Hon. H., *Hobhouse
Memoirs*, Taunton, 1927

The Worrall Family

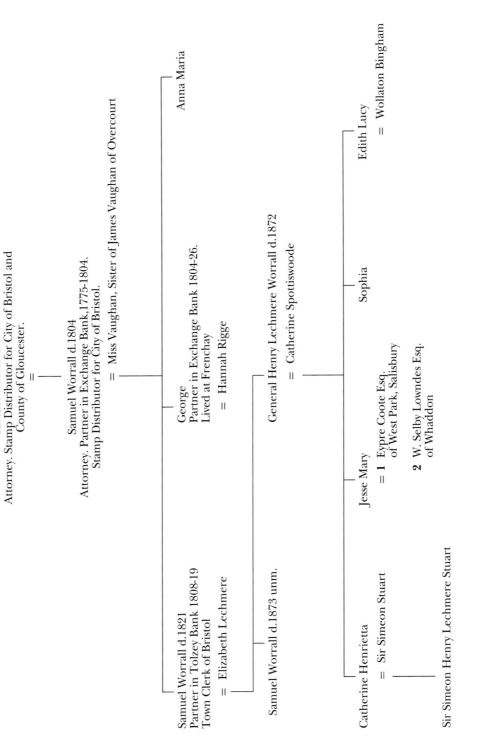

Samuel Worrall d.1746
Attorney. Stamp Distributor for City of Bristol and
County of Gloucester.
=

Samuel Worrall d.1804
Attorney. Partner in Exchange Bank, 1775-1804.
Stamp Distributor for City of Bristol.
= Miss Vaughan, Sister of James Vaughan of Overcourt

Anna Maria

George
Partner in Exchange Bank 1804-26.
Lived at Frenchay
= Hannah Rigge

Samuel Worrall d.1821
Partner in Tolzey Bank 1808-19
Town Clerk of Bristol
= Elizabeth Lechmere

Samuel Worrall d.1873 unm.

General Henry Lechmere Worrall d.1872
= Catherine Spottiswoode

Jesse Mary
= 1 Eypre Coote Esq.
     of West Park, Salisbury

  2 W. Selby Lowndes Esq.
     of Whaddon

Sophia

Edith Lucy
= Wollaton Bingham

Catherine Henrietta
= Sir Simeon Stuart

Sir Simeon Henry Lechmere Stuart

Source Cave, C. H., *A History of Banking in Bristol 1750-1899*, Bristol, 1899

The Elton Family

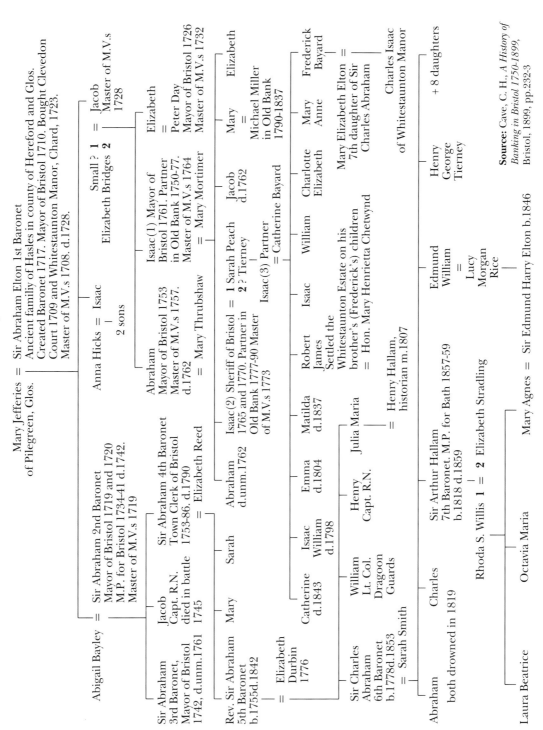

Source: Cave, C. H., *A History of Banking in Bristol 1750-1899*, Bristol, 1899, pp.232-3.

Appendix 6

The Merchants' Holdings with the Numbering of White's Plan of Clifton, 1806

		Acres	Rods	Perches
1.	Durdham Down. Lord of Manor and Tenants	250	1	22
2.	Turnpike House and Garden. Commissioners		1	0
3.	Gallows Acre. Godfrey Lowe	1	0	18
4.	The Seven Acres. Godfrey Lowe	6	3	6
5.	Three Acre Paddock. Godfrey Lowe	2	0	4
6.	Little Lippiatt. Godfrey Lowe	1	3	25
7.	Great Lippiatt. Godfrey Lowe	2	1	4
8.	Lower Cow Lease or Green. Godfrey Lowe	3	1	26
9.	Upper Cow Lease or Green. Godfrey Lowe	4	0	23
10.	Causeway Close and			
11.	Home Close. John F. Edgar	13	2	26
12a.	The Acre. Sam Worrall	1	0	27
13.	The Four Acres. Sam Worrall	4	0	13
14.	The Seven Acres. Sam Worrall	8	0	22
15.	Deans. A. P. Collins	2	3	36
16.	Road Close. Edward Elton	6	0	32
17.	HoneyPen Hill Field. A. P. Collins	4	0	14
18.	Broadmoor and Larridge. Edward Elton	9	1	33
19.	Ferney Close. Edward Elton	6	0	12
20.	Parts of Ferney Close used as garden		1	37
21.	Little Ground. Edward Elton	1	0	0
22.	York Place etc. Langston, Towgood & Co.	2	1	9
23.	House, Livery, Stables and Garden. G. Bengough	0	2	3
24.	House, Garden, Stable and Paddock. T. H. Andrews	2	2	0
25.	Messuage, Garden and Tenement. D. Ward	0	2	3
26.	A Strip in her Garden. Sarah Cross			21
27.	Small plot in his Garden. Jeremiah Hill			12
28.	Bellevue Pleasure Ground. Henry Elderton	3	1	30
29.	Quarry Ground. Merchants	2	0	21
30.	Messuage, Stables, etc. W. Jefferies	1	0	36
31.	Dwelling, Stable and Garden. Sam. Atwood			21
32.	Four Dwelling Houses and a Court. Shepherd and others			24
33.	Messuage, Cold Bath, Three Tenements, Stable Buildings and Garden. Samuel Powell		2	30
34.	Messuage, Tenement and Garden. E. Watkins			12
35.	Six Tenements and Garden. Gibbons, James, etc.		1	10
36.	Old Playhouse, now 3 Tenements, Court and Garden. Samuel Powell			30
37.	Messuage, 13 Tenements and a Close called Margarets. George D. Shewing		2	20
38.	Messuage, 3 Tenements, Garden, Orchard and Powder Mill. Samuel Powell		1	38
39.	Messuages, 4 Tenements and Garden. John Bridges.			20
40.	Two Tenements and small Garden. John Bridges			6
41.	Two Tenements and small Garden. John Bridges			4
42.	House and Garden. Thomas Lewis			36

No.	Description			
42a.	One Tenement. William Haynes			1
43.	White Hart Inn. John Bayley			30
44.	Old Ship, Tenement and Garden. Adam Sixsmith			38
44a.	Two Tenements. Adam Sixsmith			4
45.	Tenements and Garden. John Barry's executors			3
46.	Tenement and Garden. Wm. Haynes, in trust for Alan			6
47.	House and Garden. Marle			4
48.	House and Garden. Thomas Lewis			3
49.	House and Garden. John Holbrook			4
49a.	House and Garden. Rowland Rice			4
50.	Anchor Inn. Thomas Edwards			6
51.	Dwelling, Dockyard etc. Robert Bush		1	22
52.	Dock House Public House			10
53.	Three Tenements and shed at back gates of Hilhouse's Yard. Merchants			4
54.	Dwelling Outhouses, Court, Gardens, Shipyard Buildings and Dock. Merchants			
55.	Floating Dock and Premises. Merchants			
56.	The parts of Rownham Mead not granted to Dock Co.			
57.	Salutation Inn, Buildings, Yard etc. William Jones		2	20
58.	Houses, Gardens, Courts and other Premises from the Saluation to the middle of Dowry Parade. Bottington and others	1	3	11
59.	Houses and Garden on Dowry Parade and garden at West end thereof. Edward Daniel		3	28
60.	Mead Close, with the Messuages, Stables, Gardens etc. extending from Mead Lane to the New Inn Stables. Richard and Thomas Coombe	4	0	25
61.	The Upper and Lower Grounds with the Houses			
62.	and Gardens on the Southwest side thereof			
63.	and the unfinished buildings of Cornwallis			
64.	Cres. except the Eastern one. Henry Brooke	11	1	20
65.	The Eastern House of Cornwallis Crescent and way thereto. Henry Worrall			4
66.	Cornwallis House, Stable, Garden, Shrubbery and premises. Henry Brooke		2	16
67.	Dwelling, Buildings, Garden, Shrubbery and Premises. Andrew Carrick		3	22
68.	House, outbuildings, Garden and Premises. John Deverell		1	5
69.	House, outbuildings etc. Savage		3	1
69a.	A Shop on opposite side of road. Savage			1
70.	Hill Close. Gabriel Goldney	4	1	37
71.	A strip of ground granted in fee to Bleuden and Baker			25
72.	Five Tenements, outhouses, Gardens, Close and Premises. Hannah and R. Deverell	4	0	38
73.	Cecils Litfields with the road, subject to a way over the same. H. and R. Deverell	7	2	14
74.	The Five Acres. Hannah and Richard Deverell	3	1	29
75.	The Four Acres. Hannah and Richard Deverell	3	1	37
76.	Princes Buildings and Gardens, rough road above the Colonnade of shops, Powell's			
77.	Garden. St Vincent's Parade and Houses			
78.	Ice House, King David's Inn, Sam Powell	7	3	31
79.	The Rock House. Samuel Powell			2
80.	Colonnade of shops, Garden and Billiard Room. Dinah Emery			24
81.	The Pump Room, outbuildings and several tenements. Merchants			30
82.	New Hotwell House and Garden. Merchants	400	3	1

Appendix 7

Francis Freeman's Estates in Clifton

Fields named on De Wilstar's map of 1746		Acres	Rods	Perches
Uv	Batton's Grove	4	3	25
Uvi	Frimmer's	4	3	10
Uvii	Littlefields	5	2	38
Uviii	Batton's Ground	7	3	19
Uix	Nutt's Eastfield	7	1	10
Ux	Nutt's Three Acres	2	3	0
Uxi	Pool Close Lane	1	0	5
Uxii	Pool Close	4	2	28
Uxiii	Rownham Mead, Inclosed land	5	2	0
Uxiv	The Eleven Acres	10	3	18
Uxv	Nutt's Five Acres	5	1	0
Uxvi	West Ground	2	3	2
Uxvii	West Ground	4	2	16
Uxviii	East Ground	4	1	10
Uxix	Lippiatt Three Acre Paddock	3	1	8
Uxx	Inner Lippiatt Paddock, The Three Acres	3	1	18
Uxxii	Inner Lippiatt Paddock, The Two Acres	1	3	38
Uxxiii	The Two Acre Paddock	1	3	16
Uxxiv	Westfield Eight Acres	7	1	18
Uxxv	Ambrose Close	6	0	30
Uxxvi	The Long Legged Paddock	2	3	0
Uxxvii	The White Ladyes, One	3	0	0
Uxxviii	Tenement with three	3	2	0
Uxxix	paddocks	3	0	25
Uxxx	Flower Hill, Eleven Acres	11	2	10
Uxxxi	Honeypenn Hill along the Browhill claiming three styles	2	0	15
Uxxxii	The Eight Acres	8	0	2
Uxxxiii	The Long Legg, Nine Acres	9	1	11
Uxxxiv	The Road Close	4	0	8
Uxxxv	Pitt Close	4	0	10
Uxxxvii	The Ell, Five Acres	4	3	27

Unnamed Fields

AO	Several Tenements from opposite the Dockyard to the Churchyard	6	0	10
Viv	The one acre paddock by Gallowshill Rd.	0	3	30
U	The Brickkiln Ground by the Riverside and the Hotwell Road	3	3	16
Ui	One tenement, Orchard, Garden and Paddock where Mr. Knight lives	1	2	20
Uii	One tenement, Orchard, Garden field of pasture, let to Mr. Cann	9	2	20
Uiii	One tenement, Garden and Penn adjoining to Brimley lett to Mr. Pedlar	1	0	14
Uiv	One tenement and Garden, to Mr. Parcker	0	2	0
		189	1	17

References

References to Chapter One

1. Seyer, p.60. *See also* Lloyd Morgan, 'Notes on Clifton, Burwalls and Stokeleigh Camps', *P.C.A.C.*, Vol.5, 1900, p.16.
2. Ibid., p.62, but this does not appear in J. H. Harvey, *William Worcester – Itineraries*, Oxford, 1969.
3. Ibid., p.65.
4. Caesar, *The Gallic War. Book V*, trans. H. J. Edwards, p.261.
5. Birch, *Cartularium Saxonicum*, No.1335, quoted by Jones, 'The Growth of Bristol. The Regional Aspect of City Development', *Trans. of the Institute of British Geographers*, Vol.11, 1946, p.67.
6. Douglas and Greenaway (eds.), *English Historical Documents*, II, 1953, pp.123-4.
7. Seyer, p.66.
8. Ibid., p.159.
9. Suetonius' biography of Vespasian in *Lives of the Caesars*, trans. J. C. Rolfe, p.287.
10. P. Ellis, 'Sea Mills, Excavations, 1965-68', *T.B.G.A.S.*, Vol. 105, 1987, p.100, and W. H. Manning, *Report on the Excavations at Usk, 1965-76; the fortress excavations 1968-71*, Cardiff, 1981. *See also* A. Trice Martin and E. K. Tratman, 'Excavations at Sea Mills, Bristol', *T.B.G.A.S.*, Vol.XLV, 1923, pp.193-201; Frederick Ellis, 'Roman remains near Bristol, Sea Mills', *P.C.A.C.*, 1893-96, Vol.III, p.16-; D. P. Dobson, 'Excavations, Sea Mills, near Bristol', *T.B.G.A.S.*, 1937, pp.330-2; G. C. Boon, 'The Roman Site at Sea Mills', *T.B.G.A.S.*, 1945, Vol.LXIV, pp.258-95; G. C. Boon, 'A Claudian Origin for Sea Mills', *T.B.G.A.S.*, 1949, Vol.68, pp.184-8.
11. P. Ellis, *op. cit.*, p.103.
12. A. T. Martin, 'On the Roman Road between Bath and Caerwent', *P.C.A.C.*, Vol.1, 1885, pp.58-66. *See also* Bishop Clifford, 'Some remarks on the ancient passage across the Severn', *T.B.G.A.S.*, Vol.III, 1878-9, pp.83-9.
13. A. T. Martin, 'The Roman Road on Durdham Down, Bristol', *P.C.A.C.*, 1900-3, Vol.V, pp.75-7.
14. St Clair Baddeley, 'The Battle of Dyrham, A.D.577', *T.B.G.A.S.*, Vol.51, 1929, pp.95-101.
15. *Anglo-Saxon Chronicles*, Everyman Edition, 1953.
16. J. S. Moore (ed.), *Domesday Book, No.15, Gloucestershire*, Phillimore, 1982, p.170b.
17. E. S. Lindley, 'The Anglo-Saxon Charters of Stoke Bishop', *T.B.G.A.S.*, Vol.LXXVIII, 1959, p.98.
18. C. S. Taylor, 'Bristol and its Neighbourhood in Domesday', *P.C.A.C.*, Vol.II, 1888-93, pp.67-82.
19. J. S. Moore, 'The Gloucestershire section of the Domesday Book: geographical problems of the text', Part 1, *T.B.G.A.S.*, Vol.105, 1987, pp.118-21. *See* R. Atkyns, *The Ancient and Present State of Glostershire*, 1712, p.187; A. F. Ellis, 'On the manorial history of Clifton', *T.B.G.A.S.*, Vol.3, 1878-9, p.212; Lewis Upton Way, 'The 1625 survey of the smaller manor of Clifton', *T.B.G.A.S.*, Vol.36, 1913, p.220; C. S. Taylor, 'Note on the entry in Domesday Book relating to Westbury-on-Severn', *T.B.G.A.S.*, Vol.36, 1913, pp.182-90.
20. Lindley, *op. cit.*, pp.96-109.
See also S. Everett, 'A Reinterpretation of the Anglo-Saxon Survey of Stoke Bishop', *T.B.G.A.S.*, 1961, Vol.LXXX, pp.175-8; C. S. Taylor, 'The Parochial Boundaries of Bristol', *T.B.G.A.S.*, 1910, Vol.XXXIII, pp.126-39; G. B. Grundy, 'The Saxon Charters and field names of Gloucestershire', *T.B.G.A.S.*, Vol.LVII, 1935-6, pp.223-31.
21. A. J. Green-Armytage, *Concerning Clifton: A Historical Narrative*, 1922, p.29.
22. L. Upton Way, 'The 1625 Survey of the smaller manor of Clifton', *T.B.G.A.S.*, Vol.36, 1913, p.224.
23. A. S. Ellis, *op. cit.*, p.213.
24. Abbey Reg., quoted by T. D. Fosbrooke, *Abstracts of Records and Manuscripts respecting the County of Gloucestershire*, 2 vols, 1807, quoted by A. S. Ellis, *op. cit.*, p.216.
25. Ibid.fol.25, and A. S. Ellis, *op. cit.*, p.216.
26. Ibid.fol.212, and A. S. Ellis, p.217.

27. *Bristol Journal*, No.465, 25 June 1987, p.1.
28. Seyer, Vol.II, p.19.
29. W. Barrett, *The History and Antiquities of the City of Bristol*, 1789, p.367.
30. *Rotuli Hundredorum*, I, Record Commission, p.177, quoted by A. S. Ellis, *op. cit*, p.218.
31. All this section is based on the work of A. S. Ellis, *op. cit.*, pp.211-29.
32. *Victoria County History of Gloucestershire*, Vol.II, 1907 edition, reprinted 1972, ed. W. Page, p.108, quoting *Worces. Episcop. Regis.*, Carpenter, I, fol.183d.
33. C. S. Taylor, 'The Church and Monastery of Westbury-on-Trym', *P.C.A.C.*, Vol.IV, p.36.
34. *Victoria County History*, Vol.II, p.108, quoting Tanner, *Notitia Monastica*, 1744 edition, p.142.
35. Ibid., Vol.II, p.108, quoting Deputy Keeper's Rep., viii, App.ii, p.48; *also Worces. Episc. Registers*, Carpenter, I, fol.231; *also Valor Ecclesiasticus*, Rec. Comm., Vol.II, 1835, p.434. *See also* Taylor, *op. cit.*, p.20.
36. A. S. Ellis, *op. cit.*, p.227.
37. P. McGrath, *Records relating to the Society of Merchant Venturers of the city of Bristol in the 17th century*, Bristol Record Society, Vol.XVII, 1952, p.132, No.269.
38. H. J. Wilkins, *Some Chapters in the Ecclesiastical History of Westbury-on-Trym*, 1909, pp.11-12.
39. J. H. Bettey, *Bristol Parish Churches during the Reformation c.1530-1560*, Bristol branch of the Historical Association, 1979, p.11.

References to Chapter Two
1. G. Baskerville, *English Monks and the Suppression of the Monasteries*, Cape, 1937, p.132.
2. G. A. J. Hodgett, 'The unpensioned religious in Tudor England', *Journal of Eccles. Hist.*, XIII, ii, 1962.
3. B.R.O. 4984/1-5.
4. B.R.O. 32226, Box 39, Clarke, Gwynne and Press, Victoria Rooms, unsorted.
5. R. Atkyns, *Glostershire*, p.359.
6. S.M.V. Box 14B, Bundle 5, No.1, 20 October 1596, 38th Eliz.I, Indenture between William Clarke of Barrow ... and ffrances his wife, and others ... to John Satchfield and others.
7. B.R.O. 32835(s) AC/M15 Survey of the Manor, 1625.
8. S.M.V. Box 14B, Bundle 2, No.1, 22 April 1690 between the Merchants and Joanne George (widow). The same evidence re. 'Greatfield alias Northfield' is at S.M.V. Box 14B, Bundle 2, Nos.2, 3 and 4. Also Box 14B, Bundle 1, No.1, 18 June 1652 and Box 14B, Bundle 1, No.2, 26 Feb. 1676.
9. B.R.O. 05178 Marriage Settlement of Edw. Freeman of quarter of manor of Clifton, 30 July 1698.
10. B.R.O. 32835(s) AC/M15 Survey of Manor 1625.
11. J. S. Moore, *Clifton and Westbury Probate Inventories, 1609-1761*, Bristol, 1981, p.xxvi and footnote B.R.O. EP/A/32/41 field nos.558-9, 997-9.
12. Ibid., p.xxvii.
13. D. Hollis (ed.), *Calendar of the Bristol Apprentice Book 1532-42*, Bristol Record Soc., Vol.XIV, 1949, pp.199-200.
14. Moore, *op. cit.*, p.iv, using Smyth, *Men and Armour*.
15. J. S. Moore, *Probate Inventories*, p.202, example 230.
16. Ibid., p.xvi, Table 3.
17. S.M.V., *Abstract of Leases, 1665-1716*, p.1, No.2, pp.22-3, No.28, pp.26-7, No.30.
18. S.M.V., *Chancery Papers*, S.M.V. versus Lambe, Deane et al., Bundle marked Legal Papers, 1682-84, The plea and answer of John Lambe, the defendant. Purchased from Edward, Thomas, Nicholas and Christopher Clark.
19. S.M.V. Estates, *Abstract of Leases, 1752-1783*, p.62, 17 April 1757. S.M.V. and John Wakley Phippen, Gent.
20. B.R.O. 32835(s) AC/M15 Survey of Manor 1625. *See* L. Upton Way, 'The 1625 Survey of the smaller manor of Clifton', *T.B.G.A.S.*, Vol.36, 1913.
21. S.M.V., *Abstract of Grants, 1665-1716*, p.1.
22. U.B.D. Goldney House deed box, Bundle 1.
23. Ibid., 20 April 1694, Lease for 99 years, Roland Baugh and Thomas Goldney the younger.
24. Atkyns, *op cit.*, 1712, reprinted 1970, p.360.
25. T. B. Howell, *A Complete Collection of State Trials*, 1817, Vol.iv, p.229, quoted by P. McGrath, *Bristol and the Civil War*, 1981, p.3.

26. McGrath, *op. cit.*, p.10.
27. Sir B. de Gomme, 'Journal of the Siege of Bristol', printed in E. Warburton, *Memoirs of Prince Rupert and the Cavaliers*, London, R. Bentley, 1849, Vol.2, p.237.
28. J. Latimer, *The Annals of Bristol in the 17th C*, 1900, p.191.
29. Ibid., p.192.
30. Ibid., p.196.
31. E. Warburton, *Memoirs of Prince Rupert*, p.168.
32. Col. J. Bramble, 'Ancient Bristol Documents', No.VIII, in *P.C.A.C.*, Vol.2, 1888-9, p.155.
33. Moore, *Probate Inventories*, No.99, pp.93-4, No.101, pp.95-6, No.116, pp.105-6.
34. T. Carlyle, *Oliver Cromwell's Letters and Speeches*, 1908, p.185.
35. Latimer, *Annals of the 17th C*, p.206, quoting Hist. MSS. Commission, Report XIII, 8 Oct. and 12 Nov.
36. P.R.O. E179/113/31, 4 Rich.II, 1381 Poll Tax, also E179/113/13a and E179/113/35a.
37. P.R.O. E179/113/4 6 Edw.II, Assessment of Tallage, 15ths and 10ths. The list is undifferentiated for the hundreds and there are no headings for tythings.
38. P.R.O. E179/113/55 3 Hen.IV, Inquisitions. Within the Glos. return King's Barton is included, but Clifton is not differentiated.
39. P.R.O. E179/113/189 16 Henry VIII, Lay Subsidy 1524-5. Subsequent lay subsidy assessments give full listings of individuals, but Clifton within King's Barton is not particularised, e.g. E179/114/221 28 Hen.VIII, E179/114/251 37 Hen.VIII, E179/114/249 37 Hen.VIII, E179/115/311 4 Edw.VI, E179/115/342 5 Edw.VI, E179/115/353 2 Eliz.I, E179/115/367 6 Eliz.I, E179/115/407 30 Eliz.I, E179/115/430 36 Eliz.I.
40. P.R.O. E101/58/26 26 Hen.VIII, Militia Muster Roll 1535.
41. P.R.O. E179/116/554 13 and 14 Charles II, 1662 Michaelmas Hearth Tax and P.R.O. E179/277/13 and 14, 23 Charles II, the 1671-2 Hearth Tax. There is also a photostat copy of the 1672 Michaelmas return in the Glos. County Record Office, Clarence Row, Alvin St. GRO D/383 (Part 2 for King's Barton), p.165.
42. GRO D/1762/6 Parliamentary Survey of Church Livings in the diocese of Glos., 1650.
    See C. R. Elrington, 'The Survey of Church Livings in Glos., 1650', *T.B.G.A.S.*, Vol.83, 1964, p.96. 'Clifton – Impropriated, not more than £6 allocated to m. No settled m. 30 families. Fit to be united with W-on-Trym'. Particularly frustrating is the disappearance of Bishop Cheyney's returns to the Queen's Privy Council for 1563. Richard Cheyney, 1562-79, held Bristol 'in commendam'. In question 5 the Privy Council asked each diocese:
    'Fifthlie, How manye howsholds are within every parishe or within anye suche member of anye parishe, that hathe suche Churches or Chappells of ease?'
    See Bodleian Library, MSS Rawlinson, C790, re. Glos.
    See Richard Furney's MSS, 1721, 4 notebooks by a master at the Crypt School, Glos. 1719-21. MSS.B *Collections from the Original Records, Deeds, in the Office of the Bishop's Register of Gloucester made in the year 1721* in the Gloucester Room, Gloucester City Library.
43. J. Smyth, *A Description of the Hundred of Berkeley*, p.9, quoted by A. J. and R. H. Tawney, 'An Occupational Census of the Seventeenth Century', in *Econ. Hist. Rev.*, Vol.V, 1934-5, p.30.
44. In Clifton in 1535 only four men between 16 and 60 turned up for the Muster. *See* P.R.O. E101/58/26. 26 Hen.VIII.
45. Atkyns, *op. cit.*
46. J. S. Moore, *Clifton and Westbury Probate Inventories*, 1609-1761, Bristol 1981, pp.xx-xxi. Moore's findings are that the average size of household ranges between 3·85 (Horfield) and 5·71 (Alveston). The average for all the parishes he looked at was 4·43. This is the basis for using the multiplier 4·5.
47. P.R.O. E179/113/189 Lay Subsidy Roll, 16 Henry VIII (7 taxpayers $\times$ 4½)
48. Militia Muster Roll, 1608, J. Smyth, Men and Armour (Fit adult males aged 16-60 $\times$ 3½. Assume males = 50% of pop.; that adult pop. = 60% of fit pop.; that pop. over 60 or unfit = 5% of total). *See* J. S. Moore, *Goods and Chattels of our Forefathers*, Chichester, 1976, p.11.
49. G.R.O. D/1762/6 Parliamentary Survey of church livings in diocese of Glos., *T.B.G.A.S.*, Vol.83, 1964, p.96 (30 families $\times$ 4½).
50. P.R.O. E179/116/554 Hearth Tax, 13 and 14 Charles II, 1662, Michaelmas. (Heads of households 25 $\times$ 4½, but within the houses, 103 hearths.)

51. P.R.O. E179/277/14 Hearth Tax, 23 Charles II, 1672 reveals 72 households, including those discharged from paying and 174 hearths. (72 × 4½.)

52. Atkyns, *op. cit.*, gives population estimates for each parish.
    See J. Moore, *Probate Inventories*, 1609-1761, Bristol, 1981, pp.xx and xxi for average size of households for parishes in S. Glos. (4·43).

53. B.R.O. 29174(1).

54. E. Ralph (ed.), *Marriage Licence Bonds for the Diocese of Bristol*, Vol.1, Records Section, B. and G. Arch. Soc. 1952.

55. M. V. Campbell, *Registers of St Andrews, Clifton, Transcripts*, Vol.1, pp.71 and 72.

56. P. McGrath, *Merchants and Merchandise in 17th C Bristol*, p.ix.

57. J. S. Moore, *Probate Inventories*, p.xxii.

58. S.M.V., *Abstract of Leases, 1665-1716.*

59. J. Latimer, 'The Manor of Clifton', *T.B.G.A.S*, Vol.16, 1891-2, p.206.

60. S.M.V. Chancery Papers, S.M.V. versus Lambe, Deane and others, Bundle marked Legal Papers 1682-4.

61. E. Kerridge, *Agrarian Problems in the 16th C and after*, 1969, p.93.

62. B.R.O. 32835(s) AC/M 15 Survey of Manor, 1625.

63. S.M.V. Box 14B, Bundle 5, No.1, 20 Oct. 1596.

64. B.R.O. 32835(s) AC/M 15.

65. Ibid.

66. S.M.V. 26 July 1603, Bargain and sale from William Clarke of Barrow Minchin, Esq., to John Young of one Quarter part of the manor.

67. B.R.O. 32835(s) AC/M 15.

68. S.M.V. 26 July 1603, *op. cit.*

69. S.M.V. Chancery Papers, S.M.V. versus Lambe, Deane and others, Bundle marked Legal Papers 6182-84.

70. S.M.V. Box 7, Bundle A, Part 2, 7 Nov. 1965, between Stephen Stringer, of the parish of Clifton, vintner, and Samuel Price, now Master of the M.V.s and others.

71. B.R.O. 7837(25) 5 June 1690. Indenture bet. William Weare of Hinton in the parish of Dyrham ... yeoman and Stephen Stringer of the City of Bristol vintner.

72. Ibid.

73. S.M.V. Box 7, Bundle A, Part 2, 7 Nov. 1695.

74. B.R.O. 05178 Marriage Settlement of Edward Freeman of one quarter of manor of Clifton, 30 July 1698.

75. S.M.V., *Abstract of Leases, 1665-1716*, fol.4, No.7. My attention was drawn to this reference by Moore.

76. Ibid., fol.12, No.17. Also noted by Moore.

77. Ibid., fol.20, No.26, Similar warnings were given to Thomas Cuffe, 23 Jan. 1679, fol.23 and to John Boarporker in 1708, fol.315, No.360.

78. J. S. Moore, *Probate Inventories*, p.xxix, quoting his own research in Moore, *The Goods and Chattels of our Forefathers*, Chichester, 1976, p.30, Table 10.

79. S.M.V., *Abstract of Leases, 1665-1716*, fol.7, No.13 re. Anthony Hodges and Box 14B, Bundle 5, No.1 20 Oct. 1596.

80. B.R.O. 12964 (1)-(2), *Collections Relating to Somersetshire, MSS, 1672-1741*, p.34, Kingsweston, 18 May 1696.

81. Ibid., p.30 to Sir Robert Southwell, 24 Nov. 1694.

82. Ibid., p.34, from John Plomley, 18 May 1696, Kingsweston. (French grass is of course cinquefoil.)

83. Ibid., p.32.

References to Chapter Three

1. S.M.V. Legal Papers, Chancery, S.M.V. versus Lambe et al. 8 Jan. 1685, 1st.Js.II.

2. Latimer, *Merchant Venturers*, p.203.

3. S.M.V. Box No.7, Bundle A, Part 1, 11 and 12 May 1674, Lease and Release, being a Conveyance by Richard Christmas and Peter Saunders to John Huie and Richard Lane, in Trust for Thomas Moore and Roger Bathron, Executors of John Bowen, of ¾ parts of the manor of Clifton.

4. A. E. Ellis, 'On the manorial history of Clifton', *T.B.G.A.S.*, Vol.3, 1878-9, p.231.

5. S.M.V. Chancery Papers, S.M.V. versus Lambe, Deane and Others to discover their rights and titles. Bundle marked 'Legal Papers', 1682-4.

6. Sir Robert Cann's deposition 'to whom and to whose heires two of the said daughters remitted and released their respective properties in fee'.
7. S.M.V. 26 July 1603, 1 James I, Bargain and sale from William Clarke to John Young.
8. S.M.V. Chancery Papers, S.M.V. versus Lambe et al. The plea and answer of John Lambe, the defendant.
9. S.M.V. Box 14B, Bundle No.5, 20 Oct 1596, Lease from William Clarke of Barrow in the County of Somerset, and his wife, to John Satchfield and others.
10. S.M.V. Box 7, Bundle 2 (Part), 12 Jan 1615, Settlement by John Young.
    See also Abstract of the Merchants' Title.
11. Ibid., 22 Oct 1668, Articles of agreement for the sale by William Whittington to Isaac Morgan.
12. Ibid., 16 and 17 May 1670, Lease and Release, being a conveyance of the said 3/4ths of the Manor of Clifton by the said Isaac Morgan to Richard Mountney of London, Esq.
    See also Abstract of Title. Legal Papers, 1682-84.
13. Ibid., 17 May 1670, 22 Chs.II, Indenture between Isaac Morgan Esq. and Richard Mountney of London Esq., for His Majesty's Collectors of the Customs.
14. S.M.V. Chancery Papers, S.M.V. versus Lambe et al. Abstract of Title.
15. Ibid.
16. McGrath, Records, p.131.
17. S.M.V. Lease Book, Abstract of Grants, Manor of Clifton 1665-1716, fol.76, 6 and 7 July 1676, Indentures of Lease and Release, Roger Bathron, merchant, to Roger Hart, Master and the Merchants' Society.
18. B.A.O. 6609(11) The Conveyance of the Manor of Clifton, 4 May 1668.
19. Ibid.
20. Descendants of Gabriel Deane, Merchant – Stephen Watts and Mary, his wife, Arthur Hart and Martha, his wife, and Sarah Deane, kinswoman.
21. S.M.V. Lease Book, fol.81.
22. Ibid.
23. Ibid., fol.82.
24. Latimer, Merchant Venturers, p.167.
25. S.M.V. Chancery Papers, S.M.V. versus Lambe, Deane et al. Bundle marked Legal Papers, 1682-84, The Pleas and answer of John Lambe, the defendant.
26. S.M.V. Box 9, Bundle 10, The Home Ground and Messuage, being No.14 on the Survey. The 'Old Castle' or Manor House, 'heretofore burnt down by fire'.
27. J. Latimer, 'The Manor of Clifton', T.B.G.A.S., Vol.16, 1891-2, p.201.
28. Ibid., p.206.
29. Ibid., p.205.
30. S.M.V. Chancery Papers, Bundle marked Legal Papers, 1682-84, The Joint and several answers of Martha Deane ... and Stephen Watts, Mary his wife, and Sarah Deane.
31. S.M.V. Chancery Papers, Mr. Lambe's title to Clifton and Francis Pemberton's opinion.
32. S.M.V. Chancery Papers, The Joint and several answers of Martha Deane, etc.
33. S.M.V. Chancery Papers, Legal Papers, 1682-84, Between the Master, Wardens and Society of the mistery or Art of Merchant Adventurer of the City of Bristoll, Pltfs., John Lamb Esq., Martha Deane, widow, Ellis Kelly and several other Defts. 1683.
34. S.M.V. Chancery Papers, Legal Papers, 1684-86, Order to Dismiss, 10 Nov. 1685.
35. S.M.V. Chancery Papers, Letter dated 21 Sept 1686.
36. S.M.V. Deed, 15 Oct. 1686 between Edw. Tocknell, Master, and Mr. Arthur Hart and Stephen Watts.
37. B.R.O. 05178 Marriage settlement of Edward Freeman of one quarter of the Manor of Clifton, 30 July 1698.
38. S.M.V. Chancery Papers, S.M.V. versus Lambe, Deane et al., 1682-4, shelf M, bundle marked 'Legal Papers, Surveys'.

References to Chapter Four
1. J. Latimer, 'Clifton in 1746', P.C.A.C, Vol.V, 1900-3, p.26.
2. W. Stubbs, Select Charters, Illustrative of English Constitutional History, 1890, pp.68-73, Ordinance of the hundred, A.D.959-75, Edgar, for origin of the Hundred.
3. R. Atkyns, Glostershire, pp.359-60.

4. J., Wilstar, 'A Survey of the Manor of Clifton in the County of Gloucester; part of the estates belonging to the Merchants' Hall, Bristol', 1746, S.M.V.
5. Jefferies MSS., Vol.V, Bristol Central Reference Library, quoted in J. Latimer, *Annals of the 18th C*, 1893, p.245.
6. Latimer, 'Clifton in 1746', p.27.
7. Bryan Little, 'The Georgian Houses of Clifton', *Country Life*, 6 Sept. 1962, p.520.
8. University of Bristol Deeds, Goldney House Deed Box, Bundle 3, Nos.4-6, 8-9, 11; E 1-2; Bundle 4, No.A1; Bundle 7, Nos.C1-2: Bundle 12, No.B11; Bundle 13, No.A3; Bundle 14, No.A6; Bundle 15, No.A5; for complete references to these Deeds see J. S. Moore (ed.), *Clifton and Westbury Probate Inventories, 1609-1761*, 1981, Introduction, p.xi.
9. Ibid.
    See 13 Sept. 1692, Marriage Settlement, Lord Folliott to Trustees to uses.
    See 20 April 1694, Lease for 99 years.
    See 15 and 16 June 1705, Lease and release.
10. P. K. Stembridge, *Goldney, A House and a Family*, 1969, p.15.
11. S.M.V. Estates, *Abstracts of Leases, 1752-1783*, fol.168, 1764, S.M.V. and Thomas Goldney, fol.181, 1765, S.M.V. and Thomas Goldney, reversion of a lease. Thomas Goldney II had begun to build and extend his estate as early as 1719.
    See S.M.V., *Minute Books*, Index to Proceedings, Nos.4 and 5, 28 Aug. 1717, 'Mr. Goldney proposes to take and build on a piece of waste ground on which Mr. Speed built a coach house'. 9 July 1719 and 7 Oct. 1719, 'Cttee to view ground purchased by Mr. Goldney'.
12. D. Richardson, *Bristol, Africa and the Eighteenth Century Slave Trade to America*, Bristol Record Soc. publ. Vol.XXXIX, 1987, pp.25, 47 and 67.
13. A. B. Beavan, *Bristol Lists, Municipal and Miscellaneous*, 1899.
    See Minchinton, W. E., *The Trade of Bristol in the Eighteenth Century*, Bristol Record Soc. publ. Vol.XX, 1957, pp.20, 30, 31, 185, 189, 'Paul Fisher Junior, Co-partner to Slade Baker and William Griffin, linen drapers'.
14. J. W. Daymer Powell, *Bristol Privateers and Ships of War*, 1930, pp.147, 150 and 156.
15. A. J. Green-Armytage, *Concerning Clifton: A Historical Narrative*, 1922, p.29.
16. B.R.O. 32173/2c Abstract of Title to premises at Clifton, late Mrs. Cross's, 23 Feb. 1822.
17. Russell Mortimer, *Early Bristol Quakerism, The Society of Friends in the City, 1654-1700*, Bristol Branch of the Historical Assoc., 1967, p.14.
    See also J. Latimer, *Annals of the 17th C*, p.431.
18. Stembridge, *op. cit.*, p.5.
19. Daymer Powell, *op. cit.*, p.94.
20. Stembridge, *op. cit.*, p.7.
21. Latimer, *Annals of the 18th C*, p.54.
22. Daymer Powell, *op. cit.*, pp.103-22.
23. Latimer, *Annals of the 18th C*, p.75.
24. Daymer Powell, *op. cit.*, p.121
25. Latimer, *Annals of the 18th C*, p.76.
26. Stembridge, *op.cit.*, p.9
27. Ibid.
28. C. H. Cave, *A History of Banking in Bristol, 1750-1899*, 1899.
29. Stembridge, *op. cit.*, p.13.
30. Daymer Powell, *op. cit.*, p.183.
31. Stembridge, *op. cit.*, p.13.
32. Ibid., p.23.
33. Ibid., p.25.
34. Daymer Powell, *op. cit.*, p.144.
35. Ibid., p.150.
36. Ibid., p.154.
37. Ibid., p.170.
38. Ibid., p.182.
39. Ibid., p.154.

40. Bristol Society of Friends, *Minutes of Men's Monthly Meetings*, Vol.210, p.548.
    See W. E. Minchinton, *The Trade of Bristol in the Eighteenth Century*, Bristol Record Society Publ., Vol.XX, 1957, p.28.
41. J. Day, *Bristol Brass: The History of the Industry*, 1973, p.83.
42. Latimer, *Annals of the 18th C*, p.67.
43. B. Little, 'The Georgian Houses of Clifton', *Country Life*, 6 Sept. 1962, p.523.
44. Latimer, *Annals of the 18 C*, p.362
45. C. Wells, *A Short History of the Port of Bristol*, 1909, p.3, quoted in W. E. Minchinton, *Politics and the Port of Bristol in the Eighteenth Century*, B.R.S.Publ., Vol.XXIII, 1963, p.138.
    See McGrath, *Merchant Venturers*, p.154.
46. A. F. Williams, 'Bristol Port Plans and Improvement Schemes of the Eighteenth Century', *T.B.G.A.S.*, Vol.LXXXI, 1962, p.150.
47. Daymer Powell, *op. cit.*, p.227.
48. Day, *op. cit.*, p.90.
49. Ibid., p.85.
50. D. M. Olsen, 'Richard Champion and the Society of Friends', *T.B.G.A.S.*, Vol.102, 1984, p.173.
51. B.R.O., SF/A1/13 *Minutes of the Men's Meeting*, p.368.
52. Ibid.
53. Olsen, *op. cit.*, p.176, using B.R.O. SF/F1/2, *Records of Collection from 1763*.
54. W. Savadge, 'The West Country and the American Mainland Colonies, 1763-1783, with special reference to the merchants of Bristol', unpublished B.Litt. thesis, University of Oxford, 1952, p.57, quoting Society of Friends, *Minutes of Men's Monthly Meeting*, Vol.209, pp.317-20.
55. D. Richardson, *The Bristol Slave Traders: A Collective Portrait*, Bristol Hist. Assoc., 1985, p.29.
56. W. E. Minchinton, *The Trade of Bristol in the Eighteenth Century*, Bristol Rec. Soc., Vol.XX, p.9, Note 7.
57. Richardson, *Bristol Slave Traders, op. cit.*, p.29.
58. Minchinton, *op. cit.*, p.190, Appendix G (ii).
59. Ibid.
60. M. Hebditch, *Blaize Castle House Museum*, 1971, p.9.
    See also D. Jones, 'The Elbridge, Woolnough and Smyth families of Bristol in the Eighteenth Century, with special reference to the Spring Plantation, Jamaica', unpublished M.Litt. thesis, University of Bristol, 1971, p.94.
61. Ibid., p.11.
62. P. T. Underdown, 'Burke's Bristol Friends', *T.B.G.A.S.*, Vol.LXXVII, 1958.
63. P. T. Underdown, *Bristol and Burke*, Bristol Branch of the Hist. Ass., 1961, pp.13, 18-19.
64. Richardson, *Bristol Slave Traders, op. cit.*, p.23.
65. Ibid., pp.16-17.
66. D. Richardson, *Bristol, Africa and the 18th century Slave Trade to America*, Vol.1, The Years of Expansion, 1698-1729, Bristol Records Society Pubs., Vol.XXXVIII, 1986, pp.148, 155, 157.
67. Ibid., pp.173, 182, 185, 186.
68. Daymer Powell, *op. cit.*, p.160.
69. Ibid., p.239.
70. Savadge, *op. cit.*, Appendix C, Bristol Exports to America, 1773, pp.12-13.
71. Ibid., pp.16-17.
72. Ibid., p.25.
73. P.R.O. Chatham Papers, Bundle 343, No.313 'List of Debts due by Citizens of the U.S.A. to Merchants and Traders of Gt. Britain, contracted previous to the year 1776, with interest on the same to January 1790', quoted by Savadge, *op. cit.*, p.461.
74. *New York Gazette*, 26 Sept. 1774, quoted in Savadge, *op. cit.*, p.451.
75. Latimer, *Annals of the 18th C*, p.414.
76. Ibid.
77. Savadge, *op. cit.*, Appendix A, Annual number of ships from Bristol trading with the American mainland colonies, 1762-75.

References to Chapter Five
 1. J. Latimer, 'Clifton in 1746', *Proceedings of the Clifton Antiquarian Club*, 1900-3, Vol.5, p.29.
 2. J. Smyth, *Men and Armour for Gloucestershire*, 1608 and 1902, reprinted 1980, p.236. Smyth mentions 21 males in Clyston, including three mariners.

3. M. Hill, 'A Plan of Clifton and Hotwells, August 11, 1787'. Copyright County Reference Library, Bristol.

4. J. S. Moore, *Clifton and Westbury Probate Inventories, 1609-1761*, Avon Local History Assoc., University of Bristol Department of Extra-Mural Studies, 1981.

5. D. Hollis (ed.), *Calendar of the Bristol Apprentice Book, 1542-52*, B.R.S., Vol.XIV, 1949, pp.199-200. E. Ralph and N. M. Hardwick (eds.), *Calendar of the Bristol Apprentice Book, 1542-52*, B.R.S., Vol.XXXIII, 1980, Appendix II, p.153-5. Anne Yarborough, 'Geographical and Social Origins of Bristol's Apprentices', 1542-65, *T.B.G.A.S.*, Vol.98, 1980, p.126.

6. R. Atkyns, *Glostershire*, pp.359-60.

7. S. Rudder, *A New History of Gloucestershire*, 1779, reprinted 1977, p.383.

8. Reports and Abstracts of the Census of Great Britain, presented to the House of Commons 29 June 1801, of the answers and returns made to the Population Act of 41st Geo.III, p.126. Bristol Central Reference Library, RR 423. Clifton appears under the hundred of Barton Regis. The 4,457 persons comprise 1,673 males and 2,784 females. Fifty-five people are chiefly employed in agriculture, while 239 are chiefly employed in trade, manufactures or handicraft.
   See also the House of Commons Report, ordered by the Population Act of 1830, dated 19 Oct. 1831, *Population, a Comparative Account of the Population of Great Britain in the years 1801, 1821 and 1831*, Bristol Central Reference Library, RR 423.

9. A. J. Green-Armytage, *Concerning Clifton*, p.27.

10. U.B.D., Bundle 159 (Rodney Lodge), also quoted by Moore, *op. cit*, p.xxiv.

11. Green-Armytage, *op. cit.*, p.28.

12. B.R.O. 32835(s) AC/M 15 Henry Lilly's survey of the manor, 1625.

13. B.R.O. 12160 (1) 30 March 1638, Robert Hooke leases 30 acres.

14. L. J. U. Way, 'The 1625 Survey of the smaller manor of Clifton', *T.B.G.A.S.*, Vol.36, 1913, p.226.

15. B.R.O. 12160 (10) 6 Feb. 1666, 'Leasee to leave 12 standers oakes on all acres'.

16. B.R.O. 12160 (2).

17. B.R.O. 3579, 'Indenture between Thos. Barnes and Wm. Barlow'.

18. B.R.O. 12160 (3) 6 Feb. 1666, Thomas Barnes to John Watts.

19. B.R.O. 12160 (4) 2 March 1668 Fee Farm grant, 'Covenant from leasee to build a dwelling house'.

20. B.R.O. 12160 (5) 10 Feb. 1675, Fee Farm grant. John Watts to David Nicholas.

21. B.R.O. 12160 (6), John Watts to William Bailey.

22. B.R.O. 12160 (10) 'except a Lease to Barnes for 99 years determinable on the deaths of Charity, Edith and Mary, daughters of Barnes'.

23. B.R.O. 12160 (8) 15 March 1688, bet. Frances Hooke, widow, relict of John Hooke, brewer, and Tobias Garland.

24. B.R.O. 12160 (10) Abstract of Title, 1711.

25. J. de Wilstar, Survey of the Manors of Clifton, 1746, attached to Map No.4, S.M.V. copy.

26. B.R.O. 12160 (10) Abstract of Title, No.13, 16 Sept., 5th Wm. and Mary, 1693, 'As to the Wood'.

27. S.M.V. Chancery Papers, Bundle marked Legal Papers, Surveys, 1682-4.
    See also S.M.V. Abstract of Grants 1665-1711, fol.1, No.3, fol.2, No.5.

28. Ibid., Survey of Edward Bond's houses, 1679.
    See also Abstract of Grants 1665-1711, fol.7, No.12, fol.6, No.11.

29. S.M.V. Abstract of Grants 1665-1711, fol.15, No.21.

30. Ibid., fol.22, No.28.

31. B.R.O. Clifton Parish Registers, St Andrew's, transcript CM6 1538-1681.

32. C. Witt, C. Weeden and A. P. Schwind, *Bristol Glass*, 1984, p.53.

33. *Sketchley Directory*, 1775, reprinted 1971, p.17.

34. Witt et al., *op. cit.*, p.54.

35. Ibid., p.27.

36. A. Raistrick, *Industrial Archaeology*, 1972, p.82.

37. A. C. Powell, 'Glass Making in Bristol', *T.B.G.A.S.*, Vol.XLVII, 1925, p.215.

38. Witt et al., *op. cit.*, pp.26-7.

39. Ibid., p.54, quoting the Commissioners of Inquiry into the Excise Tax on glass for 1832, a tax introduced in 1695 to pay for the war with France. The Limekiln Lane Glasshouse by 1838 had been replaced by the timber merchants, Thomas and Isaac Rouch, who leased the site from the cathedral authorities.

40. U.B.D. the Goldney House Deed Box.
    See Moore, *op. cit.*, for detailed references to these deeds in his introduction, p.xi. The system of numbering is not easy to comprehend but it would lead to confusion to start again. Bundle 3, Nos B 4-5, Bundle 8, No.A4, Bundle 9, Nos.J1, 3, 5-6, 8-11, 14; K 1-3, 6; Bundle 12, Nos.F, 1-4; Bundle 15, Nos.A5 and 7.
41. Ibid.
42. U.B.D. the Goldney House Deed Box, Bundle red K,6 21 Dec 1736, insurance policy, No.5357.
43. McGrath, *Merchant Venturers*, pp.187-8.
44. B. Little, 'The Gloucestershire Spas: an eighteenth century parallel', in P. McGrath and J. Cannon (eds.), *Essays in Bristol and Gloucestershire History*, for the *T.B.G.A.S.*, 1976, p.171.
45. Latimer, *Annals of the 17th C*, p.471.
46. Bryan Little, *The City and County of Bristol*, 1954, p.231.
47. V. Waite, *The Bristol Hotwell*, Bristol Branch of the Historical Assoc., 1960, reprinted 1977, pp.6-9.
48. Sketchley, *op. cit.*, p.119.
49. Waite, *op. cit.*, p.6.
50. Ibid., p.3.
51. Little, 'Gloucestershire Spas', *op. cit.*, p.172.
52. M. Campbell, 'The Strangers' Burial Ground', *Avon Archaeological Council Newsletter*, Spring 1977, pp.7-9.
53. J. Latimer, *Annals of the 18th C*, p.390.
54. Sketchley, *op. cit.*, p.70.
55. Ibid., p.87.
56. Latimer, *Annals of the 18th C*, p.245.
57. G. R. Powell, *The Bristol Stage*, 1919, p.13.
58. Latimer, *Annals of the 18th C*, pp.62-3.
59. Waite, *op.cit.*, p.11.
60. Latimer, *Annals of the 18th C*, p.64.
61. Ibid., p.497.
62. Ibid., p.439.
63. Quoted by W. Ison, *The Georgian Buildings of Bristol*, 1952, reprinted 1978, p.160.
64. Latimer, *Annals of the 18th C*, p.463.
65. Ibid., p.490.
66. Waite, *op. cit.*, p.14.
67. Moore, *op. cit.*, pp.xii and xiii.
68. *See* Moore's estimate, *op. cit.*, Introduction, p.xxiii, based on B.R.O. EP/A/2/2.
69. Abstract, presented to the House of Commons of the answers and returns made to the Population Act of 41st.Geo.III, the 29 June 1801, p.126.
70. Latimer, *Annals of 18th Century*, p.494.
71. Ibid., p.422.
72. W. Minchinton, *The Trade of Bristol in the 18th century*, B.R.S. publication, Vol.XX, p.180, Appendix D.
73. A. Buchanan and N. Cossons, *Industrial Archaeology of the Bristol Region*, 1969, p.39.

References to Chapter Six
 1. B.A.O. 12160/10 List of Leases. No.13 Rev. J. Power to Hugh Williams, 16 Sept., 5th Wm. and Mary, 1693, 'a piece of woody ground 255' × 100'', No.15, Francis Hooke to George Worth, 3 May 1705 and B.R.O. 11178(20) Francis Freeman, Gent. and Thomas Garland, 12 Nov. 1723.
 2. 25-26 March 1721.
    See W. Ison, *The Georgian Buildings of Bristol*, 1978, p.158.
 3. S.M.V. Abstracts of Leases 1752-1783, fol.3, 3 Nov. 1752.
 4. Ison, *op. cit.*, pp.47-8 for George Tully, pp.157-61 for Dowry Square, pp.201-2 for Dowry Parade.
 5. S.M.V. Inventory of Deeds, Box 10, Bundle 36, 1 May 1763, Joseph Thomas to Robert Comfort 'Daniel's Ground Lot 2', Joseph Thomas to Matthew Gilbert 'Daniel's Ground Lot 3'.
 6. J. Summerson, *Georgian London*, 1962, pp.29-31.
 7. B.A.O. AC/JS/8 for the Tinker's Close estate in the 1730s and J. Latimer, *Annals of the 18th C*, p.261 for the 'College Street' development in White's Garden.
    See also my M.Litt. dissertation 'The Elbridge, Woolnough and Smyth Families of Bristol ...', University of Bristol, 1971, p.xii, Introduction, for Jarrit Smith.

8. J. R. Ward, 'Speculative Building at Bristol and Clifton 1783-1793', *Business History*, Vol.XX. No.1, 1978.
9. S.M.V. Minute Book 4, 9 July 1719 and 7 Oct. 1719.
10. Ibid., 29 April 1723.
11. S.M.V. Minute Books 1733-97, *Index to Proceedings*, 16 Jan. 1749, p.223.
12. Ibid., 2 Nov. 1749.
    See also 19 March 1753 and 6 June 1757 for Ann Hibbs and *Abstract of Leases*, 1752-83, fol.1, states that Ann Hibbs, Joseph Lewis, Gent. and John Deverall, surgeon, and Richard Coombe, Esq. previously held leases dated 2 Nov. 13 Wm.III and 3 Nov. 13 Wm.III.
13. S.M.V. Hall Book 11, 22 May 1786, p.227.
14. Ibid.
15. Ibid., 15 May 1786, p.219.
16. S.M.V. *Index to Proceedings*, Minute Books, 17 Jan. 1750, p.223.
17. S.M.V. *Abstract of Leases*, 1752-1783, 3 Nov. 1752, fol.2.
18. Ibid., 8 Nov. 1758, fol.106.
19. Ibid., Minute Book 8, 21 Dec. 1761, p.137.
20. S.M.V. Minute Book, 20 Oct. 1764, p.233.
21. S.M.V. Box 12, Bundle 52, Part 1.
22. Ibid., 6 Jan. 1796.
23. S.M.V. Minute Books, 20 Oct. 1764.
24. Ison, *op. cit.*, pp.198-201.
25. Ibid., pp.202-4.
26. Latimer, *Annals of the 18th C*, p.400.
27. B. Little, 'The Gloucestershire Spas: an eighteenth century parallel' in McGrath and Cannon, *Essays in Bristol and Gloucester History*, 1976, p.175.
28. J. de Wilstar, Survey of the Lands of the Manor of Clifton 1746, see note in margin by 'Z', Mr. Hodges' Freehold, bought by Mr. Worrall.
29. Ison, *op. cit.*, p.204.
30. S.M.V. Hall Minutes, p.232. S.M.V. and Rev. John Davie, executor of Alexander Daniel, clerk.
31. S.M.V. Hall Book 9, 24 March 1763. Quoted by McGrath in *Merchant Venturers*, p.195.
32. *See* R. A. Buchanan, 'The Construction of the Floating Harbour in Bristol, 1804-1809', *T.B.G.A.S.*, Vol.LXXXVIII, 1969, pp.184-204.
33. S.M.V. Hall Minutes, p.226, S.M.V. and William Champion, 1767/8
34. Ibid.
35. Ibid., p.272, An Indenture of 4 parts following the bankruptcy of William Champion, 3 Sept. 1770.
36. McGrath, *Merchant Venturers*, pp.154-7 and S.M.V. Hall Book 9, 14 June 1770.
37. A. Gomme, M. Jenner and B. Little, *Bristol: An Architectural History*, 1979, Chapter 13.
38. S.M.V. Hall Book 10, 15 June 1778, 'Mr. Beames, the Heir to the late Mr. Power of Clifton'.
39. Ison, *op. cit.*, pp.225-6.
40. *Sarah Farley's Bristol Journal*, 24 May 1788. At this date the paper was owned by Rouths and Co.
41. Ibid., 30 April 1791. Quoted by Latimer, *Annals of the 18th C*, p.494.
42. P.R.O. Chancery Masters' Exhibits, C 110/151, Part 1, Examinations, Depositions and other Proceedings under Commission of Bankruptcy, 22 Oct. 1794, against William Bleuden, Carpenter, Builder, Dealer and Chapman.
43. B.A.O. 6609(57), Nov. 1797 Bankruptcy Hearing, Thomas Wiltshire, William Heard and Saml. Mereweather v. William Watt's estate. B.A.O. Corporation deeds 12746, 13625, 13942, 16133, 16305(6), 16857, 18088, 19328, 19905.
44. J. R. Ward, 'Speculative Building', p.9.
45. Ibid., quoting P.R.O. E 112/1939/658.
46. P.R.O. B1/118 f.84-7, 22 Oct. 1794.
47. P.R.O. C 110/151 Part 1, Brief for the Plaintiffs Simon Oliver and Harry Elderton, assignees of William Bleuden.
48. P.R.O. B1/118, f.86.
49. P.R.O. C 110/115 Copy of Bankrupt's last examination at the *White Lyon*, Broad Street, 27 Jan. 1795.

50. P.R.O. Court Bankruptcy Order Book B1/86, fol.189-95.
51. P.R.O. B1/86 fol.189-95 *re* Mariners' Path development for Rev. John Taylor.
52. Ward, *op. cit.*, p.11.
53. S.M.V. Hall Book 11, 9 March 1789, p.489.
54. P.R.O. Exchequer K.R. Exhibits E 140, Bundle 141-4 and 145, Letter Books and Account Books.
55. Latimer, *Annals of the 18th C*, p.505.
56. Ibid.
57. Ison, *op. cit.*, pp.228-31.
58. *Sketchley Directory*, 1775, p.60.
59. Ward, *op. cit.*, p.16.
60. Ibid., p.7, quoting B.A.O. Corporation deeds 16305(6).
61. B.A.O. 30638(1)b 30 May 1792.
62. Ison, *op. cit.*, p.228.
63. Ibid., p.229.
64. S.M.V. Hall Book 12, 27 Oct. and 24 Nov. 1791, pp.166 and 180.
65. Ison, *op. cit.*, p.231 ff.
66. S.M.V. Hall Book 12, 12 Sept. 1792, p.219.
67. Ibid., *re* Lockier's plans for Honeypen Hill.
68. Ibid., p.220.
69. Ibid., 3 Nov. 1791, p.170.
70. Ison, *op. cit.*, p.227.
71. S.M.V. Hall Book 10, 22 May 1786, p.227, 'James Cross, as Assigned of two several Indentures of Lease and bearing date 15 June 1753, granted to Paul Fisher for a Term of 99 years'.
72. S.M.V. Hall Book 12, 20 March 1792, p.189 and 22 May 1792, p.203.
73. Ibid., 12 Sept. 1792, p.219.
74. Ison, *op. cit*, p.234.
75. Sketchley, *op. cit.*, p.102.
76. F. Farley, *Journal*, 12 Nov. 1792, quoted by Ison, *op. cit.*, p.226.
77. Ison, *op. cit.*, p.226.
78. Ibid., pp.235-6.
79. Ibid., pp.213-4, 224-5, 226.
80. S.M.V. Hall Book 11, 16 Oct. 1788, 9 March 1789, p.489.
81. Ibid., 9 March 1789, p.489 and 31 Aug. 1789, p.526.
82. F. Farley, *Journal*, 29 Nov., p.469.
83. Latimer, *Annals of the 18th C*, p.469.
84. L. S. Presnell, *Country Banking in the Industrial Revolution*, 1956, Appendix 28, The Crisis of 1793: Henry Thornton's estimate of the extent of bankruptcy, 7 March 1793, pp.546-7.
85. J. R. Ward, 'Speculative Building at Bristol and Clifton, 1783-1793', *Business History*, Vol.XX, No.1, Jan. 1978.
86. C. W. Chalklin, *The Provincial Towns of Georgian England*, 1974, pp.180-7; Ward, *op. cit.*, p.16; F. Hyde, B. Parkinson and S. Marriner, 'The Port of Liverpool and the Crisis of 1793', *Economics*, Nov. 1951, Vol.18, pp.363-78.
87. Latimer, *Annals of the 18th C*, p.495.
88. Hyde et al., *op. cit.*, quoting Sir John Clapham, *The Bank of England*, 1944, p.262 and T. Tooke, *A History of Prices*, 1838, Gregory (ed.), 1928, Vol.1, who believed the outbreak of the war was less significant that the overextension of credit and the paper circulation.
89. Ward, *op. cit.*, p.14, quoting P.R.O. C 110/115.
90. S.M.V. Hall Book 13, 11 April 1805.
91. J. Latimer, *Annals of the 19th C*, p.514.

References to Chapter Seven
 1. J. Latimer, *Annals of the 18th C*, p.162.
 2. A. B. Beavan, *Bristol Lists, Municipal and Miscellaneous*, 1899.
 3. Bonner and Middleton, *Bristol Journal*, 8 Jan. 1785.
 4. W. Minchinton, *The Trade of Bristol in the Eighteenth Century*, Bristol Record Society Pbl., Vol.XX, 1957, pp.143-5.

5. J. W. Daymer Powell, *Bristol Privateers and Ships of War*, 1930, p.182.
6. D. Richardson, *Bristol, Africa and the 18th century Slave Trade to America*, Vol.1, The Years of Expansion, 1698-1729, Bristol Records Society Pub., Vol.XXXVIII, 1986, p.169.
7. H. Hobhouse, *Hobhouse Memoirs*, 1927.
8. D. Richardson, *The Bristol Slave Traders: A Collective Portrait*, Bristol Hist. Assoc., 1985, p.29.
9. Bonner and Middleton, *op. cit.*, 8 Jan. 1785.
10. M. Fedden, *Bristol Vignettes*, pp.96-101.
11. C. H. Cave, *A History of Banking in Bristol, 1750-1899*, 1899, pp.232-3.
12. Daymer Powell, *op. cit.*, p.90.
13. Ibid., pp.92-101.
14. Bristol Central Reference Library, Trade and Commerce, I, Ref. B 4140, *A List of the Company of Merchants trading to Africa ...*, 1 June 1759.
15. D. Richardson, *Bristol, Africa and the 18th century Slave Trade to America*, pp.57, 64, 89.
16. Ibid., p.26.
17. Cave, *op. cit.*, pp.232-3.
18. Earl Fitzwilliam and Sir R. Bourke, *Correspondence of Edmund Burke*, Vol.II, 1844, p.6. On 12 Jan. 1775 Burke reported to Rockingham, 'The alarm among the American merchants is strong, but as yet not strong enough to get the better of their habitual deference to administration'.
19. University of Bristol, *Brickdale Notebooks*, Book II, ff.38-58, Book III, ff.1-19 and Society of Merchant Venturers, *Letters*, quoted by W. Savadge, *The West Country and the American mainland colonies, 1763-83, with special reference to the merchants of Bristol*, unpublished B.Litt. thesis, Oxford, 1952, typescript available in Bristol Central Reference Library.
20. *Correspondence of Edmund Burke*, Vol.II, pp.28-9, quoted by Savadge, *op. cit.*, p.449.
21. Latimer, *Annals of the 18th C*, *op. cit.*, p.537.
22. Ibid., p.462, quoting Bonner and Middleton, *op. cit.*, 8 Jan. 1785.
23. Ibid., pp.142-6.
24. Minchinton, *op. cit.*, Vol.XX, pp.82-101, 150-1.
25. H. Hobhouse, *Memoirs of the Hobhouse Family*, 1927.
26. S.M.V. Minute Books 1733-97, 16 Jan. 1749, p.223, and 2 Nov. 1749, 19 March 1753 and 6 June 1757.
27. Ibid., 4 Feb. 1767.
28. Farley, *op. cit.*, 26 May 1792, Vol.XLIII.
29. Hobhouse, *op. cit.*, p.7.
30. Ibid., p.15.
31. Minchinton, *op. cit.*, Vol.XX, pp.18 and xvi.
32. Richardson, *Bristol, Africa and the 18th century Slave Trade*, p.xxi.
33. Ibid.
34. Richardson, *Bristol Slave Traders*, p.16.
35. Hobhouse, *op. cit.*, 21.
36. Ibid.
37. Ibid.
38. Richardson, *Bristol Slave Traders*, p.29.
39. Hobhouse, *op. cit.*, p.22.
40. Bristol Central Reference Library, Ref B 4140, Trade and Commerce I, *A List of the Company of Merchants trading to Africa*.
41. Richardson, *Bristol Slave Traders*, p.3.
42. Hobhouse, *op. cit.*, p.24.
43. Ibid., p.26.
44. Ibid. Henry Hobhouse, born 25 April 1742, educated Winchester and Brasenose College, Oxford, B.A. 1762, M.A. 1764, Middle Temple 1762, called to the Bar 1766.
45. Ibid., p.20.
46. Latimer, *Annals of the 18th C.*, p.537.
47. *Sketchley Directory*, 1775, p.11.
48. Bonner and Middleton, *op. cit.*, 8 Jan. 1785.
49. Daymer Powell, *op. cit.*, p.182.

50. Richardson, *Bristol, Africa and the Slave Trade*, p.169.
51. Minchinton, *op. cit.*, pp.8, 143.
52. P. T. Underdown, 'Henry Cruer and Edmund Burke: Colleagues and Rivals at the Bristol Election, 1774', *William and Mary Quarterly*, Vol.XV, Jan. 1958.
53. Latimer, *Annals of the 18th C*, p.3.
54. G. E. Weare, *Edmund Burke's connection with Bristol from 1774 till 1780*, 1894, p.67.
55. W. Minchinton, *Politics and the Port of Bristol in the 18th century*, p.111.
56. Ibid., p.112.
57. Underdown, *op. cit.*
    See also Bristol Central Reference Library, scrapbook *Bristol Elections, 1774-90*.
58. Latimer, *Annals of the 18th C*, p.410.
59. Ibid., p.411.
60. Ibid., p.445.
61. Ibid., p.456.
62. Beavan, *op. cit.*, pp.211-5.
    See also Savadge, *op. cit.*, Appendix E, 'Length of Service on the Common Council of Bristol, 1720-'.
63. Fedden, *op. cit.*, pp.96-101.
64. Bonner and Middleton, *op. cit.*, 8 Jan. 1785.
65. Daymer Powell, *op. cit.*, p.146. Letter of Marque ships had the right to attack enemy vessels. They were merchantmen whose crews were paid prize money in addition to their wages. The owners had to apply for a warrant to the Commissioners of the Admiralty.
    See Daymer Powell, *op. cit.*, p.xvii.
66. Ibid., p.150, 182.
67. Ibid., p.188.
68. Ibid., p.197.
69. Ibid., p.237.
70. Latimer, *Annals of the 18th C*, p.535.
    See also Savadge, *op. cit.*, Appendix E.
71. Ibid., p.536.
72. Fedden, *op. cit.*, pp.96-101.

References to Chapter Eight
1. B. Little, *The City and Council of Bristol*, 1954, Appendix 1, p.327.
2. J. Latimer, *Annals of the 18th C*, pp.306, 323, 324.
3. R. Atkyns, *Ancient and Present State of Glostershire*.
4. B.R.O. EP/A/2/1-2, using a multiplier of five.
    See J. S. Moore, *Clifton and Westbury Probate Inventories*, p.xxiii.
5. S. Rudder, *A New History of Gloucestershire*, 1779.
6. B.R.O. EP/A/2/2 Nos. of families × 4.9 – the multiplier based on a comparison of average family size for nearby parishes in 1801 census.
    See Moore, *op. cit.*, p.xxiii.
7. *Census of Great Britain in 1801*, Vol.2.
8. Census.
9. Census.
10. Census.
11. Census.
12. Census.
13. Moore, *op. cit.*, 1981, p.xxxv.
14. Dr. A. B. Prowse, *Notes on St Andrew's, Clifton*, together with a transcription of the registers of Births, Marriages and Deaths, *c*.1991, pp.20 and 21.
15. J. Leech, *Rural Rides of the Bristol Churchgoer*, 1843-45, reprinted 1982, pp.12-13, quoted by M. V. Campbell, Introduction, p.iv.
16. A. Yarborough, 'Geographical and Social Origins of Bristol Apprentices, 1542-65', *T.B.G.A.S.*, Vol.98, 1981, pp.113-29.
17. I. M. Kirby, *Diocese of Bristol; A Catalogue of the Records of the Bishop and Archdeacons, and of the Dean and Chapter*, Bristol Corporation, 1970.

18. B.R.O. EP/A/31/22.
19. B.R.O. DC/E/3/8, pp.55-86, quoted by Moore, *op. cit.*, p.xxxvii.
20. G. T. Clark, *Report to the General Board of Health on the Sewerage and Supply of Water and the Sanitary Condition of ... Bristol*, 1850, pp.91-3.
21. S. R. Woods, 'Shirehampton: the 1851 Census', *T.B.G.A.S.*, Vol.LXXXIX, 1970, p.147.
22. Ibid., p.153.

References to Chapter Nine
 1. S.M.V. Hall Book 18, p.113, 13 Oct. 1837; p.125, 3 Nov. 1837.
 2. R. A. Buchanan, 'The Construction of the Floating Harbour in Bristol, 1804-9', *T.B.G.A.S.*, Vol.LXXXVIII, 1969, pp.184-204.
 3. A. F. Williams, 'Bristol Port Plans and Improvement Schemes of the 18th Century', *T.B.G.A.S.*, Vol.81, 1962, pp.138-88.
 4. J. Latimer, *Annals of the 19th C*, pp.16-7.
 5. *Reports and Abstracts of the Census of Great Britain*, presented to the House of Commons, 29 June 1801, of the answers and returns made to the Population Act of 41st Geo.III, p.126, Clifton appears under Barton Regis, *Reports and Abstracts of the Census 1861-1951*, Sessional Papers.
 6. B.R.O. 31660 (1) Abstract of Title to 26 The Mall.
 7. S.M.V. Box 7, Bundle 2, Part 1, 1602-1674, Indenture 24 Oct. 1668, Lease and Release, being a Conveyance of three-quarters of the Manor of Clifton, except such parts thereof as had been lately sold to Aycliffe Green by William Whittington.
 8. B.R.O. 7837 (30), 4 Oct. 1749, Settlement on the marriage of Edward Maddocks and Mrs. Elizabeth Bevan. This Indenture mentions a previous Lease and Release between John Power and James Bevan and Edmond Rogers describing a plot immediately behind the houses in Dowry Square lately erected by Thomas Oldfield, Gent. and George Tully.
 9. B.R.O. 31660 (1) 24 and 25 April 1787, Lease and Release, John Beames to Henry Dupont, Gent.
10. Ibid.
    See also B.R.O. 31660 (1) 18 and 19 June 1788, Lease and Release, John Beames and John Hughes, Gent.; 22 and 23 Dec. 1788, Lease and Release, John Beames and Robert Bayley; 23 and 24 June 1791, Lease and Release, Robert Bayley and Thomas Coates, wine merchant, and Samuel Powell and Thomas Morgan.
11. W. Ison, *The Georgian Buildings of Bristol*, p.223.
12. B.R.O. 31660 (1) Abstract of Title to No.26 Clifton Mall.
13. B.R.O. 38521 The West Mall, 22 Dec. 1795 to Rev. Thos. Exon, 1 April 1795 to Miss Sarah Whippie, 25 Feb. 1807 to Miss Catherine Chappell.
14. L. Wright, 'Regency Clifton II', *Somerset Countryman*, Jan./March, 1947, p.149.
15. B.R.O. 35716 (1) Clifton Club, notes on its history, 1793-1882.
16. B.R.O. 19488 (1-10) Mortgages *re* Windsor Terrace, John Drew and Isaac Cooke.
17. B.R.O. 32420 29 March 1830, Indenture between Isaac Cooke, Gent. and John Clark of Clifton, Esq.
18. B.R.O. 19590 (1-9), Isaac Cooke and John Drew *re* No.5 Royal York Crescent.
19. S.M.V. Box 14B, Bundle 3, Leases, 1 Oct. 1705, 16 Sept. 1745, 25 Aug. 1756, 11 Nov. 1766, 18 April 1800, 24 June 1808, 9 Dec. 1824.
20. S.M.V. Hall Book 20, 28 Jan. 1846, pp.193-4, Report of the Ferney Close Cttee. Letter from Samuel Hemming to S.M.V.
21. S.M.V. Chancery Papers, S.M.V. versus Lambe, Deane et al. Bundle marked Legal Papers 1682-84. The plea and answer of John Lambe, the defendant.
22. B.R.O. 12149 (5)b Indenture 7 Feb. 1777, Conveyance to Samuel Worrall.
23. Latimer, *Annals of the 18th C*, p.261.
24. B.R.O.12149 (29) 12 March 1875, Miss Sophia Worrall to James Bigwood. (31) 15 May 1875, Miss Sophia Worrall to James R. Shorland, (34) 18 Oct. 1876, Miss Sophia Worrall to John Davies.
25. S.M.V. Map 221 N, Cornwallis House, showing ash pit, well and pump.
26. G. T. Clark, *Report to the General Board of Health*, 1850, p.37.
27. Sir H. T. de la Beche and Dr. L. Playfair, *Report on the Sanitary Condition of Bristol. Health of Towns Commission*, 1845, p.13.
28. Latimer, *Annals of the 19th C*, p.134.

29. P.R.O. B1/118 f.86.
    See also Gentleman's Magazine LXXI, 1806, p.1080.
30. S.M.V. Hall Book 15, 13 March 1821, pp.139-42.
31. S.M.V. Hall Book 17, 11 Feb. 1835, p.292.
32. S.M.V. Hall Book 16, 9 Sept. 1825, pp.72-3.
33. Ibid., 4 Dec. 1829, p.363.
34. S.M.V. Hall Book 14, 3 Jan. 1810, p.94.
35. S.M.V. Hall Book 15, 17 April 1822, p.228.
36. S.M.V. Hall Book 16, 9 Nov. 1825, p.92.
37. Ibid., 5 June 1829, p.332.
38. S.M.V. Hall Book 13, 3 June 1805, p.336.
39. B.R.O. 21782, Box VI, 104/B 21 Feb. 1828.
40. B.R.O. 21782, Box VI 104/B 9 May 1839.
41. S.M.V. Deeds, Box 11A, Bundle 46, 1 June 1728, Lease from the Society to Robert Smith of
    Cecills Littfields.
42. S.M.V. Hall Book 16, 10 Dec. 1824, p.7.
43. Ibid., 10 Nov. 1825, p.104.
44. S.M.V. Hall Book 18, 26 Nov. 1839, p.401.
45. R. and A. Warin, *Portrait of a Zoo, 1835-1985*, 1985, p.9.
46. Bristol, Clifton and West of England Zoological Society Rules and Regulations, Bristol, 1836.
47. A. Green-Armytage, *The Story of Bristol Zoo*, 1964, pp.5-9.
48. Warin, *op. cit.*, p.11.
49. J. E. King, *Clifton College Annals, 1860-1912*, p.xxii.
50. *Illustrated Bristol News*, Vol.21, No.166, Aug. 1973.
51. O. F. Christie, *A History of Clifton College*, 1860-1934, 1935, p.20.
52. Ibid., pp.21-2.
53. C. Crick, *Victorian Buildings in Bristol*, 1975, pp.30, 32.
54. Indenture, 30 Oct. 1844. Conveyance of a Freehold Estate in Clifton, George Rooke Farnall and
    John Kemp and John Swayne, masons. Also citing an Indenture of 25 Nov. 1842 of nine parts.
    Deeds in possession of owners on Vyvyan Terrace.
55. Ibid.
56. Crick, *op. cit.*, p.54.
57. S.M.V. Hall Book 18, 8 Sept. 1837, p.97; 12 Oct. 1838, p.239; 8 May 1840, p.441.
58. S.M.V. Hall Book 19, 11 Feb. 1842, p.214; 13 May 1842, p.240.
59. Ibid., 9 Feb. 1844, p.420.
60. S.M.V. Hall Book 20, 18 Oct. 1844; 22 Nov. 1844, p.71.
61. Ibid., 14 March 1845, p.106.
62. Ibid., 5 June 1845, p.116.
63. Ibid., 16 Oct. 1845, pp.157-68.
64. Ibid.
65. Ibid., 28 Jan. 1846, pp.193-4.
66. Ibid., 26 May 1848, pp.378-9.
67. Ibid., 13 Aug. 1847, pp.315-16.
68. Ibid., 26 May 1848, pp.378-9.
69. S.M.V. Hall Book 21, 14 Dec. 1849, p.37.
70. S.M.V. Hall Book 20, 26 March 1847, p.296.
71. S.M.V. Hall Book 21, 3 Aug. 1855, p.509.
72. S.M.V. Hall Book 23, 13 Dec. 1861, p.171.
73. Ibid., 5 June 1863, p.284.
74. Ibid.
75. S.M.V. Hall Book 24, 15 June 1866, p.92.
76. Ibid., 22 June 1866, p.102.
77. Ibid., 24 Feb. 1869, p.323.
78. Ibid., 21 Jan. 1870, pp.395-6.
79. Ibid., 5 Aug. 1870, p.440.
80. S.M.V. Hall Book 25, 21 Oct. 1870, p.8.

81. Ibid., 27 March 1874, pp.317-8.
82. B.R.O. 32226 Box 39, Unsorted Papers, Clarke, Gwynn and Press. Appointment by Francis Adams, 3 Feb. 1838, to A. G. H. Battersby, H. Bush, Charles L. Walker and Richard B. Ward, Esq.
83. Latimer, *Annals of the 19th C*, pp.320-1.
84. S.M.V. Deeds, Box 11A, Bundle No.46, 29 March 1836.
85. Ibid., 18 Feb. 1853, Deed of Arrangement with respect to various lands belonging to the Society and Francis Adams the Younger and his Trustees.
86. Crick, *op. cit.*, p.54.
87. S.M.V. Hall Book 22, 12 March 1858, p.213; 14 May 1858, p.251; 16 Feb. 1859, p.333.
88. S.M.V. Hall Book 24, 22 June 1866, p.102.
89. Latimer, *Annals of the 19th C*, p.281.
90. Ibid. pp.284-6.
91. McGrath, *Merchant Venturers*, p.426.
92. Latimer, *Annals of the 19th C*, pp.131-4, 375-7.
93. Crick, *op. cit.*, p.55.
94. S.M.V. Hall Book 25, 26 July 1872, p.164ff.
95. Ibid.

References to Chapter Ten
 1. B.R.O. 35831 Plans and Terrier of the Clifton Estate of Francis Adams, Esq., 1884, Map A.
 2. S.M.V. Deeds, Box 14B, Bundle No.2, 27 Oct. 1864 with a plan, 26 June 1865, with a plan and 4 June 1866.
 3. Ibid., 28 April 1865, with a plan and 13 May 1865.
 4. S.M.V. Deeds, Box 14B, Bundle No.5, 25 March 1864.
 5. Ibid., Bundle No.2, 13 May 1865 and Box 14B, Bundle No.1, 1 May 1865.
 6. C. Crick, *Victorian Buildings in Bristol*, 1975, pp.25-7 and T. H. B. Burrough, Bristol, City Heritage Series, 1970, p.88.
 7. S.M.V. Hall Book 24, 15 May 1868, p.256.
 8. S.M.V. Hall Book 25, 7 Dec. 1870, p.25; also Hall Book 24, 3 June 1870; Hall Book 25, 29 Dec. 1871, p.118 and 26 Jan. 1872, p.122; 26 April 1872, p.143; 28 June 1872, p.157.
 9. S.M.V. Hall Book 25, 9 June 1871, p.59.
10. S.M.V. Hall Book 24, 6 May 1870, p.432.
11. S.M.V. Hall Book 26, 31 May 1878, p.180 and 26 July 1878, p.193.
12. Ibid., 28 Feb. 1879, p.239 and 21 Jan. 1881, p.340.
13. *The Builder*, 12 Sept. 1868, p.675, noted by Crick *op. cit.*, p.55.
14. Dr. W. Kay, *Report on the Sanitary Condition of Bristol and Clifton*, 1844, p.3.
15. Ibid., p.6.
16. S.M.V. Hall Book 25, 22 March 1871, p.43.
17. S.M.V. Hall Book 26, 31 Dec. 1875, p.23.
18. H. Reid in J. Belsey et al., *Bristol: The Growing City*, 1986, p.20.
19. J. Latimer, *Annals of the 19th C*, p.516.
20. P. Guedalla, *The Second Empire*, 1922, p.188-9.
21. 'Clifton's Eugenie house', *Bristol and West Country Illustrated*, No.25, June 1979.
22. Reid, *op. cit.*, p.22.
23. *The Jubilee Book of the Clifton High School, 1877-1927*, 1927, pp.14-15.
24. N. Glenday and M. Price, *Clifton High School, 1877-1977*, 1977, p.11.
    See also B.R.O. 40170, Records of Clifton High School (6 boxes), Box 1.
25. Glenday and Price, *op. cit*, p.34.
26. Ibid., p.74.
27. C. M. MacInnes and W. F. Whittard (eds.), *Bristol and its Adjoining Counties*, 1955, p.329.
28. T. H. B. Burrough, *Bristol*, p.93.
29. D. Carlton, *A University for Bristol*, 1984, p.132.
30. S.M.V. Hall Book 27, 27 Sept. 1889, p.303.
31. Ibid., 26 Sept. 1890, p.350.
32. Ibid., 27 Feb. 1891, p.379.
33. S. Jones, *Whiteladies Walks: 5 Town Trails in a Victorian Conservation Area*, 1976, p.5.
34. S.M.V. Hall Book 9, 24 March 1763.

35. B.R.O. 12149 Schedule of Deeds, 28 and 29 Nov. 1790.
    See 12149(17) Deed of partition, 10 April 1815 between the Devisees, in trust for Saml. Worrall deceased, and Mr. Thomas Sime, to Andrew Pope Esq.
    See also 12149(27) for a map.
36. B.R.O. 12149 (29) 12 March 1875, Miss Sophia Worrall and John William Miles (banker), to James Bigwood for £2,280 10s. for ground between Belgrave Rd. and Worrall Rd.
    B.R.O. 12149 (30) 12 March 1875, Miss Sophia Worrall and John William Miles (banker), to John T. Jackson for £500 for ground off Worrall Rd.
    B.R.O. 12149 (31) 15 May 1875, Miss Sophia Worrall and John William Miles (banker), to J. R. Shorland for £8,000, four acres along Worrall Rd. below Anglesea Place.
    B.R.O. 12149 (34) 18 Oct. 1876, Miss Sophia Worrall and John William Miles (banker), to John Davies. Ground in Pembroke Rd.
    B.R.O. 12149 (35) 9 March 1878, Miss Sophia Worrall and John Williams Miles (banker), to John Davies. Ground near Pembroke Rd.
37. Latimer, *Annals of the 19th C*, p.318.
38. Jones, *op. cit.*, 26.
39. Latimer, *Annals of the 19th C*, pp.71-3, 100-1.
40. S.M.V. Hall Book 29, 22 May 1903, p.47, and 31 March 1905, p.129, and 29 Sept. 1905, p.152, and 30 March 1906, p.184.
41. McGrath, *Merchant Venturers*, p.471.
42. *Clifton Digest*, Vol.6, Issue 2, 11 August 1989, p.1.
43. Crick, *op. cit.*, p.57.
44. Reid, *op. cit.*, p.29.
45. Latimer, *Annals of the 19th C*, pp.383-4.
46. Ibid., pp.387-9.
47. Ibid., pp.462-5.
48. Crick, *op. cit*, p.6.
49. S.M.V. Hall Book 16, 5 March 1830, p.378, and 16 April 1830, p.382; Hall Book 17, 20 April 1836, pp.389-90, and 11 May 1836, p.394, and 17 Aug. 1836, p.418.
50. Latimer, *Annals of the 19th C*, p.199.
51. S.M.V. Hall Book 16, 2 April 1828, p.273; Hall Book 17, 17 Dec. 1834, p.282.
52. E. Ralph, *The Downs, 1861-1961*, 1961, p.11.
53. S. Hutton, *Bristol and its Famous Associations*, 1907, and a fuller bibliography see B. Little, *The City and County of Bristol*, 1954, pp.374-6.
54. A. Carter, 'The Crescent to beat all Crescents', *Illustrated Bristol News*, Oct. 1963.

References to Appendix One
1. S.M.V. Chancery Papers, 1682-4, The Plaintiffs' Title to the three fourths parts of the Manor of Clifton, 28 April 1683.
2. S.M.V. Chancery Papers, S.M.V. versus Lambe, Deane et al. Bundle marked Legal Papers, 1682-4, the plea and answer of John Lambe, the defendant.
3. B.R.O. 32835 (s) AC/M 15 Survey of Manor, 1625.
4. B.R.O. 05178 Marriage Settlement of Edward Freeman 30 July 1698.
5. U.B. Deeds *re* 'Hollylands' for Duncan House Cottage, Francis Freeman to Sir Thomas Daniels of Bristol, Merchant, Conveyance in Fee Farm, 15 Feb. 1750, 'by him the said Francis Freeman and Edward Freeman Esq., his late uncle, deceased ...'.
    See also B.R.O. 21782, Box XVI, 115/1 Deeds of Manilla Hall *re* 'Hollylands', 20 Dec. 1736, Indenture of Lease and Release between Francis Freeman, Gent. and Edward Parker, Yeoman.
6. S.M.V. Box 'A', Bundle No.2, by Indenture enrolled in Chancery, 3 Nov. 1758, Michaelmas Term, 32 Geo.II.
7. S.M.V. Miscellaneous Papers Box, 18th and 19th centuries, 26 May 1761, Shute Adams to S.M.V.
8. Sir Francis Hyett, 'Sir George Onesiphorus Paul', in *T.B.G.A.S.*, Vol.51, 1929, p.143-68. Onesiphorus Paul married three times. Catherine Freeman (d.20 Oct. 1766) was his second wife and there were no offspring. By his first marriage with Jane Blackburn (d.26 May 1748) he had three children, Sir George Onesiphorus Paul, Elizabeth and Jane, but Sir George never married and Elizabeth (d.1772) and Jane had no children.

9. S.M.V. Box 'A', Bundle No.2, 3 Nov. 1758, Abstract of Title of Francis Adams Esq. to Messuages, Lands, Tenements, Rents, Pews, Hereditaments and Premises in the Parish of Clifton.
    See also Box 'A', Bundle No.2, 1850, Abstract of Title to a Close of land called Lower Lidfield.
10. Bristol Central Reference Library, B.31723, Adams Estate Act, 15 and 16 Vict. Cap. 8., 1852.
11. B.R.O. 35831 Plans and Terrier of the Clifton Estate of Francis Adams, Esq., 1884.
12. A. A. Dibben, *Title Deeds*, The Historical Association, 1968, pp.9-11.

References to Appendix Two
1. P.R.O. C 104, Creagh v Rogers, Boxes 36-40 and 160-1. Boxes 36, 37 and 40 are divided into two boxes each.
2. Ibid., Box 36, Part 2, Articles of Agreement, 10 May 1708, 'part owners of the New-built Shipp called the Duke, burthened about 350 tons', similarly, 'the New-built Shipp called Duchesse'.
3. Lt. Col. B. M. H. Rogers, 'Woodes Rogers's Privateering Voyage of 1708-11', *Mariner's Mirror*, Vol.19, No.2, 1933, pp.196-211.
4. E. Cooke, *Voyage to the South Sea and round the World*, 2 Vols., 1712, Introduction, p.13 for list of subscribers. Also for the *Constitution of a Council* for directing the affairs fo the ships *Duke* and *Dutchess* and for the *Agreement* between the owners and the crew.
5. P.R.O. C 104, Box 36, Part 2, Orders and Instructions to Captain Woodes Rogers.
6. P.R.O. C 104, Box 36, Part 2, Thomas Goldney to the owners and proprietors of the ships *Duke* and *Dutchess*.
7. Captain Woodes Rogers, *A Cruising Voyage round the World first to the South Seas, thence to the East Indies, and homewards by the Cape of Good Hope. Begun in 1708, and finish'd in 1711, containing a Journal of all the remarkable Transactions ...*, London, 1712, Introduction, p.iv.
8   C. D. Lee, 'Alexander Selkirk and the last voyage of the Cinque Ports Galley', *Mariners' Mirror*, Vol.73, No.4, Nov. 1987, pp.385-99.
9. Woodes Rogers, *op. cit.*, p.125.
10. P.R.O. C 104, Box 36, Part 2, Captain Courtney's Committee Book, June 1710.
11. Ibid., 8 Aug. 1707.
12. P.R.O. C 104, Box 37, Part 2, Orders and Instructions to Capt. Woodes Rogers.
13. Edward Cooke, *Voyage to the South Sea*, p.345.
14. P.R.O. C 104, Box 37, Account Book of the *Duke* and *Dutchess*, fol.40-7.
15. Woodes Rogers, *op. cit.*, pp.329-31.
16. P.R.O. C 104, Box 36, Part 2, *John Parker's Minute Book*, from Aug. 1708-Aug. 1711, of all Committees held on board the *Duke* and *Dutchess*, together with copies of all letters and other communications, p.137, 14-25 Aug. 1711.
17. P.R.O. C 104, Box 37, Part 2, Orders and Instructions, 14 July 1708.

Bibliography

PRIMARY SOURCES

Manuscripts

The Merchants' Hall
Although the Merchants' Hall was destroyed by bombs in the Second World War, there was no fire and the unique records of the Society survived. They were temporarily housed with the Corporation of Bristol, and were then moved to the Merchants' Hall, The Promenade, Clifton.

Abstract of Leases, 1716, 1752-83, 2 vols.
Bill in Chancery, S.M.V. v. Lambe, Deane et al. 1682-4, Depositions and Answers and later papers to 1686.
Indexes to Proceedings of the Hall, 1708-1925, 11 vols., referred to as Minute Books.
Legal papers relating to S.M.V. and the Adams family.
Letter Books, 1747-1845, 1851-63, 13 vols.
Maps and plans of the manor, roads and buildings, 18th and 19th centuries.
Proceedings of the Hall, 1639 onwards. 28 vols., referred to as Hall Books. These have been microfilmed and copies are available in Bristol Reference Library.
Property Deeds of the Manor, 1596-1960. *See* Elizabeth Ralph's separate catalogue of this magnificent collection at the Merchants' Hall. Property Deeds relating to the Hotwells, 1652-1925. *See* Elizabeth Ralph's separate catalogue at the Merchants' Hall.
Miscellaneous Papers, 1761-92, 1810-1926.
Registers of Leases, 1665-1850, 1716-1852, 10 vols., referred to as Abstract of Grants.
Samuel Worrall's enclosure of land called Shortgrove, believed to be part of Durdham Down, 1788-95.
Survey of lands held on lives, 1822, 1 vol.
Valuation of Clifton 1826, 1 vol.
1746 Survey and Plan of Clifton, de Wilstar.
1806 White's Plan and Terrier of Clifton.

University of Bristol
Brickdale Notebooks, 1771-4. Matthew Brickdale's minutes of debates in the House of Commons.
Property Deeds relating to Goldney House, Rodney Lodge, Duncan House, Clifton Hill House, Mortimer House, Callendar House.

Public Record Office
Chancery Masters' Exhibits (Master-Tinney), P.R.O. C 104/ Box Nos.36-40, Creagh v. Rogers (36, 37, 39 and 40 are usable but 38 is not) relating to distribution of Prize Money of *Duke and Dutchess*, Privateers, Bristol, 1708-15.

Chancery Masters' Exhibits, P.R.O. C 110/151, Examinations depositions and other proceedings under Commission of Bankruptcy, 22 Oct 1794 v. William Bleuden. Bankrupt's last examination at White Lyon, Broad Street, Bristol, 27 January 1795. B1/86, f.189-95, B1/88, f.16-19, B1/118, f.84-7.
Exchequer K.R. exhibits, P.R.O. E 140, Bundles 141-5, relating to Harry Elderton's bankruptcy. Letter Books and Diaries.

Bristol Record Office
B.R.O. 32835(s)AC/M 15 Henry Lilly's 1625 Survey of the Smaller Manor of Clifton.
B.R.O. 6609(11) The 1668 Conveyance of Manor of Clifton.
B.R.O. 7837(25) Stephen Stringer acquires Edmond Watt's estate.
B.R.O. 05178 Marriage Settlement 1698 by Edward Freeman of one quarter of Manor of Clifton.
B.R.O. 12149(1-35) for Sam Worrall's estates.
B.R.O. 21782 (Clarke, Gwynn and Press, Solicitors, Boxes VI and VII) for Hurle and Shore estates.
B.R.O. 32173/2c Abstract of Paul Fisher's will.
B.R.O. 35831 Plans and Terrier of Francis Adams' estates in Clifton.
B.R.O. 21782, Box XVI,115/1, Deeds of Manilla Hall, 1736-1902, originally Freeman's Ground.
B.R.O. 35716(1) Clifton Club Notes 1793-1882.
B.R.O. 32226 (Clarke, Gwynne and Press, Solicitors, Box 39, unsorted), Deeds *re* Victoria Rooms.
B.R.O. 32131 Deeds *re* 'The 8 Acres' – Pembroke Road.
B.R.O. 39524 Deeds deposited by Messrs. Meade-King, Solicitors, *re* Richmond Place, Manilla Road, Upper Belgrave Road and Anglesea Place.
B.R.O. 6609(62)s 1811 Deed *re* Clifton Place.
B.R.O. 32420(5) Deeds *re* Royal York Crescent 1817-1966.
B.R.O. 19488(10) Isaac Cooke's mortgages with John Drew *re* Windsor Terrace.
B.R.O. 19590(9) Isaac Cooke's mortgage with John Drew *re* 5 Royal York Crescent.
B.R.O. 40170 Records of Clifton High School for Girls, 1877-1959.
B.R.O. 4045 Records *re* Clifton College.
B.R.O. 22938(6) Maps and plans *re* Clifton National Schools.
B.R.O. 31660(1-22) Deeds *re* The Mall (*See* (1) for Ayliffe Green's Will, dated 17 Oct 1690).
B.R.O. 38251 Deeds *re* West Mall.
B.R.O. 32173/23, 35(e)s, Rownham Meads excavation 1804.
B.R.O. 3579 and 12160(1-10) Lease of small holdings in Lower Clifton by Robert Hooke and John and Francis Hooke.
B.R.O. 11178(20) and (21)s 1723 Lease of house by Limekilns, Francis Freeman and Thomas Garland.
B.R.O. 6682(1)(3)(7)(11-13)s Clifton Deeds 1653-78, 1712.
B.R.O. 32173 2(a-c)s Abstract of Title to Clifton Manor, 1712-1822.
B.R.O. 13250 Deed of Settlement, Rodney House, Clifton.
B.R.O. 05178 and 7837(25-35) Clifton Manor.
B.R.O. 8930(7) Indenture 1741 Francis Freeman and Ivyleaf Russ.
B.R.O. 11177(3) Clifton Hill House.
B.R.O. Transcript CM6 1538-1681, Clifton Parish Registers, St Andrew's.
B.R.O. SF/A1/13 Minutes of Men's Meeting, Society of Friends.
B.R.O. SF/F1/2 Records of Collection from 1763, Society of Friends.

B.R.O. 38640/26 Goldney family tree.
B.R.O. 38640 Documents deposited by the Goldney family.

Gloucester City Library
Furney, R., Four Manuscript Notebooks by a master at the Crypt Grammar School (1719-24), made in 1721 from original records and deeds and particularly a copy of MSS Rawlinson, C 790, in the Bodleian library, Oxford.
Hockaday Collections 5(4) Administrations for Glos. and Bristol, 1567, extracted from Diocesan records.
Hockaday Collections 5(5) Articles of enquiry and injunctions for dioceses, 1253-1707.
Hockaday Collections 13(3) Manuscripts in Lambeth Palace library, the P.R.O. and British Museum relating to the dioceses of Bristol and Gloucester.
Hockaday Collections 13(4) Abstracts of documents in the Bodleian library relating to Gloucestershire.

Bristol Reference Library
Proceedings of the Merchant Venturers' Hall from 1639 on microfilm.
Jefferies' manuscripts, Vol.XIII, *re* African slave trade, particularly Isaac Hobhouse, pp.1, 7, 9-158; Vol.X, pp.17-135 Matthew Brickdale, particularly the collection of Election Manifestos; Vol.VIII, Farr family, Vol.IV and XI, Elton family; Clifton Manor, Vol.II, p.17, Vol.V p.97, Vol.XII, pp.143 and 211, Vol.XII Clifton Churches, p.131.
Microfilms of P.R.O. 435, HO 107/(2) 1952, the Census of 1851, 2 reels B 23916 and B27294.

Edited Material

Caley, J. and Hunter, J., *Valor Ecclesiasticus*, 6 vols., Records Commission (1810-34).
Campbell, M. V., *Transcripts of the Memorials of the Church and Churchyard of St Andrew's, Clifton*, Bristol Record Society and University of Bristol Extra-Mural Dept. (1987).
Carlyle, T., *Oliver Cromwell's Letters and Speeches*, 1846, Everyman (1908).
Chadwyck-Healey, C., *Bellum Civile*, Somerset Record Society, XVIII (1902).
Douglas, D. C. and Greenaway, G. W., *English Historical Documents*, Vol.II (1946).
Fosbrooke, T. D., *Abstracts of Records and Manuscripts respecting the County of Gloucestershire*, 2 vols. (1807).
Garmonsway, G. N., *Anglo-Saxon Chronicle*, Everyman (1960).
Hollis, D., *Calendar of the Bristol Apprentice Book*, 1532-42, Bristol Record Society Publ., Vol.XIV (1949).
McGrath, P., *Records Relating to the Society of Merchant Venturers of the City of Bristol in the Seventeenth Century*, Bristol Record Society Publ., Vol.XVII (1952).
Minchinton, W. E., *Politics and the Port of Bristol in the Eighteenth Century*, Bristol Record Society Publ., Vol.XXIII (1963).
Minchinton, W. E., *The Trade of Bristol in the Eighteenth Century*, Bristol Record Society Publ., Vol.XX (1957).
Moore, J. S., *Clifton and Westbury Probate Inventories 1609-1761*, University of Bristol (1981).
Moore, J. S., *Domesday Book, No.15, Gloucestershire*, Gen. ed. John Morris, Phillimore, Chichester (1982).
Ralph E. and Hardwick, N., *Calendar of the Bristol Apprentice Book 1542-52*, Bristol Record Society Publ., Vol.XXXIII (1980).

Richardson, D., *Bristol, Africa and the Eighteenth Century Slave Trade to America*, Vol.I, The Years of Expansion, 1698-1729, and Vol.II, The Years of Ascendancy, 1730-45, Bristol Record Society Publ., Vols.XXXVIII and XXXIX (1986/7).

Stubbs, W., *Select Charters, Illustrative of English Constitutional History*, Clarendon, Oxford (1890).

Books and Pamphlets

Atkyns, Sir R., *The Ancient and Present State of Gloucestershire* (1712).

Barret, W., *The History and Antiquities of the City of Bristol* (1789).

Caesar, J., *The Gallic War*, Book V, trans. H. J. Edwards, Loeb Classical Library (1917).

Clark, G. T., *Report to the General Board of Health on a Preliminary Inquiry into the Sewerage, Drainage and Supply of Water and the Sanitary Condition of the Inhabitants of the City and County of Bristol* (1850).

Cooke, E., *Voyage to the South Seas and round the World*, 2 vols., London (1712).

De la Beche, Sir H., *Report on the Sanitary Condition of Bristol Health of Towns Commission* (1845).

Fitzwilliam, C. W. and Bourke, R., *Correspondence of the Rt. Hon Edmund Burke*, 4 vols., London (1844).

Harvey, J. H., *William Worcester, Itineraries*, Oxford (1969).

Kay, Dr. W., *Report on the Sanitary Condition of Bristol and Clifton*, Bristol (1844).

King, J. E., *Clifton College Annals, 1860-1912*, Bristol (1912).

Rudder, S., *A New History of Gloucestershire*, Cirencester, (1779).

Seyer, S., *Memoirs, Historical and Topographical, of Bristol and its Neighbourhood*, 2 vols., Bristol, (1812-23).

Sketchley, J., *Bristol Directory of 1775*, Kingsmead, Bath (1971).

Smyth, J., *Men and Armour for Gloucestershire*, 1608 and 1902, Alan Sutton, 1980.

Sprigg, J., *Anglia Rediviva*, Oxford (1854).

Suetonius, *Lives of the Caesars*, Book 3, Biography of Vespasian, 2 vols., trans. J. C. Rolfe, Loeb Classical Library (1917).

The Tragedy of the King's Armies Fidelity since their entry into Bristol, Together with the too late repentance of the Inhabitants, Wherein is set forth the Extreme Plunderings, Rapes, Murthers and other Villanies, London (1643).

Warburton, E., *Memoirs of Prince Rupert and the Cavaliers*, Vol.II (1849).

Woodes Rogers, Capt., *A Cruising Voyage round the World first to the South Seas, thence to the East Indies, and homewards by the Cape of Good Hope. Begun in 1708 and finish'd in 1711, containing a Journal of all the remarkable Transactions ...*, London (1712).

Newspapers and Journals

Felix Farley's Bristol Journal
Bonner and Middleton Bristol Journal
Gentleman's Magazine (1806)

SECONDARY SOURCES

Articles and Theses

Baddeley, St Clair, 'The Battle of Dyrham, A.D.577', *Trans. of B. and G.A.S.*, Vol.51 (1929).

Bramble, Col. J. R., 'Three Civil War Returns' in *Proc. of Clifton Antiquarian Club*, Vol.2 (1888-93).

Buchanan, R. A., 'The Construction of the Floating Harbour in Bristol: 1804-1809' in *T.B.G.A.S.*, Vol.88 (1969).

Bush, G. W. A., 'The Old and the New: The Corporation of Bristol, 1820-1851', University of Bristol, unpublished Ph.D. thesis (1965).

Campbell, M., 'Recording a Churchyard – The Strangers' Burial Ground' in *Avon Archaeological Newsletter*, (Spring 1977).

Carter, A., 'The Crescent to beat all Crescents' in *Illustrated Bristol News* (October 1963).

Ellis, A. S., 'On the Manorial history of Clifton' in *T.B.G.A.S.*, Vol.3 (1878-9).

Ellis, P., 'Sea Mills, Excavations 1965-68' in *T.B.G.A.S.*, Vol.105 (1987).

Everett, S., 'A Reinterpretation of the Anglo-Saxon Survey of Stoke Bishop' in *T.B.G.A.S.*, Vol.80 (1960).

Guttridge, G. H., 'The American Correspondence of a Bristol Merchant: Letters of Richard Champion, 1766-1776' in *University of California Pubs. in History* (1934).

Hyde, F. E., 'The Port of Liverpool and the Crisis of 1793' in *Economica*, Vol.18 (1951).

Jones, S. J., 'The Growth of Bristol: The Regional Aspect of City Development' in *Transactions of the Institute of British Geographers*, Vol.11 (1946).

Latimer, J., 'The Manor of Clifton', *T.B.G.A.S.*, Vol.16 (1891-2).

Latimer, J., 'Clifton in 1746', *Proceedings of the Clifton Antiquarian Club*, Vol.5 (1900-3).

Lee, C. D., 'Alexander Selkirk and the last voyage of the 'Cinque Ports' Galley' in *Mariners' Mirror*, Vol.73 (Nov. 1987).

Lindley, E. S., 'The Anglo-Saxon Charters of Stoke Bishop' in *T.B.G.A.S.*, Vol.78 (1959).

Little, B., 'Clifton's Eugenie House' in *Bristol and West Country Illustrated* (June 1979).

Little, B., 'The Georgian Houses of Clifton' in *Country Life* (Sept. 1962).

Little, B., 'The Gloucestershire Spas: An Eighteenth Century Parallel' in McGrath, P. and Cannon, J., *Essays in Bristol and Gloucester History*, Bristol (1976).

Morgan, L., 'Notes on the Clifton, Burwalls and Stokeleigh Camps' in *Proceedings of the Clifton Antiquarian Club*, Vol.5 (1900).

Martin, A. T., 'The Roman Road on Durdham Down, Bristol' in *Proceedings of Clifton Antiquarian Club*, Vol.5 (1900-3).

Minchinton, W. E., 'The Virginia letters of Isaac Hobhouse, merchant of Bristol' in *Virginia Magazine of History and Biography*, Vol.66 (1958).

Moore, J. S., 'The Gloucestershire Section of the Domesday Book: geographical problems of the text', Part 1 in *T.B.G.A.S.*, Vol.66 (1987).

Olsen, D. M., 'Richard Champion and the Society of Friends' in *T.B.G.A.S.*, Vol.102 (1984).

Oswald, A., 'Goldney House, Clifton' in *Country Life*, Vol.104 (6 and 13 August 1948).

Powell, A., 'Glass Making in Bristol', *T.B.G.A.S.*, Vol.47 (1925).

Ralph, E., 'The Heritage that is Clifton' in *Bristol and West Country Illustrated* (April 1978).

Ralph, E., 'Victoria Square' in *Bristol and West Country Illustrated* (January 1982).

Rogers, B. M. H., 'Captain Woodes Rogers' Voyage' in *Mariner's Mirror*, Vol.19.

Savadge, W., 'The West Country and the American mainland colonies 1763-1783, with special reference to the Merchants of Bristol', unpublished B.Litt thesis, University of Oxford (1952).

Taylor, C. S., 'Bristol and its Neighbourhood in Domesday' in *Proc of Clifton Antiquarian Club*, Vol.2 (1888-93).

Taylor, C. S., 'Note on the entry in Domesday Book relating to Westbury-on-Severn' in *T.B.G.A.S.*, Vol.36 (1913).

Taylor, C. S., 'The Parochial Boundaries of Bristol' in *T.B.G.A.S.*, Vol.33 (1910).

Underdown, P. T., 'Henry Cruger and Edmund Burke: Colleagues and Rivals at the Bristol Election, 1774' in *T.B.G.A.S.*, Vol.15 (January 1958).

Ward, J. R., 'Speculative Building at Bristol and Clifton' in *Business History*, Vol.20 (January 1978).

Way, L. U., 'The 1625 Survey of the smaller manor of Clifton' in *T.B.G.A.S.*, Vol.36.

Williams, A. F., 'Bristol's Port Plans and Improvement Schemes of the Eighteenth Century' in *T.B.G.A.S.*, Vol.81 (1962).

Wilson, E., 'The Bone Cave or Fissure of Durdham Down' in *Proc. of Bristol Naturalists Society*, Vol.5 (new series).

Wright, L., 'An Account of the Bristol Society of Architects' in *Journal of the British and Somerset Society of Architects* (June 1950).

Wright, L., 'Regency Clifton' in *Somerset Countryman* (July-Sept. 1946, Jan.-March 1947).

Yarborough, A., 'Geographical and Social Origins of Bristol's Apprentices', 1542-1565, *T.B.G.A.S.*, Vol.98 (1980).

Books

Beavan, A. B., *Bristol Lists, Municipal and Miscellaneous*, Bristol (1899).

Belsey, J. et al., *Bristol: The Growing City*, Bristol (1986).

Bettey, J. H., *Bristol Parish Churches during the Reformation, c.1530-1560*, Bristol Branch of the Historical Association (1979).

Buchanan, A. and Cossons, N., *Industrial Archaeology of the Bristol Region*, Newton Abbot (1969).

Buchanan, A. and Williams, M., *Brunel's Bristol*, Redcliffe, Bristol (1982).

Butcher, E., *Clifton Hill House, the first phase 1909-1959*, Arrowsmith (1961).

Carlton, D., *A University for Bristol*, Bristol (1984).

Cave, C. H., *A History of Banking in Bristol, 1750-1899*, Bristol (1899).

Chalklin, C. W., *The Provincial Towns of Georgian England* (1974).

Challenger and Edward, E., *Illustrated Guide to Bristol and Clifton*, Bristol (1911).

Chilcott, J., *New Guide to Clifton and the Hotwells*, Bristol (1853).

Christie, O. F., *A History of Clifton College, 1860-1934*, Arrowsmith, Bristol (1935).

Claridge, A. and Williamson, B., *Clifton, Not so Long Ago*, Bristol (1986).

Crick, C., *Victorian Buildings in Bristol*, Bristol (1975).

Daymer Powell, Cmdr. J. W., *Bristol Privateers and Ships of War*, Bristol (1930).

Day, J., *Bristol Brass; The History of the Industry*, Newton Abbot (1973).

Dibben, A. A., *Title Deeds*, The Historical Association (1968).

Foster, J., *Alumni Oxonienses*, Vols. IV and V, Oxford (1891).

Glenday, N. and Price, M., *Clifton High School, 1877-1977*, Bristol (1977).

Gomme, A. and Jenner, M., *Bristol, an Architectural History* (1979).

Green-Armytage, A., *Concerning Clifton. A Historical Narrative from Saxon Times until the Present Day*, Bristol (1922).

Guedalla, P., *The Second Empire* (1922).

Hobhouse, H., *Hobhouse Memoirs*, The Wessex Press, Taunton (1927).

Hutton, S., *Bristol and its Famous Associations*, Arrowsmith, Bristol (1907).

Ison, W., *The Georgian Buildings of Bristol* (1952).

Jones, S., *Whiteladies Walks; Five Town Trails in a Victorian Conservation Area*, Bristol, Redland and Cotham Amenities Society (1976).

Knapp, A. J., *Handbook to Clifton and its Neighbourhood*, Bristol (1867).

Latimer, J., *Annals of Bristol in the Seventeenth Century*, Bristol (1900).

Latimer, J., *Annals of Bristol in the Eighteenth Century*, Bristol (1893).

Latimer, J., *Annals of Bristol in the Nineteenth Century*, Bristol (1887, Part II, 1907)

Latimer, J., *The History of the Society of Merchant Venturers of the City of Bristol*, Bristol (1903).

Little, B., *The City and County of Bristol* (1954).

McGrath, P., *The Merchant Venturers of Bristol*, Bristol (1975).

McGrath, P., *Bristol and the Civil War*, Bristol Branch of the Historical Association, Pamphlet 50 (1981).

MacInnes, C. M. and Whittard, W. F., *Bristol and its adjoining Counties*, Bristol (1955).

Manning, W. H., *Report on the Excavations at Usk, 1965-76; the fortress excavations 1968-71*, Cardiff (1981).

Markham, C. R., *Life of the Great Lord Fairfax*, London (1870).

Matthews, *Directory*, Bristol (1839).

Moore, J. S., *Avon Local History Handbook*, Phillimore, Chichester (1979).

Mortimer, R., *Early Bristol Quakerism, The Society of Friends in the City, 1654-1700*, Bristol Branch of the Historical Association (1967).

Norris-Mathews, E., *Bristol Bibliography*, Bristol (1916).

Pascoe, M., *The Clifton Guide*, Bristol (1980).

Powell, G. R., *The Bristol Stage*, Bristol (1919).

Pressnell, L. S., *Country Banking in the Industrial Revolution*, Oxford (1956).

Raistrick, A., *Industrial Archaeology*, Paladin Books (1973).

Ralph, E., *The Downs, 1861-1961*, Bristol (1961).

Ralph, E., *Guide to the Archives of the Society of Merchant Venturers of Bristol*, Gloucester (1988).

Richardson, D., *The Bristol Slave Traders; A Collective Portrait*, Bristol Branch of the Historical Association (1985).

Robinson, R., *The Sieges of Bristol*, Bristol (1868).

Rolt, L. T. C., *Isambard Kingdom Brunel*, Pelican Books (1970).

Stembridge, P., *Goldney, A House and a Family*, Bristol (1969).

Summerson, J., *Georgian London*, Pelican Books (1962).

Taylor, J., *Guide to Clifton and its Neighbourhood*, Bristol (1868).

Underdown, P. T., *Burke and Bristol*, Bristol Branch of the Historical Association (1961).

Venn, J. and J. A., *Alumni Cantabrigienses*, Vols.IV and V, Cambridge (1927).

Victoria County History of Gloucestershire, Vol.II (1907).

Waite, V., *The Bristol Hotwell*, Bristol Branch of the Historical Association (1960).

Ward, J. R., *The Finance of Canal Building in Eighteenth Century England*, Oxford (1974).

Warin, R. and A., *Portrait of a Zoo, 1835-1985*, Bristol (1923).

Wilkins, H. J., *Some Chapters in the Ecclesiastical History of Westbury-on-Trym*, Bristol (1909).

Witt, C., Weeden, C. and Schwind, A. P., *Bristol Glass*, Bristol (1984).

Index

(Compiled by Auriol Griffith-Jones)

Note: Tables are shown by **bold** page numbers. The appendices are not indexed except as a reference under their main subjects, e.g. Hobhouse, family, **Appendix** 5

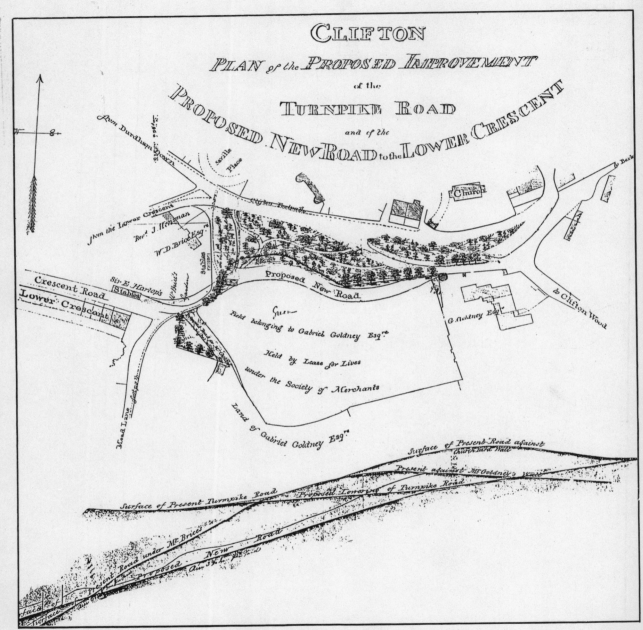

S.M.V. map drawn in March 1834 by W. Hicks Townsend. It shows the proposed improvement to the turnpike road and new road to Lower Crescent (Cornwallis), Clifton. Prospect House and Beresford House are shown opposite the Green in front of Goldney House. The church nave was destroyed in the Blitz, and the tower demolished in 1954 for no good reason. The gateway to the churchyard remains today.